Contents

Prologue v

Part I
WINNING THE BATTLE FOR CONTROL OF YOUR MONEY / 1

1 Your Money Attitudes 1
2 Seven Steps Toward Developing a Positive Money Attitude ... 15
3 Taking a Realistic Look at Past and Present Finances 24
4 Determining Current Income and Expenses 33
5 Four Basic Steps to Take Control of Your Money 44

Part II
CONQUERING DAILY LIVING EXPENSES / 55

6 Your Shopping Style 55
7 Give Me Shelter 69
8 Stretching Your Grocery Dollars 102
9 The Road to Lower Transportation Costs 120
10 The Emperor's New Clothes 147
11 Dieting Tips for Utility and Maintenance Bills 162
12 Reducing the High Cost of College Tuition 180
13 Cleaning Cents 188
14 Health and Beauty Savings 204

15 Say Hello to Good Buys 222

16 A Diaper Bag of Tricks 245

17 Wrap Holidays in Good Wishes and Merriment 252

18 Pinch a Penny and Make It Smart 267

19 Pennywise Gardening and Pest Control 273

The Frugality Network 293

Index 294

Prologue

Stop and smell that crisp dollar bill in your hand before you spend another cent. You are not just holding a mere piece of paper with monetary significance; you are holding your dreams, aspirations, shortcomings, fears, and future security. Do you control your money, or does your money control you? Are you currently debt-free and saving money for retirement, or are you working as hard as you can just to pay your expenses? Together we will explore your personal relationship with money and learn powerful methods to break through the self-imposed barriers that hold you back from realizing your full financial potential.

Taking control of your money goes beyond penny-pinching and living like a cheapskate. It does not result in living a life of deprivation and sacrifice. However, it does require a true appreciation of the life force (i.e., the precious moments you have here on earth) you exchanged for the money. The appreciation of all you currently possess as well as the full utilization of your resources are integral components to your success in controlling your money. By embracing the concept of spending your money consciously and deliberately, you will reduce your living expenses, enhance your self-reliance, and increase your self-respect. Most importantly, by spending money in a respectful manner, it will go further and last longer. You will even have money left over at the end of the month.

This is not an investment or financial planning book. Instead, it goes directly to the heart of a question frequently asked of investment counselors, "How do I come up with extra money to invest?" Together we will explore in Chapter 1 "Your Money Attitudes," the power that money has in your life and the reasons for your inability to control it. We'll discuss the following topics.

- Why you are compelled to spend money you have yet to earn by charging a purchase on a credit card.
- How you can stop your impulse shopping.
- Money as your drug of choice.
- Why the opinions of others might have excessive influence on your spending decisions.

To be in full control of your money, you must examine and come to terms with the psychological and emotional impact that money has on your life. It is only after these misconceptions and distortions are revealed that you can effectively deal with them and begin to put more money in your pocket.

In Chapter 2 "Seven Steps Toward Developing a Positive Money Attitude," you will learn to take the steps that will empower you to conquer debt and reduce your living expenses to provide a more financially secure future for you and your family. This information is not presented as abstract principles but in a specific, concrete, and easy to follow format.

Armed with these newly acquired skills, you will be ready to take an honest look at your finances in Chapters 3 and 4. Through examples and sample worksheets, you will bring your past and present financial picture into clear focus. Specific debt reduction strategies provide the knowledge and motivation necessary to successfully pay off debt more quickly and painlessly. A new technique to base all purchase decisions on previously identified goals and your own personal mission statement is presented and explored. Using this new strategy, you will find it easy to prioritize and reduce your spending on nonessential items. You will be taking the first stride toward regaining a sense of control over the money you earn. Instead of feeling powerless over your money, you will begin to understand and enjoy the benefits of using your money in a positive, productive way.

The American dream of getting married, having a child, owning a home with a white picket fence, and a car parked in the driveway costs more today than at any other time in history. In fact, from the mid-1970s until today, the price of this American dream has risen by more than 320 percent! There would be little cause for concern if wages had kept up with these increases. Unfortunately, the national per capita income has increased by little more than 135 percent. Is there any wonder why you frequently feel as though you are unable to get ahead financially?

Yes, the rules have changed, but I will share with you the simple, logical instructions to this new version of the game of "Life" as we explore "Four Basic Steps to Take Control of Your Money" in Chapter 5. Examples and worksheets are provided for you to use in evaluating and monitoring your living expenses. You will learn new, simple methods to reduce your living expenses. These methods are additional weapons in your arsenal to further empower you to take control of your money. Various uplifting and motivational techniques are included to facilitate the attainment of your goals.

After you have sewn up the holes in your financial pocketbook, you will be ready to seek out specific ways to reduce your living expenses. In Part II, "Conquering Daily Living Expenses," you can choose from many battle plans to beat the high cost of living. Savor the money-saving strategies as they explode from the pages of the book and enjoy the thrill of seeing your pockets become increasing plump each month. Do you really need two incomes to maintain your current standard of living? Maybe not! Together we will examine your current living expenses. You will be able to choose from many new, sometimes innovative, ways to reduce these basic expenses. You will learn ways to save not only money, but also time. A variety of money saving and timesaving ideas are presented, so you can determine those that are the most viable ones to use based on your family's values, lifestyle, and goals. Discussed in detail are definitive ways to reduce costs on all major expenses encountered by a family including home ownership, food, health and beauty, clothing, cleaning, transportation, child raising, holidays, gardening, and utilities.

For most of my life, I have been perceived as the "Pied Piper of Frugality." I have diligently sought and practiced methods to reduce the cost of various living expenses for my *typical* family. "A penny saved is a penny earned," truly sums up the philosophy by which I live. As a wife and mother, I worked full time for many years as a registered nurse. I know firsthand the impact that working full time can have on a family's budget and quality of life, so I understand the problems faced by many families today. I have confronted the challenges presented by rising costs and have developed creative, easy methods to dramatically reduce my family's daily living expenses. I am pleased to share with you various methods and techniques I use to compensate for a busy schedule and limited time. You will learn, as I have over the years, the power of knowledge as you implement the information within the pages of this book.

Part I
Winning the Battle for Control of Your Money

1
Your Money Attitudes

What are your thoughts and assumptions about the driver of a brand new car as it speeds past you on a crowded street? Do you immediately assume that this driver is returning to an expensive home filled with luxuries reserved only for the wealthy? Although this might have been a safe assumption years ago, car leasing now allows those who could otherwise not afford this luxury to drive a new car. Driving the latest model vehicle is no longer a luxury reserved only for the rich. This particular driver may very well be returning to a modest apartment furnished with rented furniture and clothing purchased with a credit card. The only thing this driver may be able to claim ownership of is a large debt and an overdrawn bank account.

As you navigate along the road of life, consider whether you are riding on a firm, secure surface or a slippery, muddy one made of false assumptions, beliefs, and attitudes. A car, like your finances, needs a solid foundation upon which to navigate. A car cannot attain satisfactory traction on a slippery surface. When a slick spot is encountered, the car wheels spin helplessly out of control. A firm, secure surface provides optimal traction and control. Likewise, your finances can spin out of control if decisions are based on false beliefs and attitudes about money.

Many of us have a distorted or unrealistic view about our money. We believe money is responsible for our moods, our success, our failures, and even our self-worth. On occasion it is our best friend, and at other times, it seems to turn on us and become our worst enemy. How we think about money and the importance we give it in our lives reflects our attitudes and beliefs about money. These opinions about money are one of the pivotal forces steering our financial actions or inaction. Falsely held beliefs or attitudes about money can lead to financially damaging decisions and negative behaviors. These false opinions can only be replaced with beliefs based on truth and positive behaviors if they are uncovered and recognized for what they are. Decisions made on sound financial knowledge and principles can net large financial rewards. In reality, our money is not responsible for our happiness, our problems, our successes, or our failures. Each of us is responsible for our own financial decisions and their consequences. Of course, it is much easier to blame our problems or unhappiness on an inanimate object, such as a dollar bill. Money should not control us, we must be in control of our money.

Defining your attitudes and beliefs about money is the first step in developing a new relationship with money. Most of the seeds of these beliefs were planted at an early age and have been growing and developing throughout your lifetime. What is your first memory about money? Was it when you were given a quarter by a loving grandparent to buy some candy? What feelings were evoked when you had your allowance withheld for some wrongdoing as a child? Do you recall the emotions you felt when your parents told you they could not afford to purchase a toy you dearly wanted? Were you raised in a family of modest financial means or one with excesses? Your current perception about money has been shaped throughout your life and has become an integral part of your basic belief system and values. Although these attitudes and beliefs by themselves are not "bad," if they are taken to extremes, negative or financially damaging behaviors can result. Together, we will examine some commonly held beliefs and attitudes about money, so that you can begin the process of building a secure foundation on which you can safely navigate your finances.

IF I ACT RICH, I WILL BE RICH

This attitude is based on the notion that money is attracted to money. People with this attitude may feel compelled to dress in designer clothes, eat at expensive restaurants, and drive leased luxury cars. Too often, they pay for this false façade with credit cards or by living from paycheck to paycheck. Their financial reserves are limited or nonexistent because all of their money goes toward maintaining the appearance of a high social status. The notion that money will somehow come knocking on their door as a consequence of dressing and looking like they are "rich" has no basis in fact. Although money is attracted to real money, money is repelled by debt. In other words, if you have an excess of money in the bank, you have the financial means to take advantage of an investment opportunity. If your wealth is only an illusion, you are unable to take advantage of these opportunities. Instead of providing the means to make more money, living on borrowed money actually inhibits your ability to become wealthy and attain your financial or personal goals.

In the long term, trying to "act rich" without genuine wealth ultimately reduces your self-esteem and leads to increased feelings of frustration and resentment. Acting rich does not improve your ability to become financially secure. If anything, it dramatically reduces your ability to attain your financial dreams.

Studies show that most often people attain genuine wealth as a result of a lifestyle of hard work, perseverance, planning, self-discipline, and sacrifice. An interesting finding by Stanley and Danko as reported in their book, *The Millionaire Next Door,* is the fact that most genuinely wealthy people do not "act rich." Most live rather modest lifestyles and intentionally do not display their wealth.

Therefore, if you truly desire to "act rich," do not live a lavish lifestyle. Instead, live a frugal lifestyle, and live below your means. Stanley and Danko confirmed in their research that the majority of millionaires today attained their wealth the old-fashioned way—they earned it, saved it, and invested it, so their money worked for them. Consequently, you should *act* rich by *being* frugal.

MONEY IS A NECESSARY EVIL

People maintaining the belief that money is inherently evil do not feel the need to control or respect their money. They seem to be trying to demonstrate to themselves and to others around them that money is not important in their lives. They believe that because money is evil, those who have it are sinister, insensitive, dishonest, corrupt, or greedy. As a result, living on a modest income allows them to remain pure and virtuous. In fact, some feel that the less money they have, the more virtuous they will become. They treat their money with disrespect and spend it frivolously with little regard for their future financial security. Few, if any attempts are made to control their money. Their checkbook is seldom balanced, and it is common for them to pay late fees for past due bills.

In reality, their lack of control over their money allows money to control them. This realization is felt when they want to buy something of genuine value, and they find themselves with insufficient financial resources. This attitude prohibits them from providing a sound financial base for their family and certainly provides no financial security for their future.

Money is not evil. However, people can act in evil ways with their money. People can also do wonderful things with the money they control. For example, schools and hospitals have been built with donated money, and thousands of students attain a college degree each year as a result of money donated for scholarships.

If you do not take control of your money and your living expenses, they will control you. Unless you are in control of your money, you will never be able to attain your full potential, and your ability to accomplish your life's purpose will be dramatically reduced.

MONEY IS POWER, MONEY IS WORSHIPPED

From a very early age, you have seen and experienced the power of money. Money can be used to secure the physical necessities and luxuries of life. Yet money cannot buy happiness, love, fulfillment, or a sense of inner peace. Unfortunately many people become trapped in the endless quest to make more money. In reality, the amount of money we make has no relationship to the level of happiness, love, fulfillment, or sense of inner peace we feel in our lives. Problems occur when people become trapped, like a hamster running inside an exercise wheel, in this endless quest to make more money. "More, more, more" has become the mantra of many today. Getting more money becomes the central focus and driving force of their every action. They want more money, more power, more respect from their peers, more perks from their job, and more possessions. Unfortunately, instead of feeling more satisfaction, contentment, and genuine happiness, they find that the more they have, the more they want.

Let's face reality, no one can "have it all." No single person can "own" the entire world. He who dies with the most toys *does not* win. Studies show that true happiness and inner peace cannot be bought at any price and are unrelated to your net worth. More is *not better*. While trapped in this attitude, you will never fully appreciate the gifts you have been blessed with. You will be unable to see what you have—you will only be able to see what you *do not* have.

To break out of this vicious cycle, you must come to terms with what you perceive to be "enough." In their book, *Your Money or Your Life*, Dominguez and Robin explain that enough is the point where your needs are met without creating excess and clutter. Enough is the point where you not only have what is necessary for survival, but adequate comforts and little luxuries, so you continue to feel a sense of success and fulfillment in your life. Will a larger house bring you more contentment and a greater sense of fulfillment or just a larger mortgage along with more pressure to maintain a high income and more rooms to keep clean?

To determine your *enough* point, you must balance your needs with your desires. Evaluate what is truly required to maintain your comfort and security. Work on developing an appreciation for those things that you already own as they relate to fulfilling your physical needs. Consider also the consequences associated with buying more than you need: decreased financial security, working long hours to pay for a big mortgage, increased stress, less time with the family, both parents working outside the home, and more "stuff" to dust and keep organized.

A good method to use to start breaking out of the cycle of wanting more and determining your enough point is to begin a thankfulness journal. Every day, add five items to your journal for which you are grateful. They should be things that your money cannot buy: the laughter of your child, a sunset, a clean kitchen, a hug from a friend. As you add more to your journal, you will begin to develop a clear understanding of what is enough in your life. For perhaps the first time, you will see what is truly important in your life and what is just clutter.

Once you have defined and implemented the concept of enough in your life, you will find an inner calm and peace. You will have finally found the "more" that you were searching for. Your purchases will be based on their ability to fulfill your needs, not some distorted attitude about money. You will have enough of those things you need without excess clutter to weigh you down or take up valuable space in your life.

Implement this new "enough" philosophy the next time you buy a car. Write down your needs on a sheet of paper. Carefully examine everything you write down to confirm that it is a need and not a desire. Air conditioning is a need if you live in a warm climate, it is a desire if you live in a cool climate. Then, find a car that will meet those needs without creating excess. Although you might like the prestige of driving a new car, this prestige will be gone within a few months when a new line of cars is produced. Is it worth paying 20 to 30 percent more for a car so you can brag to your friends? A good quality used car will save you thousands of dollars and provide equally good transportation.

MONEY CAN BE USED TO CONTROL PEOPLE AND SHOW EMOTIONS

The first time your parents withheld your allowance because of an overlooked chore, the seeds for this belief began to grow within you. Many people with this belief find nothing unethical or immoral in using money as a powerful weapon to coerce or force others to do their bidding. Lavish gifts given as a demonstration of affection can also serve as a method to control another person. People who use money to control others are frequently distrusted and avoided. The respect they are shown is only out of fear, not as a result of a sincere appreciation for their talents. However, money cannot be used to control you unless you allow it to happen.

Too often, money is used in lieu of an honest and sincere exchange of your feelings. Buying flowers after an argument is easier than admitting that you were wrong. A parent called away frequently on business trips may bring gifts after each trip to make up for his or her absence. Money cannot buy love. Money cannot replace the genuine expression of your emotions through actions and words. Frequently, parents buy their children expensive gifts at Christmas because they want their children to know how much they are loved. Unfortunately, children do not equate the number of gifts they receive from their parents with the degree to which they are loved by their parents. After all, they hardly know Santa, and he brings them lots of gifts. On the other hand, a child does understand from an early age that his or her parent's time is extremely valuable. Therefore, they do equate the amount of time a parent spends with them to the love their parent feels for them.

I NEVER HAVE ENOUGH MONEY TO PAY MY BILLS

People with this attitude demonstrate a lack of control over their expenses and the money they earn. They have frequently given up trying to reduce their living expenses and have justified spending more than they make by blaming it on the fact that they are underpaid. Most are resigned to live beyond their means.

In reality, one of the primary reasons people today have problems with too much debt is not because they do not make enough money, it is because they spend too much! Those of us in the middle income tax bracket earn good incomes. Unfortunately, too often we spend it before we earn it—which leaves us in debt. A return to the philosophy that was practiced before the days of ready access to credit cards would help to modify this attitude. Instead of buying on impulse for immediate gratification, put money aside until enough is saved to purchase the item with cash. You will find that anticipation is half the fun.

Many people with this attitude have never really tried to reduce their living expenses. They justify their lack of planning and overspending on the fact that they are too busy to save money. They have convinced themselves that saving a quarter here and a dollar there will not make a difference, so why try? Frequently, they tell themselves, "My time is worth money," so it does not pay to shop around for the best price or wait until the item goes on sale. They refuse to take the time to evaluate their needs because it requires a further expenditure of their time. The belief that personal time is worth money may increase your self-esteem, but it certainly has the opposite effect on your personal bank account. After work hours, an employee receives no compensation for his or her time from an employer. You are paid for your time at work, but your personal time is not compensated. However, the money you save by comparison shopping is real money, not Monopoly™ money.

I find that people who claim to have insufficient time to plan their purchases spend more time and money than those of us who take a few extra moments to evaluate our needs and plan accordingly. For example, the planning and purchase of food for my family takes a total of one and a half hours each month. This includes the actual purchase of the food at the grocery store. Upon questioning hundreds of people in the classes I teach, I find that most people who do not plan their menus go grocery shopping three or four times per week. They spend a minimum of 30 minutes in the grocery store during each visit. Therefore, they spend one and a half to two hours each week or six to eight hours a month shopping for groceries. I spend only $50–$75 each week to feed my family of four, whereas the average family of four spends $175! Careful planning and conscious spending saves me not only money, but also time.

Too often, people make their purchases almost as a reflex. They want something, so they buy it. A candy bar at the checkout stand looks good, so they buy it, even though they are not hungry. The latest model television would be nice to have (even though they already have a perfectly good television), so they buy one. If the money is not in their checking or savings account, they simply charge it. "I needed it," is the justification for their purchase. They have few, if any, spending priorities. Their purchase decision is based primarily on the question, "Do I want it?" The very fact that they want it makes it a need. Their lack of planning or careful evaluation of their genuine needs results in excessive, careless spending and an inability to put money aside for savings. Sometimes people assume that they will be forced to live a life of deprivation if they reduce their living expenses. In reality, you do not have to deprive yourself of things you need.

Instead, approach each and every expense in a logical and intelligent manner. Separate your "needs" from your "wants." Identify those things you really need from luxury items you would like to have someday. The first of the year is a perfect time to identify your spending priorities for the upcoming year. Use common sense in evaluating your future needs. Although you might want to take a vacation to Disney World in the upcoming year, the fact that your house needs a new roof is a higher priority. Will your car need to be replaced in the next 12 months? Does one of your children need braces? Have you been putting off any repairs to your car or home? The identification of needs and wants is a personal decision. What one family may see as a need, another may characterize as a want.

Sit down and discuss these spending priorities with your spouse or significant other, and draw up a plan to put aside money regularly for anticipated expenses. Once enough money has been set aside to pay for the necessities, you can begin to save for planned luxuries. This is a very effective motivational method to reduce spending. The entire family should become involved in the planning and saving of money to fund the anticipated purchases for the upcoming year. If your children are aware of these needs, they will be more supportive and less likely to try to persuade you to spend your money on superfluous things. For example, the kids will be more willing to eat a lunch brought from home, instead of buying their lunch at school if they know that it will help fund their participation in soccer or pay for their dance lessons, and so on.

To reduce your living expenses, carefully evaluate each and every expense. Can this expense be reduced? Do I really need to spend money for this purchase or service? Remind yourself that a penny saved is a penny earned and yes, every penny does add up.

Knowledge is quickly transformed into more money in your bank account. Therefore, become knowledgeable about the things you buy with your money. Do not make purchases based on misinformation, rumors, marketing claims made by a company, or an effort to "keep up with the Jones's." Is one brand of green beans really better than another brand? You decide for yourself, and then act accordingly.

I WORK HARD FOR MY MONEY, SO I WANT TO ENJOY IT. YOU CAN'T TAKE IT WITH YOU

First of all, we all work hard for our money. Second, yes, you should enjoy your money. If you found nothing positive or enjoyable in regards to the money you earn, you would find it extremely difficult (if not impossible) to be motivated enough to return to work each day and earn more money.

Finally, no, you cannot take your money with you when you die.

Problems occur with these beliefs when you spend money that you do not have. Too often, those working in a salaried position fall into the habit of working more than 40 hours every week. As a result, they have less time to shop wisely, they eat out more often because they don't have time to prepare their meals at home, and they pay for services they do not have time to perform themselves. Working more than 40 hours a week results in no increase in pay because they are on a fixed salary. Yet, their living expenses increase dramatically. This phenomenon also occurs when hourly employees work overtime. Most hourly employees report that by the time taxes are deducted from their overtime wages, they see only a modest increase in their paycheck. They work more hours and have even less money at the end of the week because of these increased living expenses.

As a coping method to deal emotionally with the stress of working long hours, they feel the need to "reward" themselves. This emotional need is so great that they frequently buy something they cannot really afford. Their job does little to make them feel satisfied or attain a sense of accomplishment. Spending money fulfills this emotional void. Unfortunately, they charge the purchase to a credit card knowing that they will not be able to pay it off in the near future. These hardworking, dedicated employees only dig themselves deeper and deeper into debt. Unless they come to terms with the reality of what they are doing, they are destined to continue to repeat these actions.

MONEY AS YOUR DRUG OF CHOICE

Spending money is mood altering. We spend money to celebrate. We spend money to lift a mood. Temporarily, it makes us feel better, and we forget about our problems. Malls and departments stores throughout America are designed to excite the senses and entice shoppers to spend money. Spending money can make even the most humble feel important and powerful as a well-dressed salesperson caters to their needs and compliments their appearance or taste in choosing a product or article of clothing.

Marketing claims encourage us to buy the most expensive products because "we're worth it!" Do you feel depressed, lonely, unloved, or bored? Go shopping and forget your problems! The marketing techniques used by stores and manufacturers have been so successful that we even fault ourselves if we return home empty handed. It has become socially acceptable to be in debt. A high credit card balance is accepted as the norm and status quo. Over the course of time, commercials and advertisements have shaped our thinking, so we believe that spending money takes a special skill or talent and is to be valued. Well, let me be the first to tell you, shopping is not a skill! Anyone with cash in hand or a valid credit card can walk into a store and spend money. It takes no talent to spend money. However, it does take willpower, discipline, knowledge, and skill to reduce your spending and put money aside into savings.

The first step in overcoming the use of money as your drug of choice is to recognize it as a problem and admit it. Next, steps should be taken to identify the underlying reason for your depression, loneliness, boredom, and so on. Are you in a bad marriage? Are you bored and lonely at home now that the kids have left the nest? Did your best friend just move away? Spending your money on a marriage counselor instead of high-priced merchandise at the mall is a better long-term investment. Contact one of the local nonprofit organizations in your area, and volunteer your time if you are bored or lonely. Volunteering your time will increase your self-esteem and make you feel needed and wanted.

The last step in overcoming your money-spending problem is to stay out of stores and the mall. It sounds quite simple because it is. If you do not go to the store, you cannot spend money. Of course, this also includes discarding catalogs (if you are an avid catalog shopper) and turning off the television or computer (if your weakness is shopping via the television or online). Carefully plan all future purchases based on your identified needs, and only shop when you have to purchase one of these specific items.

IF I ONLY HAD MORE MONEY, I WOULD BE HAPPY

Deep inside us exists the knowledge and understanding that money cannot buy love, approval, or happiness. We inherently know that the amount of money we make is not directly proportional to the amount of happiness, love, and fulfillment we receive from life. This fact has been proven over and over in countless studies. Unfortunately, too many of us bury this knowledge so far under other false assumptions about money that we begin to believe that money can buy happiness. We think back to how happy we were when we got our very first car and believe that the same level of excitement will return if we buy an expensive new car. When this new car fails to bring the same level of happiness, we buy something else. Excessive spending does not bring excessive happiness. Instead, the subsequent debt brings only increased feelings of insecurity and inadequacy.

MONEY IS A RENEWABLE RESOURCE

How often do you write a check knowing that there are insufficient funds in your checking account in anticipation of being paid prior to the check clearing your account? Do you spend your bonus or income tax refund before it is received? Do you live from paycheck to paycheck? These actions are indicative of a "money as a renewable resource" attitude and are predicated upon the belief that you have complete control over your job, health, and future. It is unsettling to contemplate the fact that we have little, if any, control over our lives. You could die unexpectedly, be laid off with little notice, or be diagnosed with a terminal illness.

Many employees in the 1990s experienced the pain of losing a job firsthand. Call it downsizing, reorganization, corporate restructuring, or any of several other terms, but a new fact of life is that most corporations place a higher value and priority on maintaining their profits than on the quality of their workforce. In the twenty-first century, job security is no longer a benefit offered in the workplace. Regardless of your personal opinion about your importance within your company, if another person comes along who can do your job in an adequate manner for less money, you will be shown the door. Profit takes precedence over quality. Employee wages reduce profits.

To cope with these changes in the workplace, you should always be alert to new employment opportunities. Maintain your skills in the latest technology and training in your field to keep yourself marketable to potential employers. Network with others in your profession or trade to learn of job opportunities. Contact employment agencies representing those in your field to evaluate the job market and learn of potential job opportunities. Re-evaluate the job market on an annual basis to confirm that your job pays the highest wages and offers you the best opportunity. To do less, leads to complacency. Complacency leaves you vulnerable to being "downsized."

IF I ASK FOR A DISCOUNT, PEOPLE WILL THINK I AM CHEAP OR POOR

I hear this attitude stated frequently. Those who share this attitude with me express concern regarding how a salesclerk, waitress, repairman, or some other person representing a specific business will perceive them. If you consider the consequences and realities of this situation, you will quickly come to the same conclusion that I do each and every time.

Fact. You will probably never see this salesperson again.

Fact. What if the salesperson does think you are cheap or poor? Is this attitude on his or her part going to cause you any physical, emotional, or financial hardship or pain? Of course not!

Fact. The research done by Stanley and Danko in their book, *The Millionaire Next Door,* confirmed that the average millionaire is very frugal. Therefore, if you did ask for a discount, the salesperson may think you are wealthy because his or her personal experience has probably been that only rich people ask for discounts. A more appropriate attitude is, "If I ask for a discount, people will think I am wealthy."

Fact. The worst thing that can possibly happen if you ask for a discount is that the salesperson will say "no."

Fact. Chances are pretty good that you will be given a discount and save money. Frequently, a clerk is allowed to discount a product, but only after an inquiry is made by the customer. This is particularly relevant if the customer is not paying for the item with a credit card because many stores provide a discount if the item is paid for with a check or cash.

The conclusion that I come to each and every time I consider these facts is, who cares what the salesperson thinks. Ask for a discount because it is your hard-earned money that you are going to save.

MONEY WORRIES AND FEARS

Almost everyone has some fears or anxieties about money: Worries that an unexpected expense will prevent you from paying your bills; fear of being laid off from your job; anxiety about the economic security of your family if the primary wage earner died suddenly or suffered from a debilitating illness; and apprehension about an enormous credit card debt. Financial anxieties can serve to bind you into an emotional knot. They leave you feeling vulnerable, weak, and helpless. Consequently, you remain in a state of suspended animation, unable to take action. To overcome these fears and prevent them from continuing to control you, you must identify your money worries and confront them. If you continue to hide them or deny their existence with the hope that they will go away, they will only become compounded.

Take, for example, anxiety caused by an enormous credit card debt. As this anxiety becomes more profound, it can lead to a fear that you will not be able to pay your other bills. Then, concern might be raised that you will not be able to make your house payment. This might escalate into you becoming anxious that you will lose your house, go bankrupt, and end up in a homeless shelter on public assistance. Your anxieties can spiral out of control as you feel increasingly helpless in your ability to alleviate or manage your money worries.

What are your money worries and fears? Write them down on a sheet of paper and ponder the question over the course of the next few days. Once you have identified all of your fears, look at them in very realistic terms. Identify a specific course of action to take control of each concern. Every money worry has a logical course of action that can be taken to eliminate its control over your life.

For example, if you are concerned about the economic security of your family should the primary wage earner become ill, take out a life and/or disability insurance policy on this person. A dear friend of mine had this concern regarding her husband. Upon investigating his life and disability insurance policy, she found that he already had more than enough insurance through his employer to provide for the family's security. Her money worries immediately disappeared.

If you are concerned that you will not be able to pay for unexpected expenses, start a special savings account dedicated to this purpose. Even if you only put a few dollars a month into this account, your worries will begin to dissipate, and you will soon begin to feel that sense of financial security that had been absent from your life.

2

Seven Steps Toward Developing a Positive Money Attitude

Take off those rose-colored glasses distorting your vision, and look at your money for what it is. It is simply printed paper for which you trade your life force. It does not define the quality of your life on earth. Your self-worth is not equal to your paycheck. Furthermore, you are not powerless in controlling your money and reducing your living expenses. Within you is the ability to change and shift your focus from nearsighted to farsighted vision.

In this chapter you will learn how to replace the false beliefs and attitudes about money, which you identified with in the previous chapter, with truth and wisdom. You will embark upon a journey of seven steps that contain many detours along the way. Enjoy the journey because you will find that as you take increasing control over your money, your vision will no longer be clouded by uncertainty and financial chaos. You will see your money in a new way, and feelings of serenity and contentment will once again find a place in your life.

STEP 1 **DEVELOP A NEW WAY TO LOOK AT THE MONEY YOU EARN AS IT RELATES TO THE LIFE FORCE YOU EXCHANGED FOR IT**

Upon entering the world, you can claim ownership to only one thing, your life force. Your life force is the amount of time you have here on earth. It is a finite period of years, months, days, hours, minutes, and seconds. The moment at which your life force will be extinguished remains one of the biggest mysteries of life. Although you might expect to live a long healthy life, experience has proven that with little, if any notice, we can quickly be taken from this world. The thought of this uncertainty, our vulnerability, and our inability to control the inevitable fact of our mortality can be very frightening and unsettling. Therefore, we tend to push this reality from our stream of conscious thought.

Everyday we hear about people who have gone to extreme measures to save another person's life. These actions serve to illustrate the high value we place on our lives and the lives of others. How much is your life force or that of your loved ones worth? Most people will clearly and emphatically state, "priceless!" Yet, what do your actions actually reveal? How you choose to spend your life force during your brief period of time here on earth ultimately defines the quality and the very purpose of your life.

Think back to a previous job interview at the point when wages were discussed. During these negotiations, you discussed the number of hours you would be required to work. Your potential employer offered to pay a specific amount of money in exchange for these hours. Sound familiar? In reality, you were in the position of placing a price tag on your life force. For example, you agreed to give your employer 40 hours of your life force every week and in exchange, the company would pay you $500. In this instance, you sold 40 hours of your life force for $12.50 per hour.

In the conversion of your life force to a monetary figure, the true value we place upon our life force then rests, in large part, upon how we spend this money for which it was "sold." Dominguez and Robin explore this concept in their book, *Your Money or Your Life*. It is a profound, simple truth of life today. We sell our life force for money.

The significance of this action and the genuine value of your life force is not realized until the money is spent. Do you spend your money prudently and in a manner that is respectful of the life force you gave in exchange? Is your spouse the primary wage earner? Do you spend the money that your spouse exchanged for his or her life force in a manner that will serve to further honor and respect the precious gift he or she has given to you and your family? Do you spend your money with no regard for its true value, but instead, base your spending on some false beliefs and attitudes? Treating your money with disrespect and in a careless manner demeans the value of your life.

You further devalue your life force by selling it at a discount to your employer. Too often, when employees are paid a salary to work 40 hours a week, they actually work well over 40 hours each week on a regular basis. The employer gladly accepts this action because the company receives more of your life force at no additional cost. Instead of receiving $12.50 an hour for working 40 hours, you would only receive $10 an hour if you had, in fact, worked 50 hours during the week. Even though this may be an acceptable situation on rare occasions, too often it becomes the norm.

When you regularly work more than 40 hours, dire far-reaching consequences occur. Not only are you selling your life force at a dramatic discount, but your living costs increase in proportion to the amount of extra hours worked. Working overtime on a regular basis does not allow adequate free time to shop prudently or to plan your purchases in advance. Consequently, you spend more on groceries, eating out, clothing, and other expenses of daily living. You may feel the need to pay others to do those things you cannot do yourself, such as clean your house, cut the grass, launder your clothes, walk the dog, and so on. Your finances suffer because you do not have time to balance your checkbook, monitor your investments, or even pay bills on time. The accrued late fees, bounced check fees, increased debt, and loss of interest income can quickly add up over the course of a year. By working overtime, you not only sell your life force for less, but actually force yourself to spend more of your hard-earned money on those things necessary to enable you to work overtime. In other words, you are paying money for the privilege to work overtime!

Let's say you work 50 hours in one week. As a consequence, you eat out every night and pay someone to do your laundry for the week. This results in spending $60 more during that week on these items. Deduct the costs you incur as a result of working overtime from your weekly salary. Then, divide this resulting figure by the total number of hours you actually work to arrive at your genuine hourly wage (or the value placed upon your life force) for the week. Instead of receiving $12.50 per hour, your net income per hour was only $8.80.

Long hours on the job cause emotional, psychological, and physical stress. As a consequence, you may have to seek medical help or counseling to deal with the ill-effects on your relationships and health. Both of which come at a monetary cost. Once again, you are paying for the privilege to work overtime.

Increase the value of your life force by maximizing the compensation you receive when it is expended. Treat the money you receive in payment for your life force with great care. Spend your money in a responsible, respectful manner, and get full value for every dollar. Do your best at work during the 40 hours of your employment. Then, go home and give your best to your friends and family to receive maximum compensation in terms of emotional support and love. You will be happier, healthier, and wealthier both spiritually and monetarily.

STEP 2 ACCEPT RESPONSIBILITY FOR YOUR CURRENT FINANCES

Acknowledge and accept that you are responsible for the current state of your finances. Only you are to blame because—it's your money! Stop blaming previous situations, unexpected problems, or excessive spending on your current debt or lack of financial reserves. Admit that you made mistakes in the past. Learn from those mistakes and go forward. Everyone makes mistakes now and then because no one is perfect. Unless we learn from our mistakes, we are only destined to repeat them. Mistakes are opportunities to learn. You are not the sum of your debts. Your bank balance does not define who you are. Your creditors do not own you. The past is behind you. You now have the opportunity to go forward with newfound knowledge and confidence to take the necessary steps to ensure a debt free, financially secure future.

STEP 3 IDENTIFY AND USE EFFECTIVE COPING STRATEGIES TO DEAL WITH YOUR SHOPPING STYLE(S)

Recognizing and admitting specific problems associated with your shopping style(s) is a significant step in the right direction to change them. Work on making the recommended changes to have a more positive impact on reducing your living expenses and controlling harmful shopping behaviors. Refer to Chapter 6 for specific methods you can use to deal more effectively with your shopping style(s).

STEP 4: IDENTIFY YOUR FEARS, ATTITUDES, AND BELIEFS ABOUT MONEY AND REPLACE THEM WITH A NEW REALITY AND TRUTH

In Chapter 1, you identified your fears, attitudes, and beliefs about money. At this point in your life, you can either continue to spend your money in the same manner based on previously held beliefs, attitudes, and habits, or you can begin to replace them with new, effective, and more appropriate attitudes, beliefs, habits, and truth. You have within you the ability to change and take control of your actions. You are not powerless.

New habits are created in the same manner that old habits are established, by repeating specific actions over and over until they become automatic responses. New habits take three weeks to create and another three weeks to establish for a lifetime. Positive thinking (through the use of positive messages) can open your mind to new creative solutions for what were previously considered problems. The process is quite simple. Create a positive, motivational message for yourself and instill it in your subconscious to replace a negative attitude or belief.

To develop your own positive message, use the guidelines in the following list.

1. Make your positive message short and concise, so you can repeat it word for word. For example, "My self-worth is not dependent upon the brand of clothing I wear," or "I will do my job to the best of my ability in 40 hours this week," or "I make more than enough money to support my family."
2. Use the present tense because your intention is to begin implementing this change immediately. "I will pay off my credit card debt within the next 12 months."
3. Write the message in positive, open-ended, measurable terms. Do not say "up to $100" instead write "at least $100." For example, "I will spend at least $100 less for groceries and food this month."
4. Repeat your new truth dozens of times each day: on your way to work, when you feel anxious about your money, when you are tempted to buy something you do not need, when you pay bills, the first thing in the morning, and the last thing at night. Post it on the

bathroom mirror, so you can see it when you comb your hair. Put notes with your positive message in various locations—in your car, in your billfold, and on the refrigerator door—so you can see them throughout your day. Actually write your positive message down 25 times a day.

Soon you will find that your positive message has become a self-fulfilling prophecy. Attaining your new truth will allow you to feel more confident and self-assured in the management of your money and your expenses. You will soon find that your money fears decrease. For perhaps the first time in a long time, you will begin to know genuine feelings of empowerment.

STEP 5 DETERMINE WHAT MAKES YOU FEEL FULFILLED AND IDENTIFY A PURPOSE FOR YOUR LIFE

Does it seem that the more you have, the more you want? You have a new house, but you wish it were bigger. You have a great running car, but you would prefer the latest model. Do you frequently feel a restlessness deep inside because you want more? You may be caught up in the endless cycle of desire begets desire. When trapped in this vicious, tumultuous cycle, you try to buy your way to happiness, contentment, and self-fulfillment. However, you will never arrive at the point where you feel that you have it all because no one can "own" it all.

Stop trying to reach a goal that is unattainable. Instead, set a purpose that is higher than that of getting more and getting ahead. Reach for the highest goal in life, that of achieving your life's mission or purpose. Too often, people work their lives away with little regard for what would truly bring them inner peace and happiness. They are so focused on their jobs and getting ahead that they forget to stop, take a deep breath, and ask themselves the most vital question of all, "What do I really want to accomplish during my lifetime?"

Figure 2-1 provides specific tasks in writing your personal mission statement. Complete these tasks honestly and with much thought to your inner feelings and needs. Your spouse or significant other should complete his or her own personal mission statement(s). Upon completion of your personal goal and mission statement, share them with one another. Together you can write your family's personal mission statement and goals.

> **FIGURE 2-1**
>
> ### Identifying Your Personal Goals and Writing a Personal Mission Statement
>
> Identify short-term and long-term priorities in your life.
>
> Write several things (goals) that you consider are of the highest priority in the next 1–12 months.
>
> Write several things (goals) that you consider are of the highest priority to attain within the next 10–20–30 years. (Choose a time frame based on your own personal situation.)
>
> List the most important people in your life.
>
> Evaluate how these important people relate to your short-term and long-term priority list.
>
> If necessary, change the previous item(s).
>
> Write a personal mission and/or goal statement for your life. (You do not have to limit yourself to one).

Too often, a mother or father's only goal or purpose is to help their child to attain his or her goal(s). However, each of us has our own personal, unique goal(s) and purpose in life. As we mature and experience more in life, our goal(s) and purpose change. Therefore, this exercise should be repeated periodically throughout your life, so you never lose sight of your goal(s).

It is important to take your loved ones into consideration when determining your priorities in life. For example, if being home with your children is important to you, your short-term goal can be modified to include changing your work hours from full-time to part-time or to stop working altogether.

Define and quantify your personal definition of success and fulfillment in your mission statement. If desired, write more than one personal mission statement. One can address your current goal(s), whereas the second can focus on your long-term goal(s). You will feel a great sense of satisfaction in the consideration and development of your personal mission. Your focus is not to please others or to try to live up to someone else's expectations. Instead, you should identify your ambitions and allow your talents to reach their full potential. Once written, it is easy to become committed and dedicated to your mission statement because it represents your heart's desire.

Your personal mission statement is a powerful tool to use in taking control of your spending. From this point forward, base your purchasing decisions on your personal mission statement. Ask yourself, "Will purchasing this item add to my ability to attain my personal mission?" If the answer is "No," you can easily resist the urge to spend your money because of the importance that is given to attaining your personal mission in life.

STEP 6 MAKE A COMMITMENT TO TAKE CONTROL OF YOUR MONEY AND REDUCE YOUR LIVING EXPENSES

Do you have a clear understanding of your finances, or do you simply cross your fingers and hope that you will have enough money in your checking account to cover your bills each month? Do you have more than enough money to accomplish your goals? Do you know the total amount of your debt? Are you so much in debt that you must declare bankruptcy? Will you be able to retire as you have planned?

Carefully evaluate your current finances, and take steps now to prepare for a financially secure future. Are you living from paycheck to paycheck and spending everything you earn? If so, you must implement methods to reduce your living expenses. Accept responsibility for your debt and pay it off. Modify your spending habits to ensure that you won't go into debt again.

Commit to a new way of life, one of total integrity, where you refuse to spend more money than you have. Track all expenses. Maintain an accurate record of the money in your checking account and balance your account monthly. Pay bills on time to avoid late fees. Do not spend money you do not have. Do not charge a purchase unless you have the money to pay the balance in full at the end of the month. Better yet, cut up your charge cards and only pay for purchases with cash or a debit card!

Anticipate your needs, and plan your purchases accordingly. Do not wait until December 1 to begin to shop for your holiday gifts. Always be alert to sales and discounts of those things on your list of needs. To have money available for the purchase of more expensive items, put money aside on a regular basis until you have saved enough to pay for them with cash. Spending money recklessly with little regard for the consequences is not respecting yourself or the life force you gave in exchange for it. Once again, if you do not take control of your money and your expenses, they will control you!

STEP 7 ACT IN A SOCIALLY RESPONSIBLE MANNER WITH YOUR MONEY

A woman in one of my classes stated quite proudly, "I feel like I am doing my part to help the economy by spending money." I was a bit surprised at the grandiose position she had assigned herself. I pointed out to her that even if she spent every penny she and her husband made, she would not be able to help the national economy. The economy is too large for her retail spending to have a positive impact. However, her spending can have a negative impact upon her personal finances and her community. Her reckless spending was, in fact, a socially irresponsible act. Each and every one of us must act responsibly with our money. Excessive consumerism contributes to the overflowing landfills, tainted rivers, contaminated soil, and polluted air.

Instead of spending excess money on unnecessary items in a misguided attempt to "help the economy," help your community in definitive, concrete ways by making a donation to the various nonprofit groups that provide one-to-one assistance to the people who live and work in your community. In lieu of buying a new car every year, save or invest the extra money you would have spent. The money you place in a savings account or invest in a company is put back into your community. Companies use your investments to expand and create new jobs. Banks use your savings to fund mortgages and new businesses. Your investments and savings, no matter how small, are important components to the financial strength of our nation!

3

Taking a Realistic Look at Past and Present Finances

Do you sometimes feel like Chicken Little with the sensation that the sky is about to fall on top of you? Are you working long hours or two jobs to keep the sky from falling? Is your spouse also employed full time?

Is the sky really falling? Are you getting very far in your marathon run to get ahead? Or, are you running on the money treadmill? Do you feel like you are running as fast as you can, but never seem to get anywhere? Does it seem like the more you make, the more you spend? What do you have to show for your last raise or bonus?

You must break out of the pattern and rhythm that has lulled you into believing various facts about yourself and your finances. Stop! Unplug the treadmill, and take a step onto the firm earth. Remove your specially designed cross-training sneakers and feel the cool grass under your toes. Take a deep breath, and clear your mind of worries and distractions. Open your thoughts and heart and allow yourself to see your finances for what they really are.

HOW MUCH ARE YOU WORTH?

Have you ever considered how much money you have already earned in your lifetime? You might be surprised to learn how much money has passed across the palm of your hand during your life. How much do you have to show for this money? Complete the "How Much Are You Worth" worksheet in Figure 3-1 to determine this for yourself. Review old tax records to help you recall the total amount you have been paid. If this information is unavailable, use your best recollection.

Figure 3-1

How Much Are You Worth?

Subtract your current age from the age when you got your first job.
Total the gross wages you earned during this time.
Determine your spouse's wages using the same method.
Combine both incomes to obtain the gross income realized since you began working.
Estimate your net worth by adding together the equity in your home, cars, and so on, plus all of your financial assets (stocks, bonds, etc.).
Subtract your net worth from the combined gross incomes.

Any surprises?

In the completed example (see Figure 3-2), the current age of the husband is 35. He received his first job at the age of 17, so he has worked a total of 18 years. The total amount he earned in gross wages (before taxes) during this time was $614,000. His wife is currently 33 years old and started working at the age of 14 when she began to baby-sit for neighbors. Consequently, she has worked a total of 19 years. Her gross wages earned during this 19-year period are $334,000. Their combined wages total $948,000. Note that even if the couple was not married during this time, the wages should be combined. This family estimated the net worth of all their assets by combining the equity of their home, the value of their furniture and personal possessions, the current blue book value of their cars, the value of their IRA/mutual fund, 401(k) retirement plan, and life insurance policy. Finally, they subtracted their net worth ($100,000) from their gross income ($948,000). The resulting figure of $848,000 represents the total amount of money they earned during their lifetimes for which they have nothing of monetary value to show.

Of course, a significant portion of this figure was paid directly to the government in the form of local, state, and federal taxes. However, the primary reason pretax wages and not after tax wages are considered, is to allow you the opportunity to look at the unabridged version of your finances. To control your money, you must look at all of the money you earn. Steps should be taken on your part to reduce your taxable income as well as the total amount paid out in taxes. Consult with your tax specialist to discuss specific tax reduction strategies you can employ. Act in a socially responsible manner

Figure 3-2
How Much Are You Worth?

Subtract your current age from the age when you got your first job.
 35
 −17
 18 years

Total the gross wages you earned during this time.
 2K x 2 years =   4K
 3K x 2 years =   6K
 35K x 9 years = 315K
 55K x 3 years = 165K
 62K x 2 years = 124K
           $614,000

Determine your spouse's wages using the same method.
 33         $350 x 2 years = $700
 −14   2K x 2 =   4K
 19 years   3K x 2 =   6K
             4K x 1 =   4K
             6K x 1 =   6K
             22K x 6 =   132K
             35K x 4 =   140K
             42K x 1 =   42K
                           $334,700

Combine both incomes to obtain the gross income realized since you began working.
 $614,000
 +334,000
 $948,000

Estimate your net worth by adding together the equity in your home, cars, and so on, plus all of your financial assets (stocks, bonds, etc.).
 $75K home, furniture
 $15K stocks, bonds, CD, retirement, life insurance
 +$10K cars
 $100,000

Subtract your net worth from the combined gross incomes.
 $948,000
 −100,000
 $848,000   Any surprises?

as a taxpayer. Contact your elected officials regarding any and all legislation that will impact the amount of taxes you pay and express your opinion. Let them know if you support specific legislation and why. Notify them of your concerns if you do not support the legislation. Do not let other people make these important decisions for you. Voice your opinion further by voting in all local, state, and national elections. If you do not write, call, or e-mail your elected official, he or she will assume that no one has any concerns and will vote his or her conscience. Worse yet, he or she may vote consistent with the desire of some special interest group providing financial support to his or her reelection campaign.

This worksheet exercise might be a somewhat sobering exercise for some of you and serve as a wake-up call to reduce needless spending. Others may find that careful spending and investing has resulted in providing a financially secure future. Regardless of the outcome, let this serve to further challenge and motivate you to continue on the path of taking control of your money and expenses.

HOW MUCH MONEY SHOULD YOU BE "WORTH" BASED ON YOUR AGE AND INCOME?

As you attain years of experience in your career, you expect an increase in your income and net worth. In their book, *The Millionaire Next Door,* Thomas J. Stanley, Ph.D. and William D. Danko, Ph.D. give us a simple equation that they developed based on these expectations and supported by their years of research. Refer to Figure 3-3 to compute your expected net worth as it relates to your age and current pretax income.

In the example shown in Figure 3-4, Mr. Gerard is 50 years old. His gross income (before taxes are deducted) is $40,000. After multiplying his age by his annual income, we arrive at a total of $2,000,000. By dividing this total by 10, we arrive at his expected net worth of $200,000.

Figure 3-3
Wealth Determination Factor

Multiply your age by your pretax income from all sources *except* inheritances.
To determine your expected net worth, divide the total by 10.

> **FIGURE 3-4**
>
> **Wealth Determination Factor**
>
> *Multiply your age by your pretax income from all sources except inheritances.*
>
> Example: Mr. Gerard is 50 years old and currently makes $40,000 per year.
> $$\begin{array}{r}\$40,000 \\ \times\ 50 \\ \hline \end{array}$$
> Total $2,000,000
>
> *To determine your expected net worth, divide the total by 10.*
> $2,000,000 ÷ 10 = $200,000
> $200,000 = expected net worth

What is your actual net worth and how does it compare to Stanley and Danko's calculation of your expected net worth? Case studies given in their book serve to further illustrate the fact that regardless of your income, living a high-consumption lifestyle allows for very little, if any, money to be put aside for saving and investing. Most people with genuine wealth (i.e., millionaires) live well below their means and limit their expenses, so they can regularly invest a portion of their incomes. The intent of providing this equation is to quantify your financial goals and provide another incentive to reduce your living expenses.

OWNING UP TO YOUR TOTAL DEBT

Many people have no idea of the total amount of their debt. Denial, fear, or shame prohibits them from facing this reality. However, unless specific steps are taken to control your debt, it will control you.

Your debt cannot be managed until it is quantified. Therefore, the first step is to arrive at a total. Only then can you recognize it and make a commitment to control it. Refer to Figure 3-5 for a worksheet that can assist with this process. Write down all of the credit card companies, banks, relatives, department stores, and so on to whom you owe money. Then, include the current balance as well as the interest rate that you are being charged. At the very bottom of the form, total all of the amounts owed to arrive at the grand total of your debt. Surprised? Ashamed? Pleased? Relieved? Proud? Embarrassed? Debt is the cause of much worry, stress, anxiety, and fear about the future.

Figure 3-5
Debt Worksheet

Date prepared _____

Credit cards

Card #1 _____

Outstanding balance _____ Interest rate _____

Card #2 _____

Outstanding balance _____ Interest rate _____

Card #3 _____

Outstanding balance _____ Interest rate _____

Car loan

Outstanding balance _____ Interest rate _____

Student loans

Outstanding balance _____ Interest rate _____

Home mortgage

Outstanding balance _____ Interest rate _____

Installment loans

Outstanding balance _____ Interest rate _____

Medical Bills

Outstanding balance _____ Interest rate _____

Other

Outstanding balance _____ Interest rate _____

TOTAL DEBT: _____

If you have excess debt, accept responsibility for the fact that you are in this position. Don't make excuses or justify your debt. Acknowledge mistakes you made in the past as a result of careless spending, weak self-discipline, or lack of planning. This may not be pleasant to admit. As these emotions come forth take them and turn them inward. Transform and ignite them until they form the basis of a firm commitment to revolutionize your spending and saving habits. Make a commitment to never allow this to happen again. Get mad at your debt. Make it your foe in your battle to become debt free.

The first step in managing your debt is to stop incurring more debt. Stop charging purchases. Do not spend money you do not have. Then, set up your own payment plan for each creditor. Pay the minimum amount required to those creditors charging the least interest. Pay as much as you possibly can above the minimum payment requirement to the creditor charging the most interest. As the high interest account is paid off, take the money that you paid toward it each month and apply it to the creditor with the next highest interest rate. Continue to pay off your creditors in this manner until they are all paid off. As you see your total debt decrease each month, you will gain an increased sense of control. You will no longer be on the money treadmill. You will be on the straight and narrow road to debt freedom.

If you find that you simply cannot manage your debt problems alone, contact the Consumer Credit Counseling office in your area. The counselors at this nonprofit organization will work with you individually to get your finances back on track. They charge only a nominal fee for this service. Call their toll free information line at (800) 388-CCCS for a referral to the office in your area.

Another solution to paying off a credit card debt more quickly is to transfer the balance to a credit card with a lower interest rate. Any credit card balance can be transferred including those issued by gas stations, department stores, banks, and so on. When a balance is transferred, the new credit card company sends full payment to the previous credit card company, and then debits your new account for the same amount. Some credit card companies issue checks for you to use to pay off other debts with a higher interest rate than that being charged by the credit card company. College loans, installment loans, or personal loans can be transferred to a lower interest rate credit card in this manner.

Refer to the credit card payment chart in Figure 3-6 to determine the amount of interest paid on a $2,500 balance when charged 5.9%, 12%, and 18% interest. Even if you continue to pay the same amount, $200 per month, you will save $244 simply by transferring the $2,500 balance from a card charging 18% to one charging 5.9%. Paying $400 per month will save an additional $41 in interest charges and you will pay off the debt five months earlier.

Figure 3-6
Credit Card Payment Chart

Total debt	Interest rate	Monthly payment	Total time to pay off debt	Total amount paid	Total interest paid
$2,500	18%	$100	32 months	$3,156.80	$656.80
2,500	18%	200	14 months	2,789.24	289.24
2,500	12%	100	29 months	2,891.48	391.18
2,500	12%	200	13 months	2,683.96	183.96
2,500	5.9%	200	12 months	2,586.46	86.46
2,500	5.9%	400	7 months	2,545.45	45.45

Periodically, credit card companies offer low "introductory" rates to encourage new customers. These rates remain in effect for a specific period of time, which varies from three to 12 months. To pay off a credit card debt more quickly, take advantage of this low rate. Then transfer your balance to another card offering an equally low interest rate before the low rate on the first card expires.

Be certain you understand the terms of the new credit card plan before accepting the card. Carefully evaluate the fine print listing the terms of the credit card to ensure that there are no hidden costs that are unacceptable.

Use the following guidelines to find an acceptable low interest credit card.

- Make sure you can transfer balances from another credit card and still pay the low rate on these transferred balances.
- Look for a credit card offering no more than 5.9% interest on the transferred balances for at least six months.
- Look for a credit card with no annual fee.
- Make certain that the credit card company does not charge a fee to transfer the balances. This is sometimes referred to as a "transaction fee."

Upon finding an acceptable credit card, complete the necessary paperwork to transfer the balances from your current credit cards. You may need to find more than one credit card offering a low interest rate if your debt exceeds the maximum limit for your new card.

Be certain to cancel the old credit card as soon as it is paid off and attains a zero balance, and ask the credit card company to provide written confirmation of the cancellation. Without this cancellation, the old credit card will continue to be listed as an open account on your credit report—even if it has a zero balance. An excess number of credit cards on your credit report can adversely affect your ability to obtain a loan. Therefore, cancel any credit cards that show a zero balance, so they will not pose a problem in the future. A written notice of cancellation may be needed as proof if the credit card company fails to notify the credit reporting agency of the cancellation.

You may be able to find a low interest credit card as close as your mailbox. Credit card companies aggressively market their low interest introductory rates by sending offers in the mail to prospective customers.

The Bankrate.com Web site at *www.bankrate.com* provides the interest rate of thousands of credit cards at no charge.

The Frugality Network Web site at *www.frugalitynetwork.com/calculators.html* provides various free calculators to evaluate the interest charged by credit cards and the financial impact of paying off a credit card early. These calculators make it much easier to evaluate your credit card debt.

4

Determining Current Income and Expenses

Benjamin Franklin was certainly correct when he said, "Beware of little expenses; a small leak will sink a great ship." Are small leaks in your finances preventing you from sailing into the sunset? Until you identify and fill these gaping holes, you might as well be using a bucket to bail water from the deck of the Titanic. Like a lighthouse beacon on a moonless night, this chapter will provide guidance to quickly organize and examine your finances.

DETERMINE YOUR MONTHLY INCOME

To take control of your money and begin to fill the holes in your finances, you must have a clear understanding of your monthly income. Take out a clean sheet of paper and record the necessary information. A loose-leaf binder can be used to secure the papers that you use to evaluate your income and expenses as you proceed through the next two chapters.

Total all of the monthly income you receive in the form of wages after withholding taxes and any other deductions are removed—this is your take-home pay. Include your spouse's income if he or she is also employed. Do not include bonuses or any periodic overtime pay. If you receive money from sources other than wages on a regular basis and use it toward your living expenses, include this income as well. This is the amount of money you can count on receiving each and every month, so we will refer to it as your total monthly income.

If you work on commission, use the amount that you consistently receive. Do not take your annual salary and divide it by 12. It is much easier to manage your money and spending on a month-to-month basis if you use the amount that you can almost always be assured. Then, when you receive money above this amount, place the excess money in a savings account, invest it, or place it in a special money management account to use when paying for planned purchases that are in addition to those associated with your monthly living expenses.

Illustrated in Figure 4-1 is the monthly income of the Richards family. John and Mary Richards have two children in grade school. John's regular take home pay is $3,125, whereas his wife Mary's take-home pay is $575 per month. Their total monthly income is $3,700.

Figure 4-1
Richards Family Monthly Income

John's take-home wages	$3,125
Mary's take-home wages (part-time)	+575
Total monthly income	$3,700

Monthly Expenditures

Separate your expenses into two distinct categories.

- Name the first category fixed expenses. Fixed expenses are those bills that must be paid on a regular basis. They are routine charges for nondiscretionary expenses. Installment loans, rent, mortgage payments, utility bills, and insurance premiums are examples of fixed expenses. These expenses represent purchase decisions that were made in the past with their payments spread out over a period of time. These bills are considered to be fixed because they cannot be changed without a conscious effort on your part, and they represent a predetermined financial commitment. It takes time and effort to reduce your fixed expenses.
- Name the second category daily living expenses. This category consists of incidental expenses incurred during the month. Daily living expenses are variable in nature because they represent discretionary purchases. This is the money spent for various living expenses, which include purchases at the grocery store, movie theater, clothing store,

restaurant, discount store, deli, and other locations during the month. Unlike a fixed expense, you have direct control over whether or not you spend money on a daily living expense. For example, you can choose to buy a candy bar at a vending machine or not. However, you cannot choose whether or not to pay your utility bill, taxes, or mortgage. Because you have direct control over the expenditure of money on daily living expenses, you can easily reduce your spending in this area.

The combination of both categories makes up your monthly expenditures. However, I am having you separate them into two distinct categories to facilitate the organization of these expenses and provide a means to further motivate you to reduce your spending. For the next few months, you should focus the majority of your attention on your daily living expenses. Due to uncontrolled shopping traits and false attitudes or beliefs about money, most people overspend in this area. You will not have to give up something you truly desire. Instead, you will find that you have ample money to pay for those things that are important to you because you no longer spend money on those items that do not enhance your life in a meaningful way. As you see the reduction in your monthly expenditures, you will be increasingly motivated to further your efforts to decrease your daily living expenses.

After several months, you will be able to reduce your spending on your daily living expenses to a level that is comfortable without making you feel deprived. Once you have your daily living expenses under control, turn your attention to your fixed expenses. These expenses can represent a significant source of holes in your leaking finances. Throughout Part II of this book, you will find various ways to reduce your fixed expenses. It is usually much more time consuming to reduce these expenses than it is to cut back on your daily living expenses. To make it more manageable, make a commitment to focus on reducing the expenses associated with only one fixed expense at a time. Monthly, or at less frequent intervals, choose one fixed expense that will be the focus of your attention. For example, comparison shop for lower insurance premiums on your homeowners' or car insurance. Educate yourself about other ways to reduce the cost of your premiums and implement those that are most appropriate for your circumstances. The money you save will serve to further motivate you to focus your attention next month or next quarter on another fixed expense.

Determine and Document the Money You Spend Each Month on Fixed Expenses

As discussed earlier, the first area of your monthly expenditures you should more carefully evaluate are fixed expenses. These expenses can be considered to be fixed or scheduled expenses that you agreed to pay at predetermined intervals. They may be paid monthly or on an irregular basis: yearly, biannually, or quarterly. You can develop your own fixed expenses in the form of voluntary, regular payments for savings, investments, retirement, or a special money management account (vacation account, holiday account, etc.).

On a separate sheet of paper, write down all of your fixed expenses. Refer to Figure 4-2 for the Fixed Expenses Worksheet. This worksheet is for your use in the compilation and computation of all fixed expenses. Use cancelled checks, previous utility bills, loan commitment papers, receipts, copies of bills, and so on as sources of this information. Indicate the minimum required payment for each installment loan or credit card as the monthly payment.

Most people ignore bills that are paid on an irregular basis until they become due for payment. Then, they have no choice but to charge the payment on a charge card because they do not have adequate funds in their checking or savings account. They can also have problems in the management of their money when faced with a large heating bill in the winter or cooling bill during the heat of the summer.

To control your money, you must acknowledge the existence of these situations and take steps to put money aside on a regular basis, so you have the money to pay these expenses when they become due. Your mortgage lender does this for you if you have an escrow account for the payment of taxes and insurance. However, you can set up your own account for the payment of infrequent or fluctuating bills. This separate savings account is your money management account. As an added bonus for placing the money in a savings account, interest will accumulate during the year.

Determine the annual payment for each infrequent expense. Then, divide the annual total by 12 to arrive at the amount that should be put aside monthly, so adequate money will be in the account to pay the bill when it is due. For utility bills (or any other fluctuating expense) that can change with the seasons, determine the total amount paid over the course of the year and divide this figure by 12 to determine the average. If the actual bill for a

FIGURE 4-2
Fixed Expenses Worksheet

Expense	Annual Total	Monthly Average
Mortgage/rent		
Car Insurance		
Homeowners/ renters insurance		
Credit card payment		
Cable TV		
Personal property taxes		
Telephone		
Long distance phone		
Cellular phone		
Beeper		
Oil/gas heat		
Electricity		
Water		
Car payment		
Trash removal		
Sewer		
Car tags		
Car taxes		
Medical deductibles		
Non-covered doctors/dentists bills		
Dance lessons		
Music lessons		
Tuition		
Membership fees		
Club dues		
Car maintenance		
Home maintenance		
Other:		
Savings		
Investment		
Donations		

given month is less than this average, pay the difference into your money management account for the month. When the bill is more than the average withdraw the difference from your money management account.

Some people may prefer to open a separate money management account for every infrequent or fluctuating expense. Others find it easier to maintain a single money management account in which they place all of the money to be used for these expenses. Be certain that there are no fees or charges associated with the establishment and maintenance of this account. Shop around, you will find that many banks as well as savings and loan institutions still offer passbook savings accounts to their customers at no charge. A passbook savings account works well as a money management account.

Figure 4-3 illustrates the Fixed Expenses Worksheet used by the Richards family. After including their average payment for the mortgage, utilities, taxes, and dues on the worksheet, they discussed any anticipated or expected expenses in the upcoming year. They chose to set up a money management account for car maintenance and decided to put $100 a month in this account to use for the repair and upkeep of their car. They also decided that when they pay off their credit card and their car loan, the money that is currently being used for these two expenses would be placed into this car maintenance account. This additional money ($250 more per month) in the car maintenance account would be used to buy another car when their current car needs to be replaced. Because their current car is only six years old with relatively low mileage, they are not anticipating having to replace it for at least four or five years. They also decided to establish a home maintenance account to pay for home repairs and snow removal as well as to ensure they have adequate funds to have their house painted this summer. They have already obtained some preliminary estimates and know that it will cost about $1,000 to hire someone to paint their house and about $200 if they do it themselves. The money they save by doing it themselves will allow them to buy a snow blower so they will not have to pay someone to plow their snow the following winter. Therefore, they estimate that they need to put only about $150 a month in this account to pay for these items plus any other miscellaneous repairs that might have to be performed throughout the year. They will also place $260 each month in a money management account to pay their infrequent bills: insurance, car tags, car taxes, and personal property taxes. They will place $25 a month in their "rainy day" money market savings account and $100 a month will be invested in their Roth IRA account.

FIGURE 4-3
Richards Family Fixed Expenses Worksheet

Expense	Annual Total	Monthly Average
Mortgage	$7,200	$600
Car insurance	600	50*
Homeowners' insurance	240	20*
Credit card payment	600	50
Cable TV	360	30
Personal property taxes	1,800	150*
Telephone	240	20
Long distance phone	120	10
Oil/gas heat	720	60
Electricity	960	80
Water	120	10
Car payment	2,400	200
Trash removal	360	30
Sewer	240	20
Car tags	60	5*
Car taxes	240	20*
Medical deductibles	180	15*
Dance lessons	312	26
Music lessons	480	40
Membership fees (Girl Scouts)	24	2
Car maintenance	1,200	100*
Home maintenance	1,800	150*
Other:		
Savings	300	25**
Investment/retirement	1,200	100***
Totals	**$21,756**	**$1,813**

*=money to be deposited in money management accounts
**=money to be deposited in money market savings account
***=money to be invested in Roth IRA for John and Mary

Total All Fixed Expenses

Add all of your fixed expenses for one month, including those that fluctuate or are paid infrequently. This total represents your main financial commitment each month. The total of the fixed expenses for the Richards family is $1,813, shown in Figure 4-3.

SET UP AND MAINTAIN A MONEY MANAGEMENT ACCOUNT

Deposit the monthly average for infrequent and fluctuating expenses in your money management savings account every month. Maintain a record of your deposits and payments made for each bill in your three-ring binder. This will allow you to easily track how much money is available for each expense. Use this same method to save for events, activities, purchases, or the maintenance and repair of your home, car, boat, vacation home, and so on. Figure 4-4 illustrates how Mr. Richards maintained a record of his deposits and expenses for his car maintenance money management account over a three-month period of time. You will note that in three months he deposited $100 each month and made only one withdrawal of $50 to purchase a new battery, leaving a balance of $250.

Figure 4-4
Car Expenses

Date	Deposit	Withdrawal/reason	Balance
10/1/00	+$100		$100
11/1/00	+$100		$200
12/1/00	+$100		$300
12/5/00		–$50.00/new battery	$250

Subtract Your Monthly Total of All Fixed Expenses from Your Monthly Income

This amount is very significant because it represents the money available for daily living expenses plus any excess money (i.e., savings!) Refer to Figure 4-5 to evaluate the amount of money available to the Richards family for daily living expenses.

Figure 4-5

Richards Family

Monthly income	$3,700
Fixed expenses	−1,813
Money available for daily living expenses	$1,887

Determine and Document the Money You Spend Each Month on Daily Living Expenses

The second category of your monthly expenditures is that of your daily living expenses. Daily living expenses are those remaining costs incurred during the month. Too often very little forethought or planning goes into your daily living expenses. Therein lies the primary reason many people have little, if any, money set aside for saving or investing. You have direct control over whether you spend your money on a daily living expense. You can easily reduce spending in this area. However, you must first specifically identify where the money is going.

How often do you put a $20 bill in your pocket in the morning and by that evening the money is gone, and you can't recall where the money was spent? Every nickel, dime, quarter, and dollar you spent did add up over the course of your day as evidenced by your empty pockets. You gave so little thought to the act of spending your money that you have no recollection of the act. If you had taken a few moments to consider your actions and had opened your mind to your true objective in spending the money, you probably would have been able to arrive at a less costly option or one that would not have required the expenditure of money at all.

To determine where the money is going, you must track your expenses. Keep a log of all the money spent for items *other than* those listed on your Fixed Expenses Worksheet for at least one month. Some people find it helpful to continue doing this every month. However, monitoring your expenses for even one month will provide valuable information about your habits and how your money is being spent. Use a small notebook to record these expenses, or keep all receipts for everything you purchase and record them every evening. Of course, if you are married, your spouse must also track his or her expenses.

Refer to Figure 4-6 for the daily record of the Richards family's purchases.

Figure 4-6
Richards Family Daily Living Expenses for March 1

Food (groceries)	$59.60	Rented movie	$3.00
Food (lunch @ work for John)	$5.40	Dry cleaners, shirts	$5.30
Gasoline	$22.50	Lottery tickets	$2.00
Overdue book fee	$3.00	Girl Scout cookies	$7.00
Snacks @ work soda	$.75	Parking meter	$2.00
chips	$.50	Clothing, daughter	$44.00
School lunch x 2	$4.00	Shoes, daughter	$20.00

At the End of the Month, Group Purchases of Similar Items

All money spent on lunches while at work should be grouped under the "food-work-lunch" category. All food that was purchased for the preparation of meals at home should be grouped in the "food-groceries" category. If nonfood items were purchased at a grocery store, place the expense for those items in the appropriate category. For example, hair conditioner, shampoo, and toilet paper should be placed in the "personal hygiene" category. Laundry detergent, paper towels, bleach, and so on should be placed in the "cleaning supplies" category.

Evaluate the total for each of these grouped purchases. Are there any expenses that are obviously excessive? In the next chapter, we will discuss how to evaluate, eliminate, or reduce these excessive expenses.

Figure 4-7 illustrates how the Richards family has grouped their purchases for the entire month.

FIGURE 4-7
The Richards Family Daily Living Expenses for March

Food (groceries)	$640	Rented movies x 3	$13
Long distance phone calls	$10	Restaurant, night out	
Entertainment (movie @ theater)	$32	w/friends	$87
(bowling)	$25	Fast food restaurant x 2	$20
Eating out (Friday night pizza)	$120	Parking meter	$2
Baby sitter for parents' night out	$24	Clothing + shoes	
Overdue book fees	$4	(daughter)	$64
Clothing (son—shoes)	$42	Clothing	
Clothing (wife—outfit + shoes)	$85	(husband—shoes)	$89
Football pool at work	$5	Girl Scout cookies	$7
School lunches	$64	Sports equipment	
Medicine	$27	(softball equipment)	$35
Cleaning supplies	$14	Lunches at work	$100
Lottery tickets	$5	Hobby, craft supplies	$8
Dry cleaning	$30	Personal hygiene (soap,	
Postage	$8	shampoo etc.)	$10
Birthday gift for daughter's friend	$10	Liquor (wine)	$12
Dog grooming	$20	Haircuts	$40
Gasoline	$110	Dog food	$10
Snacks @ work		Gardening supplies	$50
(soda, chips etc.)	$25	**TOTAL**	**$1,847**

5

Four Basic Steps to Take Control of Your Money

Albert Einstein is credited with saying "Insanity is doing the same thing over and over but expecting different results," and indeed, this statement applies to our ability to manage our money. As creatures of habit, we tend to use the same products, shop in the same stores, and spend money in the same way from month to month. We find this to be comfortable and convenient. Yet, every month we expect to find different results. Every month we expect to find extra money "leftover" in our bank account when we did nothing different to allow this to happen. In this chapter, you'll find the four basic steps that will enable you to attain a new outcome at the end of a month. In fact, they produce results that you can take to the bank!

STEP 1 EVALUATE YOUR MONTHLY EXPENDITURES

Refer to the total amount you spent for daily living expenses and fixed expenses discussed in Chapter 4. Then, consider how much money was spent for your monthly expenditures relative to your income for the same period of time. This is done by subtracting the total amount spent on daily living expenses plus fixed expenses from your total monthly income. Evaluate the results. Did you spend more than you earned? Did you have money leftover at the end of the month? Unless you have consistently taken into consideration and planned for infrequent or fluctuating bills, you have never been able to accurately determine this information. Using the techniques described in the previous chapter, you can easily evaluate whether you are living below, within, or beyond your means. The Richards family had a total monthly income of $3,700. Their fixed expenses and daily living expenses totaled $ 3,660. Therefore, they had $40 remaining at the end of the month. See Figure 5-1.

Figure 5-1
Richards Family Month-End Evaluation

Total monthly income	$3,700
Routine monthly bills	−1,813
Monthly purchases	−1,847
Difference	+$40

STEP 2 DEVELOP INTERNAL CONTROLS TO EVALUATE EVERY EXPENSE AND LIMIT SPENDING

Carefully review your itemized list of daily living expenses for the month. The intent of this exercise is not to find fault with the spending habits of family members. The primary objective is to take a realistic, objective look at what is happening to the money you earn. To facilitate finding less expensive alternatives, you must identify where and why your money was spent.

While reviewing your list of daily living expenses for the month, ask yourself with honesty and sincerity the following seven questions for every expense. Your spouse or loved one(s) should review the expenses for which he or she is responsible and make the same inquiry. Make note of those purchases that you determine should be eliminated or reduced by highlighting each identified item with a brightly colored marker. For example, if you find that the purchase of an extra pair of golf shoes was not necessary (question #1) because the pair you already own is still in good repair and will last at least one more season, highlight this purchase.

1. Is this expense necessary? Do I really need this product or service?
2. Can I do anything to reduce or eliminate this expense?
3. What was the objective in the expenditure of this money? Could this objective be met by some other, less expensive means?

4. Will this expense allow me to attain my personal goals? Is it in alignment with my values and what I perceive to be of genuine lasting importance in my life?
5. Did I receive value for my money? Was the service or product worth the amount of time it took me (or my spouse) to earn the money?
6. Would I have spent my money in this manner if I were on a fixed income with no chance for an increase to my income?
7. What does this expense cost me on an annual basis? Review the previous six questions based on the annual cost of the service or item. (Spending $20 per week to have your nails done at the salon actually costs $1,040 per year!)

Most married couples learn a great deal about one another after completing this exercise. To reiterate, the intent of this exercise is not to find fault with each other! As quickly as you extend a pointed finger toward your spouse, you will just as certainly have to turn it toward yourself. Reducing your living expenses is easier and more enjoyable if everyone is open-minded and supportive of the process.

Now that you have reviewed your entire list of previous purchases with a new critical eye in evaluating how and why the money was spent, consider only the highlighted purchases. These highlighted items represent excessive or needless purchases that were not in alignment with your values, goals, or the attainment of your life's mission. Do these highlighted items fall into natural categories, such as snacks purchased at work, articles of clothing for a particular family member, or a hobby? Decide which purchases can be eliminated altogether and which ones can be reduced. Be creative in considering alternative methods to reach your primary objective.

From this point forward, anytime you contemplate the expenditure of your money, make certain that it is conscious, deliberate, and in alignment with your values and mission in life. Put the purchase to the "test" by asking yourself the previous seven questions. This simple technique allows you to take direct control over your spending because you are placing the expenditure of money into proper perspective. With every purchase, you are reminding yourself of the relationship between your money and the life force you (or your loved one) gave to earn it. You are learning to treat this money in a more respectful manner, fully appreciative of what it represents.

To further motivate yourself to reduce your spending, take the money you save and place it in a separate savings account. (Be certain to get a savings account in a bank that doesn't charge initiation or maintenance fees.) Instead of spending $1 for a cup of coffee on the way to work every day, put the $5 you save each week into a separate savings account. After one year, you will have $260 in this account! You can then think about what you would do with an extra $260 at the end of the year. Considered in these terms, you may find it easier to purchase a thermos and bring your coffee from home instead of buying it from the coffee shop. You will not be depriving yourself in any way because your primary objective of drinking the coffee you desire will be met (and you will have an extra $260).

STEP 3 USE REDUCTION STRATEGIES TO PAY LESS FOR WHAT YOU DEEM ARE NECESSARY LIVING EXPENSES

To reduce your living expenses to their lowest level, you must carefully consider ways to reduce every expense. Focus your attention initially on those highlighted expenses you already determined to be excessive by responding in an affirmative manner to question #2—Can I do anything to reduce or eliminate this expense?

Refer to the regrouping of your purchases, which was completed at the end of Chapter 4. This regrouping allows other perspectives of your spending to come into focus. Expenses can be grouped together in any number of ways. For example, add all of the costs associated with a vacation, hobby, sport, or a specific car. Combine all of the costs incurred as a result of a second job or a spouse's employment outside the home, and then compare these costs with your take-home wages to evaluate the benefits or disadvantages of this employment.

When the Richards family reviewed their list of monthly purchases, they highlighted many food purchases. A separate listing of all money spent on food was made (see Figure 5-2). They were quite surprised to find that they spent almost one-third of their income on food! The Richards family's expenditure of excessive money on food is typical of most families today.

Figure 5-2
Richards Family March Daily Living Expenses—Food Purchases

Food (groceries)	$640
Snacks @ work (soda, chips etc.)	$25
Eating out (Friday night pizza)	$120
Restaurant—night out w/friends	$87
Kids' school lunches	$64
Fast food restaurant x 2	$20
Dog food	$10
Girl Scout cookies	$7
Liquor (wine)	$12
Lunches at work	$100
Total	**$1,085**

By regrouping their daily living expenses to focus on the money they spent for food, the Richards family had identified a hole the size of Texas in their finances. They decided to implement nine specific reduction strategies to dramatically reduce this living expense. Figure 5-3 illustrates the strategies they employed to save more than $7,000 a year or $595 each month. (To put these savings into perspective, Mary's take-home pay for the entire year is $6,900, and their monthly mortgage payment is $600. Yes, every penny, nickel, dime, and dollar you save does add up!)

Figure 5-3
Richards Family Food Purchases Reduction Strategies

Expenses	Annual Savings
Bring work snacks from home—save $15/month x 12	$271
Bring lunch from home instead of eating out every day at work	$780
Do not buy Girl Scout cookies	$7
Fix pizza at home instead of eating out	$1,248
Bring lunches from home instead of buying lunch at school	$476
Reduce wine consumption by 50 percent	$72
Limit going to a restaurant with friends to every other month	$522
Cut out the fast food restaurant lunches on Saturdays	$260
Plan all meals in advance using the Frugal Meal Planning Method (see Chapter 8)	$3,500
Grand Total Annual Savings	**$7,136**

The Richards family's specific reduction strategies:

- **Bring work snacks from home**: In evaluating their purchases for the month, Mary found that John spent .75 for a soda and .75 for a candy bar from the vending machine at work every day for a total of $1.50 a day or $30 each month. Although John felt that this expense might be excessive, he thought that denying himself the simple pleasure of a candy bar and soda would make him feel deprived. Therefore, he felt it was an acceptable way to spend his money. Mary suggested an alternative way to obtain the same objective (i.e., satisfy John's sweet tooth). She stocked up on the type of soda that John prefers whenever it was on sale for $1 or less for six cans (i.e., her "price point" was $1 for a six-pack of soda). She also stocked up on his favorite candy bars when they were on sale at three for $1 or less. She had already confirmed that she could buy candy bars at the local wholesale club for 35¢ each if purchased them in a case of 24. John agreed to take the candy bars and soda to work. (He also agreed that he would not excessively consume these food items and maintain his pattern of only one per day.) Their costs: 16¢ for the soda and 35¢ (or less) for the candy bar. Their new cost was no more than 51¢ per day for a savings of $1.04 per day ($1.55 minus 51¢=$1.04). Computed over the course of one year, the Richards family saved $270.40 (and John was still able to have his daily snack).
- **Bring lunch from home instead of eating out every day at work**: John spends $5 to buy lunch at the local deli every day when he is at work (a ham and cheese sandwich on a hard roll with potato chips and a diet Cola). John agreed to prepare this same lunch at home. The cost to prepare this lunch is less than $2. If John were to take leftovers for lunch, the cost of his lunch would be even further reduced. If John takes his lunch instead of buying it at the deli, he will save an additional $3 per day or $780 per year.
- **Do not buy Girl Scout cookies—make a direct financial donation instead**: When John and Mary asked themselves question #3—What was the objective in the expenditure of this money?—they recognized that their true objective for the purchase of these cookies was to support their local Girl Scout organization. Therefore, instead of buying the cookies they made a direct (tax-deductible) donation to

their local Girl Scout troop. As a result, 100 percent of their donation went to help this group. If they bought cookies, only a portion of their $7 would go to the Girl Scout troop because a significant portion of the money goes to pay the manufacturer of the cookies.

- **Fix pizza at home instead of eating out:** The Richards family had developed a habit of eating out every Friday night at their favorite pizza restaurant. Their normal cost for one large pizza, sodas, sales tax, and a tip was $30. The annual cost for this activity was $1,560. In comparing the cost of preparing a pizza at home, Mary found that it would cost her less than $5 to prepare their favorite pizza using pizza dough purchased from the local grocer and even less if she made her own pizza dough. In planning her meals, she bought a two-liter bottle of soda when it was on sale for $1 or less. As a result, the cost to prepare the same meal at home was less than $6. She deducted the cost to prepare the pizza at home from their annual expense to eat out and found that by preparing the pizza at home every Friday night instead of going to a restaurant, they would save $1,248 in one year's time.
- **No school lunches:** The cost to purchase one school lunch where their two children attend school is $1.60. The annual expense for both children to buy their lunches is $576. Mary found that she could provide a lunch for each child for about 50¢ each. She bought large containers of juice and poured them into reusable individual serving size bottles for an inexpensive, nutritious drink. Lunchmeat was purchased on sale, and she made cookies or brownies from scratch. Pretzels were found to be less expensive and lower in fat than potato chips, so she bought large bags of pretzels and placed an individual serving for each child in a plastic sandwich bag. As a result of bringing their lunches from home, the Richards family would save $476 over the course of the school year.
- **Reduce wine consumption by 50 percent:** John and Mary Richards go to a restaurant once a month with their good friends, the Case's. Instead of drinking one bottle of wine at a cost of $12 per bottle each time they go to the restaurant, they can reduce this expense by drinking wine every other month. This will save them $72 a year.
- **Limit going to a restaurant with friends to every other month:** John and Mary were amazed that their monthly dinners with the

Case's cost them $1,044 per year. When evaluating this expenditure of money, they first took question #3 into consideration—What was the objective in the expenditure of this money? In doing so, they mutually agreed that the objective of the dinner was to spend time with their good friends Jack and Jill Case. Then, they considered question #2—Can I do anything to reduce or eliminate this expense?—to develop a list of several ways to reach their main objective. One of the methods they considered was to reduce their frequency of going to a restaurant to every other month, thereby reducing this expense by 50 percent. However, this would deprive them of the company of their good friends, so their objective in question #3 would not be met. Therefore, this was not deemed to be an acceptable option. While sipping coffee one sunny afternoon, Jill and Mary arrived at an acceptable compromise. They would in fact continue to go to their favorite restaurant for dinner, but would do so only every other month. The month that they would not go to the restaurant, the couples would take turns hosting the other couple for dinner in their home. The children would go to the nonhost's house, so only one baby sitter would be required for the two families. The two women took into consideration the fact that they would only host the dinner at their home three times per year, and it would provide them the opportunity to use their good china and formal dining rooms. They further agreed that the host should not attempt to prepare gourmet food when it was her turn to host the meal. This minor change in this form of entertainment would save John and Mary $522 per year.

- **Cut out the fast food restaurant lunch on Saturdays**: Every Saturday Mary and her two children stop by a fast-food restaurant for lunch. Mary quickly recognized that this was not a necessary expense (question #1—Is this expense necessary?). It had simply become a habit that was encouraged by the kids because of commercials they had seen on television. Instead of eating lunch at a fast-food restaurant at a cost of $5 each week, she planned to return home with the children and eat the leftover pizza she had prepared the night before. As a result, there would be no additional cost for Saturday's lunch for her and the children. Her annual savings would be $260.

- **Plan all meals in advance using the Frugal Meal Planning Method:** Because Mary was making little, if any, attempt to plan her meals in advance, she was spending $160 to $175 every week on groceries. By carefully planning her meals as described in Chapter 8, she was able to reduce her spending to a maximum of $100 a week. Although her children have complained a little about the lack of expensive, over priced ready-made snacks around the house, they certainly are not undernourished. Mary now bakes homemade cookies and brownies for snacks. Extra baked goods are wrapped and frozen so she has them available when needed for snacks or school lunches. John and Mary decided that because soda provides no nutritional value, contributes to obesity and the development of cavities, purchasing soda was not an acceptable expense. The children's consumption of soda is now limited to only once a week. Mary is confident that their number of cavities along with the associated dental expenses will also decrease. The Richards family's annual grocery costs had been $8,700. With their grocery expenses now reduced to only $100 per week, they will spend no more than $5,200 per year. This reflects an annual savings of $3,500.

Step outside your usual practices and consider new ways to save money. Try shopping at consignment stores, off price stores, catalog outlets, or yard sales. Work on developing new habits. For example, instead of planning your menus as you walk though the grocery store, plan them in advance based on what you have in your kitchen cabinets as well as what is on sale at the grocery store. Always remain vigilant in seeking out new ways to reduce your living expenses. Be creative. Reduce a given expense until you have reached the point of "enough" without feeling deprived.

Any excess money that is not needed for your monthly expenses or a special money management account should be used to pay off debt. Once you are debt free (with the exception of your home mortgage), begin to invest and save the extra money.

Contained within the remaining chapters of this book are many methods to reduce or eliminate a family's primary living expenses. In reviewing these reduction strategies, you will be empowered with many new techniques to take control of these costs. However, only you can put the words printed on this paper into action. You will reap many financial rewards as you begin to find excess money remaining at the end of the month. Be persistent and focused on your goals. Even resistant family members will eventually come around when they understand the relationship between reducing expenses and the attainment of their goals.

It takes time and money to maintain a high standard of living. How much time do you spend wandering through the stores at the mall looking for things to buy? Your time is best utilized looking for ways to reduce your spending while still attaining your objectives. Use of your time in this manner is making an investment in a more financially secure future. Doing jobs around the house instead of paying someone else to do them keeps your money where it belongs—in your bank account.

STEP 4 MAINTAIN A RECORD OF YOUR TOTAL MONTHLY INCOME, EXPENSES, DEBT, INVESTMENTS, AND SAVINGS

By recording the information requested in this chapter as well as Chapters 3 and 4, you developed an up-to-date record of your current debt, expenses, and income. The only item lacking to make your financial information complete is a record of your savings, investments, and money management accounts. Organize this information in a three-ring binder so additional pages can be added as needed. Continue to monitor your expenses, debt, savings, investments, and income on a monthly basis to keep your financial records up-to-date. Maintain a monthly record of the amount spent on the previously defined categories, such as groceries, health and beauty products, transportation, gasoline, and so on. There are a variety of computer software programs that make this process much easier. However, a pencil and paper can be used with equal success.

A simple, yet powerfully motivational way to evaluate and track your money is to make a graph. Plot your total cost of living expenses, debt, wages, and investment income from month to month on the graph. Refer to Figure 5-4 for the graph that the Richards made to plot their living expenses, credit card debt, savings, and income. They used the extra money that resulted from the decrease in their living expenses to pay off their credit card debt. Once the credit card debt was paid in full, they put this extra money into a savings account.

FIGURE 5-4
Living Expenses

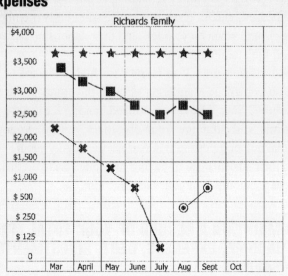

- ◉ Savings
- ✖ Total Credit card debt
- ▨ Monthly living expenses
- ★ Income

Part II
Conquering Daily Living Expenses

6

Your Shopping Style

Do you have more than one hundred pairs of shoes? Do you hate to go shopping, whereas your best friend loves to go to the mall? These actions are indicative of shopping traits or styles. Your shopping traits can be your worst enemy in trying to reduce your living expenses. A helpful method to control the amount that you spend is to understand why and how you shop. Once you have identified your personal shopping traits, you are able to take steps to modify and manage them.

Before reading this chapter, take the self-test called "What Kind of Shopper Are You?" provided in Figure 6-1. Answer each question and assign the appropriate score to each question. Total the scores for each of the four questions for each shopping trait. After you have identified your dominant and recessive shopping traits, read on to learn more about your traits and specific actions you can take to control them.

Most people have one dominant shopping trait, but traits can vary based on the emotions surrounding the purchase. For example, you may feel very comfortable and competent when shopping for groceries, so you become an extreme shopper in hunting for the best prices. Because shopping for a house is a new experience, and you have concerns about the commitment of home ownership, your style may be that of an avoidance shopper. Consequently, you are compelled to buy the first house that seems to marginally meet your needs.

You may have already compensated for some of your shopping traits. For example, your score may reveal that you are an avoidance shopper yet you do comparison shop. This is an indication that you have already learned some coping strategies to deal effectively with your avoidance shopping traits.

FIGURE 6-1

What Kind of Shopper Are You?

Reflex Shopper

1. Do you find it difficult to resist the urge to buy something on impulse?
   0=never, 1=infrequently, 2=occasionally, 3=frequently, 4=quite frequently
   SCORE_____
2. How often do you make unplanned purchases or buy things that are not on your shopping list?
   0=never, 1=infrequently, 2=occasionally, 3=frequently, 4=quite frequently
   SCORE_____
3. Do you select merchandise and place it in your shopping cart while waiting in line at the store?
   0=never, 1=infrequently, 2=occasionally, 3=frequently, 4=quite frequently
   SCORE_____
4. Do you come home with an item, only to find out later that you already have one or more of the same item (or a very similar item) at home?
   0=never, 1=infrequently, 2=occasionally, 3=frequently, 4=quite frequently
   SCORE_____

Add up your scores to see if you have reflex shopping tendencies.
TOTAL SCORE_____
   0–4 No reflex shopping tendencies
   5–10 Tendencies to be a reflex shopper
   11–16 You are a reflex shopper

Evasive Shopper

1. Do you find that spending money, even if you have to charge the purchase, lifts your spirits and makes you feel better?
   0=never, 1=infrequently, 2=occasionally, 3=frequently, 4=quite frequently
   SCORE_____
2. When you have a bad day at work or at home, do you go shopping?
   0=never, 1=infrequently, 2=occasionally, 3=frequently, 4=quite frequently
   SCORE_____

Figure 6-1
What Kind of Shopper Are You?—*continued*

3. Do you spend money because you are angry with your spouse or loved one?
   0=never, 1=infrequently, 2=occasionally, 3=frequently, 4=quite frequently
   SCORE_____
4. Do you spend more than you should on gifts for your loved ones and friends?
   0=never, 1=infrequently, 2=occasionally, 3=frequently, 4=quite frequently
   SCORE_____

Add up your scores to see if you have evasive shopping tendencies.
TOTAL SCORE_____
   0–4 No evasive shopping tendencies
   5–10 Tendencies to be an evasive shopper
   11–16 You are an evasive shopper

Avoidance Shopper
1. Do you genuinely dislike shopping?
   0=never, 1=infrequently, 2=occasionally, 3=frequently, 4=quite frequently
   SCORE_____
2. Do you comparison shop?
   0= quite frequently, 1= frequently, 2=occasionally, 3=infrequently, 4=never
   SCORE_____
3. When shopping for a specific item, do you carefully evaluate all of the items on the shelf before making your purchase?
   0=quite frequently, 1=frequently, 2=occasionally, 3=infrequently, 4=never
   SCORE_____
4. Can friends or salespeople talk you into buying an item?
   0=never, 1=infrequently, 2=occasionally, 3=frequently, 4=quite frequently
   SCORE_____

Add up your scores to see if you have avoidance shopping tendencies.
TOTAL SCORE_____
   0–4 No avoidance shopping tendencies
   5–10 Tendencies to be an avoidance shopper
   11–16 You are an avoidance shopper

FIGURE 6-1
What Kind of Shopper Are You?—*continued*

Extreme Shopper
1. Would you drive more than one mile out of your way to save less than $1?
   0=never, 1=infrequently, 2=occasionally, 3=frequently, 4=quite frequently
   SCORE_____
2. Do you comparison shop at a minimum of two stores before making a purchase?
   0=never, 1=infrequently, 2=occasionally, 3=frequently, 4=quite frequently
   SCORE_____
3. Do you get excited when you come across a great sale?
   0=never, 1=infrequently, 2=occasionally, 3=frequently, 4=quite frequently
   SCORE_____
4. Do you make your purchase decisions based on what is on sale?
   0=never, 1=infrequently, 2=occasionally, 3=frequently, 4=quite frequently
   SCORE_____

Add up your scores to see if you have extreme shopping tendencies.
TOTAL SCORE_____
   0–4 No extreme shopping tendencies
   5–10 Tendencies to be an extreme shopper
   11–16 You are an extreme shopper

Status Shopper
1. Do you wear only the latest clothing styles and brands every season?
   0=never, 1=infrequently, 2=occasionally, 3=frequently, 4=quite frequently
   SCORE_____
2. Do you go to discount stores?
   0=quite frequently, 1=frequently, 2=occasionally, 3=infrequently, 4=never
   SCORE_____
3. Do you purchase specific brands of clothing, health, and/or beauty products?
   0=never, 1=infrequently, 2=occasionally, 3=frequently, 4=quite frequently
   SCORE_____
4. Is it important to impress others with where you live, the brands and styles of clothing you wear, or the car you drive?
   0=never, 1=infrequently, 2=occasionally, 3=frequently, 4=quite frequently
   SCORE_____

> **FIGURE 6-1**
> **What Kind of Shopper Are You?**—*continued*
>
> Add up your scores to see if you have status shopping tendencies.
> **TOTAL SCORE**_____
>   0–4 No status shopping tendencies
>   5–10 Tendencies to be a status shopper
>   11–16 You are a status shopper
>
> *Excessive Shopper*
> 1. Do you buy things you do not need?
>   0=never, 1=infrequently, 2=occasionally, 3=frequently, 4=quite frequently
>   **SCORE**_____
> 2. Do you tend to spend excessive amounts of money on a hobby, collection, or a specific free-time activity?
>   0=never, 1=infrequently, 2=occasionally, 3=frequently, 4=quite frequently
>   **SCORE**_____
> 3. Is the money you spend on unnecessary or unplanned purchases causing financial problems or causing you to go into debt?
>   0=never, 1=infrequently, 2=occasionally, 3=frequently, 4=quite frequently
>   **SCORE**_____
> 4. Has your family and/or friends suggested that you decrease your spending?
>   0=never, 1=infrequently, 2=occasionally, 3=frequently, 4=quite frequently
>   **SCORE**_____
>
> **Add up your scores to see if you have excessive shopping tendencies.**
> **TOTAL SCORE**_____
>   0–4 No excessive shopping tendencies
>   5–10 Tendencies to be an excessive shopper
>   11–16 You are an excessive shopper
>
> Copyright © 1997, 1999 Frugal Publications, LLC

REFLEX SHOPPER

Have you ever purchased an item that you just had to have—only to find that a few days later it remained unopened, still in the bag from the store? This is a reflex purchase. Does this happen very often? If so, you are a reflex shopper. A reflex shopper makes purchases on impulse in a manner that can be compared to an involuntary action or response. This shopping trait is the most common of the six traits. Someone scoring highly with this trait will find it very difficult to resist the urge to buy an item that they desire. They feel a strong need for immediate gratification and frequently make unplanned, spontaneous purchases with no regard for their long-term needs or priorities. Most reflex shoppers seldom comparison shop for the best price.

Budget Coping Strategies for a Reflex Shopper

To cope with this trait, you must work on developing your self-control and self-discipline. Set clear priorities for spending based on your predetermined needs and goals. When confronted with the desire to purchase a specific item, carefully evaluate the price to determine if it reflects the best value for your dollar. Then, ask yourself the following questions:

- What is the true intent or objective in purchasing this item?
- Can this same objective be met in some other way? (Consider less expensive, more creative ways to fulfill this desire.)
- Can I do anything to pay less for this item?
- Can I buy this item or a similar item for less at another store?
- Will this purchase allow me to attain my personal goals?
- Is this item worth the expenditure of my time that it took to earn the money?
- Am I going to have to charge the purchase on a credit card? (If so, how long will it take me to pay off this expense, and what is the real cost when the interest charges are included in the total price?)

These questions will enable you to carefully evaluate a purchase and assist in developing self-control and the necessary willpower, so you can walk away from the item.

The desire to buy on impulse is a universal experience. The item is identified and immediately an urge wells up within us, "I want this," "I need this," "I must buy this." Depending on your shopping traits, this urge is stronger with some people than with others. The reflex shopper has the least amount of willpower to resist this powerful inner message. Too often this yearning is disguised as a perceived need, not a desire. Reacting with the speed of light, you begin to justify the purchase. As a result, some people have difficulty recognizing a purchase being made on reflex and impulse.

However, there is a way to recognize when this is happening, but it requires listening very carefully to your subconscious. Most of us have a mantra that we tell ourselves when confronted with such a purchase. This mantra surfaces because your subconscious has found it to be very effective in the past. Listen carefully to your thoughts, and you will hear it the next time you are tempted to buy something that you really do not need. When you hear it, the impulse purchase will be revealed for what it is, and you will immediately know to walk away. I know that my mantra is "buy it, you've had a rough week, and you deserve it." My subconscious began giving me this message when I was in high school, many years ago. My best friend and I used to stop by the local ice cream shop almost every Friday after school. We justified the purchase (and extra calories) because we "had a rough week and we deserved it!" Whenever I hear this mantra in my thoughts, I immediately know that my subconscious is trying to convince me to buy the item, so this is not a rational purchase decision. Therefore, I walk away from the item.

The perceived value of money varies from person to person. Twenty dollars to you may represent disposable income or pocket change, whereas it represents a week's worth of groceries to another. To manage our money more quickly and easily, most of us have (consciously or unconsciously) developed personal spending limits when making a single purchase. For example, one person may perceive the expenditure of $30 for a single item to be within his or her comfort zone. However, spending $50 is thought to be a significant amount of money, so it represents the upper limit of his or her comfort zone. As a result, he or she is more diligent in trying to pay less for an item that costs more than $50.

To control your reflex shopping tendencies, you must identify these purchase comfort zones. Determine the upper limit of your comfort zone. Then divide this figure in half. This is your "target amount." The target amount is significant because it represents the amount of money that you allow yourself to spend on impulse items. If, as in the previous example, $50 is the upper limit of your comfort zone, then $25 reflects your new target amount.

To deal effectively with your reflex shopping traits, you must make a commitment to this target amount. Anytime you are tempted to purchase an item that is equal to or greater than your target amount, you must stop and hold off on the purchase until you have priced the item in at least three places. Chances are very good that within the next few days or weeks, you will not only find the item at a lower price but you will find one that will better meet your needs or be of higher quality. This can greatly reduce excessive spending on reflex purchases.

EVASIVE SHOPPER

Evasive shoppers use shopping to evade the problems and everyday pressures of life. When bored, they go shopping. After a fight with their spouses or loved ones, they go shopping. Evasive shoppers frequently avoid sharing themselves and their time with loved ones. Instead, they share their money in the form of lavish gifts. After working a lot of overtime during the week, a husband with evasive shopping traits will bring home a gift or flowers for his wife. After being away all week on a business trip, a working mother with evasive shopping traits will bring home an expensive toy for her child to make up for her absence.

Budget Coping Strategies for an Evasive Shopper

To cope with evasive shopping traits, you must identify the source of stress that is causing you to seek relief at the checkout counter. Are you in a bad marriage? Do you hate your job? Are your teenage children causing increased stress and tension in your family? Are your money worries the cause of your anxiety? Review the self-help books available at the local library or bookstore to determine if there is one written to address the source of your stress. Seek out a support group in your area that addresses your concerns. Support groups located throughout the country address many different issues. These groups are usually free or, in some cases, may ask for a small voluntary donation. Yet, the support you receive from meeting and talking with other people with similar concerns and experiences is invaluable. If necessary, seek out professional help. Until you learn to deal effectively with the underlying problem, your evasive shopping will only add increased debt to your stress load.

To maintain control over your expenses, plan your purchases carefully and shop prudently for only those items on your list. Be creative and think in nonmonetary ways to show your affection during the holidays and other celebrations throughout the year.

AVOIDANCE SHOPPER

Avoidance shoppers genuinely dislike shopping. One of the main reasons they dislike shopping is because it evokes a feeling of helplessness. They feel helpless in controlling or reducing their expenses. As a result, they tend to procrastinate until the last minute. Only then do they go to the store with the primary intent of getting in and out of the store as quickly as possible. Consequently, they spend too much money because they did not take the time to compare prices or even plan their purchases. They buy a product based on the fact that they "might need it someday" and because they want to avoid the experience of having to return to the store at a later date to buy the item.

Many avoidance shoppers feel that they lack control in buying situations. They feel ill-prepared and overwhelmed. Salespeople and friends easily influence their purchase decisions. Many consider themselves to be too busy to shop wisely. They frequently justify their lack of planning and excess spending by claiming, "My time is too valuable to use it to comparison shop." They miss out on products that would better meet their needs because they do not take the time to carefully consider all of their options. Many have convinced themselves that a penny saved here and there doesn't really matter in the long run. Avoidance shoppers have frequently resigned themselves to the status quo.

Budget Coping Strategies for an Avoidance Shopper

Convincing an extreme avoidance shopper of the advantages of comparison shopping to save money with my words alone is improbable. Just like Dorothy in the *Wizard of Oz,* they need to find this out for themselves. Therefore, to cope with being an avoidance shopper, you must allow yourself to be open to considering new shopping methods and strategies. Give yourself permission to try new techniques. Remain open to finding new ways to save money. If possible, have your partner do all of the shopping until you have developed some effective shopping strategies. Unless, of course, your partner is an avoidance shopper too!

Because salespeople and friends can easily influence an avoidance shopper's purchase decision, shop alone until you become more skilled at resisting these pressures. If you must shop in a store with salespeople, dress very casually. Dressing in expensive clothing tends to attract salespeople.

Because shopping is such a dreaded activity, take steps to minimize the amount of time spent in a store by making your trip more efficient. Review the weekly newspaper advertisements and/or telephone the store to compare prices for a needed item. This takes only a few minutes of your time compared to driving to the store to comparison shop. Plan your purchases in advance, and shop only for those needed items. For example, plan your meals for the next seven days taking full advantage of items on sale at one grocery store. Then, write up a shopping list to include the items that are needed to prepare these meals. You will find that your shopping trip is more organized and efficient. You will also find that you save money. Do this weekly for an entire month. By comparing the amount of money you spent for groceries during the month that you planned your meals with a previous month, you will confirm the amount saved on your grocery purchases. The money you saved will serve to motivate you to continue to take control of your grocery bill and look for even more ways to reduce spending.

Anytime you are making a purchase of over $100, it is especially important to comparison shop. There can be significant price differences between similar products. To keep from spending too much for features you do not need, carefully consider how you plan to use the product. For example, if you are shopping for a new VCR, review various models and features. Do you need to have four heads or will two heads be sufficient. Do you need to be able to program the VCR, so you can tape a show while you are away? If you are like most people, you have probably never even figured out how to program your old VCR.

As an avoidance shopper, you must find the "joy of the hunt." Take control of the money you spend. Shopping is a battle that can be won by a well-prepared, efficient, self-disciplined shopper. The financial advantages of spending your money prudently are numerous because it is your hard-earned money that you are saving.

EXTREME SHOPPER

In many ways, extreme shoppers are the opposite of avoidance shoppers. They love to shop and save money! The main feature of this trait is the fact that extreme shoppers primarily focus their attention on the purchase of sale items. You will find them cheerfully waiting in line for a store to open the first day of a sale, running from yard sale to yard sale, and perusing outlet stores. An extreme shopper can also be referred to as a save-a-holic. In fact, everyone needs at least one friend who is an extreme shopper because they always know the best places to shop for the deepest discount. Many even report getting an emotional "high" upon finding a good sale.

Their main consideration in a purchase decision is the sale price, not the quality of the product or whether it will meet their needs. They are excited and satisfied to have paid $25 for a pair of shoes that had a regular retail price of $125. However, the extreme shopper needs to realize that they still spent $25 for a pair of shoes they did not need. Therefore, they did not save $100. In fact, they wasted $25 on a needless purchase.

Many extreme shoppers suffer from a form of denial. They deny the fact that they are spending excessively on superfluous items. Because they are saving money, they truly believe that their expenses are justified and perhaps even noble. They may drive several miles out of their way to save a few pennies. Great efforts expended to save money serve to further substantiate the expense and to motivate them.

Budget Coping Strategies for an Extreme Shopper

As an extreme shopper you must remain constantly vigilant of your tendency to rationalize a purchase because of its low price. Too often, an extreme shopper's focus is on the amount saved, not on the amount spent. Therefore, you must always remind yourself of the fact that you are, in fact, spending money. An extreme shopper could go broke saving money. Formally evaluate your needs and plan your purchases accordingly. Anytime you are presented with a purchase decision ask yourself, "Do I really need this, or am I only interested in it because it is on sale?" Work on determining your "enough point." Walk away from any purchases that will not help you attain your goals and personal life mission. (Refer to Chapter 2 for a further explanation regarding the identification of your goals and life mission). As an extreme shopper, it is best that you keep out of stores and away from sales unless you genuinely need something. The temptation to "save money" can be very strong. Work on developing your self-discipline and self-control to overcome your "urge to save."

To be a prudent shopper, you must take into consideration all of the expenses associated with the purchase. Do all of your weekly shopping on one day, and plan your trip carefully to use your time and gasoline efficiently.

STATUS SHOPPER

Status shoppers believe in displaying their perceived social prominence to everyone around them by purchasing only those items and brands that further this illusion. Most status shoppers lack self-confidence and exhibit a decreased sense of self-esteem. Having these expensive things around them enhances their self-importance and ego. They always wear the latest clothing styles from the most expensive stores and usually make it a point to relate this fact to everyone around them. Brand names carry a great deal of significance to a status shopper. Their purchase decisions are primarily based on whether or not it will impress others, not the price or the quality of the product. They frequently spend excessive amounts of money on items that are not needed and may never be used.

Budget Coping Strategies for a Status Shopper

To cope with your status shopping traits, consider the true meaning and purpose of your time here on earth as it relates to the style or brand of clothing you wear or the car you drive. What would you rather have written on your tombstone? "He wore some great Armani suits," or "The world was a better place because of him."

Is the world a better place because you use expensive styling products on your hair or because you wear clothing with a specific company logo imprinted across the front? The seeds of genuine self-esteem and self-respect do not germinate in the unfertile soil of material possessions. They can only take root and blossom in soil that has been fertilized with positive feelings of self-worth. To further develop your sense of self-worth, volunteer your time to a local nonprofit organization. Through these organizations you will be able to help make your world a better place. There are many nonprofit groups in every community desperately in need of volunteers to further their mission to help people. Contact a local nonprofit group to inquire about volunteer opportunities where you live. I assure you, they will be extremely appreciative of any time you volunteer. Within a short time, you will find that this new outlet for your time and energy allows you to grow personally and emotionally in many new and exciting ways.

Years ago, you used to be able to rely on specific brands to produce high quality, well-made clothing. In fact, many people willingly paid more for these brands because they knew that the articles of clothing would last longer and they were assured of getting genuine value for their dollar. Unfortunately, today there are few, if any, brands that constitute these characteristics. Brands today are primarily an indication of the price you pay for the article. A T-shirt with an Abercrombie & Fitch logo will cost more than one with a Gap logo. The first T-shirt does not wear better than the second shirt. Yet, many people buy the Abercrombie & Fitch shirt instead of the Gap shirt. Why? The answer is simple. Wearing the more expensive shirt is an indication that your status is higher than someone wearing the cheaper Gap shirt. Manufacturers gladly support this misguided effort to increase your self-esteem by increasing their prices (and profits) even more. Unfortunately, you are not getting anything of genuine value for your hard-earned money. The quality of the merchandise does not reflect the monetary cost.

The majority of clothing continues to be labeled by a small tag sewn into the neck seam of the garment. Therefore, you are the only person aware of the brand of clothing you are wearing. While it is true that other people evaluate your appearance, consider specifically what it is they perceive. Regardless of whether you are wearing articles of clothing from a brand-name store or items purchased at a discount store, the same criteria is used by most people to quickly evaluate your appearance and perhaps arrive at a conclusion. The manner in which you present yourself is almost always considered first. Are you standing up straight and tall in a confident manner or slouching and looking as though you are ashamed of your appearance. Is your clothing clean, neatly pressed, and in a state of proper repair? Are the articles of clothing coordinated for color, style, and appropriate for the season? In reality, a person could be wearing clothing purchased at a garage sale or a consignment store and be perceived to be dressed better than a person wearing an expensive ensemble from a specialty store.

Taking the time to properly coordinate your clothing goes a long way in enhancing your personal appearance. Instead of purchasing clothing by brand name, purchase well-constructed articles of clothing that can be worn with items you already own. Build your wardrobe, do not re-create it with every shopping trip. Conservative styles can be worn for several years. If you do find a particular brand that seems to be well-made and fits well for your body type, seek out locations where it can be purchased at a discount. Does the manufacturer have an outlet store? Visit consignment stores and discount stores. Watch for end-of-season clearance sales.

As a status shopper, you should base your purchases on your own defined needs, goals, and values and not on what you think will impress others.

EXCESSIVE SHOPPER

An excessive shopper does not shop to live; they live to shop. You can even recognize them in their cars. They are the ones with the "Shop till you drop" or "Born to shop" bumper stickers as they speed by on the way to the mall. It is quite common to find several brand new, never worn items (with the tags still hanging from the garment) in the closets of these shop-a-holics. Unfortunately, their love of shopping and lack of self-discipline causes them to waste their hard-earned money by purchasing things they really do not need.

Many of these people only exhibit excessive spending on specific items or in association with a hobby, collection, or other free-time activity. For example, they may have more than one hundred pairs of shoes or several thousand baseball cards.

Budget Coping Strategies for an Excessive Shopper

If your excessive shopping tendencies are primarily focused on a specific hobby or interest, evaluate ways to minimize the cost without depriving yourself of the joy you receive from these items. For example, if you enjoy making crafts as a hobby, seek out inexpensive crafts to make. Make inexpensive gifts for friends and families. Consequently, you can fulfill your desire to make crafts as well as provide gifts for those on your list.

If you shop as recreation, develop new hobbies, interests, and friends that do not involve shopping. Stay out of stores and malls. Volunteer your time for a nonprofit group within your community. You will receive a great deal of satisfaction and enhanced self-esteem in knowing that you are helping other people. Take up a new sport or begin an exercise program. Not only will you be developing a new interest, but you will also improve your health.

The shopping habits of an uncontrolled extreme shop-a-holic can lead to bankruptcy. If you think you are an extreme shop-a-holic, review the various self-help books in the local library and/or seek out a local support group. If you are unable to find the support necessary to modify or stop this behavior through these methods, you should seek the help of a trained professional psychologist or psychiatrist.

7

Give Me Shelter

For the average family, the monthly mortgage represents the single largest monthly expenditure. Whether you are looking for your first home or your retirement home, this chapter is a "must read" to reduce these expenses. Unless you are educated about the home buying process, you will be unable to make informed, sound decisions. Instead of purchasing the house of your dreams, this process could become a living nightmare.

SHOULD YOU RENT OR BUY A HOUSE?

Buying a home still represents a good investment in most parts of the country. Although there are exceptions in specific areas, the value of a home parallels or exceeds the inflation rate. The purchase of a home not only designates a place of residence but also represents a sound financial investment and tax advantage. In comparing the cost of buying a home with renting, the advantages become very clear. In the hypothetical example discussed in this section, we will examine the experiences of two families. Both families consist of a husband, a wife, and one child. Each household has an annual income of $40,000.

The Richards bought a 3 bedroom $100,000 house with a $10,000 down payment. They financed their $90,000 mortgage with a 9.25 percent fixed rate loan. We will assume an annual property tax rate of 1 percent and insurance of .4 percent (which are included in the monthly mortgage payment). They have a marginal tax rate of 15 percent. Their total mortgage payments over a 10-year period are $106,884. Assuming an annual appreciation rate of 5 percent, their home will be worth $163,884 after 10 years. (Of course, these figures do not represent any costs associated with maintenance and repairs.)

The bottom line: After 10 years, the Richards' $10,000 investment netted them $14,533 in tax savings and $63,612 in home equity.

The Cases decided to rent a house and invested their $10,000 in a 10-year Treasury bond paying 8 percent interest. By renting, they realized no tax benefit and spent a total of $106,551 to rent a two bedroom home for $425 a month for 10 years. We will assume a 5 percent annual increase in their rent to cover increases realized by the landlord for taxes, insurance, and so on.

The bottom line: Ten years later, the Case's investment of $10,000 in a Treasury bond netted them $9,307 after taxes were deducted.

Obviously, the Richards made the best financial decision by purchasing a home instead of renting. They realized more than $78,000 in tax savings and home equity. (Assuming an annual expenditure of $2,000 per year for maintenance and repairs, the figure would still be in excess of $58,000. Any *improvements* made in the home would cause the value of their home to further increase.) The remainder of this chapter will review the home buying process to help you make sound financial decisions and truly benefit from the joys of home ownership.

Through Careful Planning and a Little Knowledge You Will Net Big Financial Rewards and the House Of Your Dreams

Real estate agents, attorneys, and lending institutions have made the purchase of a house quite easy for the average buyer. However, buying a house should not be an impulse purchase. Before you open your first real estate book or visit your first open house, you must be certain that your credit is in good order and take steps to become educated about the home buying process. With proper planning, you can save thousands of dollars in the purchase of your home and prevent the need for costly repairs at a later date.

Separate Your Needs from Your Wants

Who wouldn't want to live in a five bedroom mansion? Living in a large, expensive home requires the monthly financial commitment of a mortgage, upkeep, taxes, insurance, and utilities. The beauty of a house quickly fades if every penny you and your spouse earn goes toward these expenses and does not allow for money to be put aside for the attainment of your personal goals or a comfortable standard of living. Worse yet, you cannot enjoy your home because you must work two jobs or work overtime to pay for the house.

Instead of buying the house of your dreams, buy the house of your needs! Carefully evaluate what you need to meet your physical and emotional needs. Although a one bedroom house might meet your physical needs, emotionally you would not feel satisfied or fulfilled. To some degree, our homes serve as monuments to our success. Buying a house to impress others is a waste of your hard-earned money because it exceeds your needs. This competitive attitude forces many to buy a house they really cannot comfortably afford. Buying the house of your needs will allow you to sleep comfortably at night secure in the fact that you can make the monthly mortgage.

The best way to determine your needs in a house is to formally write them on a sheet of paper. If the house is being purchased jointly, both partners should provide input into what they need. Draw a line down the center of a page of paper. On the left side of the line write the things you need in a house. On the right side of the line write the things you would like or desire. On a separate sheet of paper include those things that would be unacceptable. Use a pencil so items can be easily erased and moved from one area to another as you define your needs more clearly. This is an important step in finding your house. Now is the time to negotiate and resolve any conflicts regarding what is needed. As you write down your needs, keep in mind that each need carries a very real price tag that will cause you to pay more. Figure 7-1 illustrates the needs of the Richards family. The Richards family came to realize that it was not worth paying at least $10,000 more for a house with a formal dining room. Using the dining room once a year for a holiday did not represent a large enough need to them, so they moved this over to the right hand column. They felt that although it would be nice to have a walk-in closet in the master bedroom, good organization and the storage of out-of-season clothing would alleviate the need for a walk-in closet. Because they seldom have out-of-town guests, it seemed a waste of money to keep a guest room in their home just for this infrequent activity. Instead, they intend to buy a sleep sofa for their family room so guests will have a place to sleep.

The Purchase of Your Home Is a Personal Decision

In determining the house to buy, balance your need to feel successful with your need to provide financial security for your family. Too often, we decide on the size of our home (and mortgage) based on the maximum amount the bank will loan us. We go to the bank and complete the paperwork

> **FIGURE 7-1**
>
> *Things We Need in a House*
> 3 bedrooms
> ~~Guest bedroom~~
> ~~Walk-in closet in master bedroom~~
> ~~Formal dining room~~
> Eat-in kitchen
> Family room
> Deck or patio
> Fenced backyard big enough for our dog and kids to play
> 2 bathrooms
>
> *Things We Would Like to Have*
>
> Guest bedroom
> Walk-in closet in master bedroom
> Formal dining room
>
> Formal living room
>
> Guest bathroom
>
> *Things We Do Not Want in a House*
> Street with heavy traffic
> The most expensive house in the neighborhood

indicating how much we make and how much we owe. The loan processor inputs these figures into the magic computer and out pops a figure indicating how much the bank will loan us. We shop for a house based primarily on this figure. This process requires that we commit a significant amount of our income to the purchase of one item. It also makes us very dependent on maintaining our current income in order to pay our monthly mortgage.

HOW MUCH SHOULD YOU SPEND ON A HOUSE?

Lenders frequently use a housing expense ratio of 28 percent. This means that your total monthly mortgage payment (including principal, interest, taxes, and homeowners' insurance—PITI) should not be more than 28 percent of your gross monthly income. However, the amount you spend on a mortgage should be a personal decision, not one based on a calculation. Instead of spending the maximum amount your current combined incomes will allow, determine your monthly mortgage based on paying less than the amount for which you qualify. If both spouses are employed, base the purchase price on only one income. Reducing your monthly mortgage commitment allows you to have more money left at the end of the month. This additional money can be utilized to ensure your family's financial security. It can be invested for a personal goal, your child's education, or retirement.

If this figure will not buy the house of your needs, wait until you have set aside more money for a larger down payment. Increase your down payment until the monthly mortgage is within your comfort level.

How to Determine the Monthly House Payment

Your next step is to determine the total amount you can spend on a house based only on spending the previously determined amount each month. You will, of course, be working backwards. Most people determine the amount they can spend on a house based on the maximum amount they can borrow. They are then shocked to find out later that the monthly payments are too high.

How to Estimate Your Monthly Payment and Interest When Borrowing a Specific Amount of Money

A typical monthly mortgage consists of paying a portion of the loan principal, the interest, taxes, and insurance (PITI). Logically speaking, the longer the terms of the mortgage, the lower the monthly payment. That is why the majority of home loans are for 30 years instead of 15 years.

Refer to Figure 7-2 to determine the maximum purchase price for a house based on a specific monthly payment of the principal and interest. This table does not include the cost of insurance (homeowners and mortgage insurance) or property taxes. To calculate your monthly payment using this table, choose the interest rate first. Then multiply the figure listed in the column designating the desired length of your mortgage by the total amount to be borrowed (delete the last three zeros from the total amount borrowed). For example, if you wanted to borrow $95,000 at 9% interest for 15 years, the number 10.15 is listed in the 15-year loan column with an interest rate of 9%. To calculate your monthly payment to borrow $95,000, multiply 95 by 10.15. Your monthly payment for principal and interest alone would be $964.25. However, your payments would only be $764.75 each month if you borrow the same amount of money at the same interest rate but extend the length of the loan to 30 years (95 × 8.05 = $764.75).

You can also determine your monthly payment by using one of the many free mortgage calculators at the Frugality Network at Web site *www.frugalitynetwork.com/calculators.html.*

Figure 7-2

Interest rate	15-year loan	30-year loan	Interest rate	15-year loan	30-year loan
6%	8.44	6.00	10%	10.75	8.78
6¼%	8.58	6.16	10¼%	10.90	8.97
6½%	8.72	6.33	10½%	11.06	9.15
6¾%	8.85	6.49	10¾%	11.21	9.34
7%	8.99	6.66	11%	11.37	9.53
7¼%	9.13	6.83	11¼%	11.53	9.72
7½%	9.28	7.00	11½%	11.69	9.91
7¾%	9.42	7.17	11¾%	11.85	10.10
8%	9.56	7.34	12%	12.01	10.29
8¼%	9.71	7.52	12¼%	12.17	10.48
8½%	9.85	7.69	12½%	12.33	10.68
8¾%	10.00	7.87	12¾%	12.49	10.87
9%	10.15	8.05	13%	12.66	11.07
9¼%	10.30	8.23	13¼%	12.82	11.26
9½%	10.45	8.41	13½%	12.99	11.26
9¾%	10.60	8.60	13¾%	13.15	11.66
			14%	13.32	11.85

The Determination of Real Estate Taxes and Special Assessments

Real estate taxes are based on the value of the house. The more your house is worth, the more you will pay in taxes. Since taxes and special assessments are usually included in the monthly mortgage payment, they should be factored into your estimated monthly payment. Contact the tax office in the town where you are considering the purchase of a house. The tax office can also tell you which houses in the area are required to pay special assessments for sewers or other improvements. To keep your taxes low, you may be wise to steer clear of neighborhoods subject to the payment of these special fees.

Ascertaining the Cost of Insurance

Insurance rates are based on the replacement value of the house. Lenders require that a home be adequately insured as part of the loan agreement. Contact an insurance agent in the area to obtain an estimate for the annual cost of homeowners' insurance. Inquire about any special requirements for houses in the areas that you are considering. Some of the houses in a given town may be located on a flood plain and are required to carry flood insurance. An excellent way to pay less for homeowners' insurance is to shop around and compare prices for the same coverage between insurance companies. At this juncture of your home buying, you need only obtain an approximation of these costs for use in calculating your estimated monthly mortgage premiums.

When lending money for a mortgage, most lenders require private mortgage insurance (PMI) if the down payment is less than 20 percent of the property's appraised value. Paying the required down payment and alleviating the need for PMI insurance will save you thousands of dollars over the course of your loan. If you are paying less than 20 percent as a down payment, contact a mortgage lender to obtain an estimate for the cost of PMI insurance.

Saving for a Down Payment and Closing Costs

When purchasing a home, you will have several up-front expenses. The most costly of which are the closing costs and the down payment.

The required down payment amount varies with the type of loan and lender. In general, the down payment is 5, 10, or 20 percent of the sale price of the house. A larger down payment is more advantageous because it allows you to reduce the total amount borrowed. Consequently, the monthly payment and total interest paid will be less.

The purchase of a home requires the payment of closing costs. Closing costs are generally 3 to 6 percent of the sale price of the house, not the amount borrowed.

Plan to have the entire amount of your down payment and closing costs in place at least two months before applying for the mortgage. How can you come up with the money for a down payment? Reduce your living expenses. Live well below your means. Save. Save. Save. One of the primary objectives of this book is to provide specific ways to reduce your living expenses. By paying less for those necessities of daily living and eliminating those things that are not needed, you will have extra money at the end of each month. If necessary, take on a part time job or agree to work overtime and place every bit of this extra income into your house account.

Pay Off As Much Debt As Possible

As a general rule, your housing payment combined with your other monthly debt should be no more than 36 percent of your gross income. Lenders call this your debt-to-income ratio. If your debt-to-income ratio is higher than 36 percent, the lender will deny your mortgage application. The more debt you have to pay off each month, the harder it will be to save money for other goals, such as a vacation, a college fund for the kids, or retirement. Therefore, even though lenders will allow up to a 36 percent debt-to-income ratio, reduce your debt to the lowest possible amount before taking on the huge commitment of a 15- or 30-year mortgage.

Let's look at an example. Pam and Rick both work full time for a combined gross income (before taxes are deducted) of $50,000. Their housing expense ratio is $1,167 (i.e., 28 percent of their gross income). This represents the maximum amount that they can spend on their monthly mortgage. Their debt-to-income ratio is $1,500 (i.e., 36 percent of their gross income). Figure 7-3 represents the debt-to-income ratios and housing expense ratios for various gross incomes.

Get Your Credit Report in Good Shape

At least three months before you plan to apply for a house loan, review your credit report (and that of your spouse if the house is to be purchased jointly) to confirm that it is accurate and up-to-date.

Contact all three of the credit bureaus listed at the end of this section and request a copy of your credit report. You are entitled to a free copy of

Figure 7-3

Gross income	Housing expense ratio 28% of gross income	Debt-to-income ratio 36% of gross income
$20,000	$467	$600
$30,000	$700	$900
$40,000	$933	$1,200
$50,000	$1,167	$1,500
$60,000	$1,400	$1,800
$80,000	$1,867	$2,400
$100,000	$2,333	$3,000
$150,000	$3,500	$4,500

your credit report if the request is submitted within 60 days of being rejected for a loan, employment, insurance, or rental housing based on information in the credit report. If you are a resident of Colorado, Georgia, Maryland, Massachusetts, New Jersey, or Vermont, you are allowed one free report. Otherwise, you must pay a fee.

A lender will review your credit report to make a judgement regarding your character (willingness to repay), your capacity (ability to pay), and your collateral (the value of what you are buying) when deciding to grant you a loan. A credit scoring system is used in which you are assigned points based on each of several factors: monthly income, length of employment, occupation, whether you currently own or rent your home, how often you have moved, and your payment history. Some lenders have their own specific profiles. Consumers who fail to fit the lender specific profiles may not qualify or may qualify to borrow money but only if they agree to accept higher interest rates. Factors that seem to increase your score and therefore increase the likelihood of obtaining the loan include being employed in the same position for more than three years, owning your own home, and having a limit of three credit cards with a credit history of making all payments on time.

Some of the factors that cause lenders concern and lead to the denial of a loan include the following.

- One or more payments 60 days or more overdue and more than two payments 30 days overdue for revolving credit (i.e., credit cards) or installment credit (car loans)
- One or more past due rent or mortgage payments
- Recent credit inquiries
- Overextended credit
- Paycheck garnishments
- Liens
- Bankruptcy

Creditors also take into consideration the total number of credit cards issued to you and their credit limits, even if they have zero balances. Close out any credit cards that are not used. Obtain a letter from the credit card company confirming the closure of the account.

If inaccuracies are found, take immediate action to correct them. It takes time to resolve disputes. Before applying for a mortgage, your credit report should be in optimal condition. Problems on your credit report will slow down the process of getting a mortgage and may prevent your loan from being approved.

To correct a problem or inaccuracy on your credit report, consider the source. If you believe a company with whom you transacted business made an error, contact them directly. Provide the company with photocopies of any documentation that supports your claim: a copy of the canceled check, and so on. Once the problem is resolved, ask them to notify the credit bureau(s) listing the error and forward a copy of this letter to you for your files. You should also write a letter to the credit bureau(s) stating the error and how it has been resolved. Always include your name as it is listed on the credit report, your social security number, date of birth, and full address. If you feel the credit bureau has not resolved the manner in a prompt or fair manner, contact the attorney general in your state or the Federal Trade Commission in Washington D.C. or call them at (202) FTC-HELP.

Negative information can remain on your credit report for no more than seven years from the date of the last activity. Bankruptcies may be reported for 10 years.

Equifax
P.O. Box 740241
Atlanta, GA 30374-0241
Phone: (800) 685-1111
www.equifax.com

Experian (formerly TRW)
P.O. Box 2002
Allen, TX 75013-0949
Phone: (888) 397-3742
www.experian.com/icds/index.html

Trans Union Corporation
760 W. Sproul Road
Springfield, PA 19064-0390
Phone: (800) 888-4213
www.tuc.com

Pre-Qualification/Pre-Approval

Real estate agents and home sellers encourage homebuyers to go through the pre-qualification process or pre-approval process before looking for a home. A lender (mortgage company, savings and loan, bank, or credit union) will translate your finances into hard facts about the maximum amount you can spend on a home. Real estate agents can also pre-qualify you. However, I do not recommend that they be allowed access to this confidential financial information or be allowed to perform this service. Their knowledge of your personal finances can actually be used to your disadvantage in negotiating the price of the house. Go to a lender to be pre-qualified or pre-approved.

Pre-qualification is similar to generating a loan application, but no formal commitment is made on the part of the lender or homebuyer. The homebuyer provides copies of their credit report, earnings, savings, and debt for scrutiny by the lender. The lender then arrives at an estimate of the amount the homebuyers are qualified to borrow. This amount is based on the housing expense ratio and debt-to-income ratio previously discussed. If you have good credit and your expenses are in line with these ratios, there is little need to go through this formal process. You can gather the necessary information and determine your ratios while sitting at your own kitchen table. However, if you are uncertain about your ability to obtain a mortgage because of a questionable credit report, excessive debt, or simply do not want to do the math yourself, visit a local mortgage lender to undergo the pre-qualification process. There is usually no fee for this service, however, it can take anywhere from a few hours to a few days to receive a response.

The pre-approval process is much more detailed and goes deeper into the mortgage process. When pre-approving a buyer, the lender also contacts the buyer's employer, bank, and other financial institutions to verify all claims of earnings and assets. Upon acceptance for pre-approval, the buyer receives a letter stating that he or she has been pre-approved to borrow a specified amount of money.

The loan processor, employed by the lender, is an excellent source of information about mortgages and the housing market in your area. Too often, homebuyers meet with the loan processor and simply answer his or her questions to complete the pre-qualification or pre-approval paperwork. Most loan processors are more than willing to answer more in-depth questions. For example, ask them to estimate the monthly mortgage (PITI) for the total amount for which you have been pre-approved/pre-qualified. Then, ask them to recalculate the PITI if you paid $5,000, $10,000, or $15,000 less for the same house. They can determine various scenarios for you and assist you in finding a monthly mortgage that will best meet your goals. Ask them to calculate closing costs for the amount for which you have been pre-qualified or pre-approved. The lending institution is going to be your "partner" in the purchase of this house and as such, it has a vested interest in ensuring that you buy a good house that will appreciate in value and one that you can comfortably afford. Until your last mortgage payment is made, it is actually the lending institution that owns your home. Inquire about the value of homes and the history of the housing market in the area where you are considering purchasing a house. You may find that homes have been dropping in value in one area (because the ground water was recently found to be contaminated from a factory that closed 50 years ago) and appreciating in value in another area. The loan processor may even be able to tell you about some foreclosed homes in the area that are selling for well below their market value. Ask the loan processor for the name of one or two house inspectors that the lending institution uses or has found to be competent. (You will need to contact the inspector after you have found the house of your needs.) Lastly, ask for the name and phone number of the loan processor so you can call him or her if you have any further questions.

In theory, a buyer who has been pre-approved or pre-qualified (although to a lesser degree) has more credibility than one who has not undergone this formal process. However, in reality, a seller will most likely accept the highest offer for their home regardless of whether the buyer has been pre-qualified or pre-approved. Real estate agents encourage pre-approval as a means to ensure that you are a serious buyer and not wasting their time by showing you houses that you cannot afford. The potential also exists that the agent can use this information against you in negotiating the price of a house. Let's say you offered $85,000 for a house and the asking price was $92,500. You had evaluated the market in the area and believed that $85,000 was a fair price to offer for this house. However, you had previously told the real estate agent that you were pre-approved for $90,000. The agent was therefore aware that you had access to $90,000 to spend on this house. Chances are good that this real estate agent (who represents the seller, not the buyer) will inform the seller of the amount for which you have been pre-approved. The counter offer from the seller will most likely be $90,000. If, on the other hand you gave the real estate agent no indication of the amount for which you had been pre-approved/pre-qualified, your chances of having your initial offer accepted would be better. One should never let their opponent know their hand when playing poker. Telling the agent the amount of your pre-approval or pre-qualification is the same as showing your opponent your poker hand.

CHOOSING YOUR NEW HOME

Never underestimate the importance of the location of a house. Although the neighborhood may be acceptable to you, at some point you will sell your home, and the location may require that you dramatically reduce the price. Therefore, when looking for a home always be thinking—resale. Your choice in a home will affect your long-term finances positively or negatively. By taking the time now to properly research the area where your home will be located as well as the structural soundness of the house itself, you will ensure that you are making a sound investment.

You have already identified what you need in a home and the amount that you can comfortably afford. Now, you must geographically narrow down your search to specific areas, such as neighborhoods, developments, or parts of town. Locate those areas with houses within your price range, and then determine those that match your own character and style. Driving through a neighborhood can tell you a great deal. Are the yards well kept? Are the homes maintained or in need of paint? Do the stores, roads, or parks appear overcrowded? Are there an excessive number of cars parked on the street after work hours? Are there major highways or noise producing activities nearby? Go to the local library and read about the local politics. You might find that the town is building two new schools so the taxes will be rising dramatically. Ask the librarian if he or she can provide the school profiles for the area. This information will allow you to evaluate the size of the schools, the ratio of students to teachers, and the standardized test scores. The school profiles for many school systems can also be found on the Frugality Network Web site at *www.frugalitynetwork.com/school.html*. Even if you do not have any children, the quality of the schools could be an important factor in the resale of your house. You may want to narrow your search to homes in a given school district. Visit the town hall and ask the clerks if there are any plans for changes to the area. They may also be able to provide information regarding the history and trends seen in the population as well as expected changes. Stop by the police department and inquire about the crime rate. Is crime in a specific area increasing or decreasing? Identify the types of reported crimes: robberies, break-ins, murders, assaults, drug-related problems, and so on. The local Real Estate Board can provide information regarding real estate trends in specific areas and the prices of homes located in these areas. Are the prices of homes going up or down in the areas you are considering? Inquire into the reason for changes in property values and the history of these changes. Of course, you would prefer to buy a house in an area with houses that are, and have been, appreciating in value. Determine your route to work each day. Will you have to deal with heavy traffic and a long commute? Do you use public transportation? Is public transportation available within a reasonable distance?

Once you have narrowed down your search to a specific locale and price range, you are ready to begin house hunting in earnest. The Internet has made house hunting easier because many real estate firms have listed their homes for sale on their Web sites. Unfortunately, most do not provide the actual address of the home, so you must contact the realtor to secure this information. The Frugality Network provides links to Web sites listing more than 1 million homes for sale in the United States at *www.frugalitynetwork.com/housing.html.* You will also find homes listed in the real estate section of local newspapers, advertised on community bulletin boards, on television shows sponsored by a local realtor, flyers, and so on. Homes for sale by their owners are frequently advertised in local newspapers. On a regular basis, drive through your selected areas and watch for yard signs indicating "HOUSE FOR SALE." Frequently, a sign is placed in the yard before the house listing appears in the Multiple Listing Service of available homes. Homeowners selling their own homes frequently rely on yard signs as a primary advertising method.

The majority of homes are listed with realtors, so chances are you will be dealing with at least one realtor in the purchase of your home. Most often, buyers do not select an agent; instead, they acquire one when they stop by an open house or call regarding a specific home listed by the agent. The most efficient way to find the best home is to be very selective regarding your choice of realtors. An experienced realtor will be able to quickly locate a home that meets your stated needs. He or she will not waste your time showing you homes you cannot afford and will not try to convince you to buy a house that does not meet your needs. Contact the local Board of Realtors to obtain the name of realtors who have been working in the area for more than five years. Ask for references from friends, colleagues, and families among this list of experienced agents. Then, contact these agents at their offices to make an appointment to meet with them for an interview.

Through the interview process, you should try to ascertain if they would be able to meet your needs in finding a house. Use this time to evaluate their personal style, professionalism, honesty, personality, and knowledge. Do they seem to have a realistic understanding of the area? After using all these information sources, you should have developed a good understanding of the area based on your own objective, unbiased research. However, if an agent seems to be misrepresenting the facts, immediately cross him or her off your list. Do you feel comfortable with him or her? Is he or she telling you the truth or only telling you what he or she thinks you want to hear? Be up front with the agent in explaining exactly what you expect of him or her in your search for a house. Don't be afraid that you might seem too confrontational. A good, experienced agent will appreciate and respect you as a client if you go through this formal interview process. If necessary, screen several agents to find one who will be able to provide the level of service that will meet your needs.

Never forget that a real estate agent represents the seller. The seller compensates the agent by paying them a percentage of the selling price. (The national average commission is 6 percent). In fact, they are bound by a written contract to do everything possible to obtain the best price and terms for the seller. Therefore, the agent has a vested interest in ensuring that the house sells for as much as possible. Although this relationship may serve the seller well, it can (and frequently does) work against the buyer.

If you feel the need to have someone represent you in the search and negotiation for a house, hire a buyer's broker. This broker is bound by a written contract to protect your interests. The homebuyer pays a fee to the buyer's broker for his or her services. Because the buyer's broker receives no compensation based on the price of the home, theoretically he or she will be more committed to negotiating the lowest price.

Occasionally, a real estate agent represents the buyer as a buyer's agent. However, the commission a buyer's agent receives is based on a percentage of the selling price of the house. Consequently, some people find it difficult to trust a buyer's agent even though they are bound by a contract to represent the buyer.

Once you have chosen a seasoned realtor to work with, show them your list of items that are needed in a house as well as those factors to be avoided. Clearly define the geographical areas or school districts that you have identified as acceptable locations for your home. Together with the realtor you can review the houses listed for sale that meet these criteria with subsequent on-site visits to the ones you prefer.

Strategies to Buy the Best House for the Best Price

Optimally, a homebuyer purchases a home for their family residence and is able to sell it for a large profit at a later date. There are several strategies that a savvy homebuyer can employ to increase these chances.

- Buy a well-built house at less than its appraised value in a good neighborhood with good schools and escalating home values, and make some improvements that increase the value of the house.
- Buy a home that needs some TLC or is a "fixer upper" (provided the home buyer has the necessary skills to do the repairs themselves). A little paint and new carpet can dramatically increase the value of a home. Be conservative in the decorating style and choice of colors.
- Look for a house that is vacant and has been on the market for a long period of time—the seller may be highly motivated to decrease the price.
- Buy one of the least expensive homes on the block. The higher priced homes have a positive influence on the value of the less expensive houses and tend to make them go up in price faster than similar homes in less expensive neighborhoods.
- Buy a small house with a large enough lot and an architectural style that will accommodate being enlarged with an addition.
- Purchase a house that is subject to foreclosure.
- Buy a house at an estate sale, auction, or probate sale.
- Buy a multiple family home and rent out the extra apartments for added income. You may find that you are able to live in the home free because the rent you receive from the other apartments pays your entire mortgage payment.
- Buy a house from a highly "motivated" seller who wants to sell it quickly due to a job transfer, divorce, and so on.

Making an Offer

Once you have selected a house, you must make an offer to purchase. Research the selling price of comparable homes in the area to be better prepared to make a reasonable offer. The town clerk or Board of Realty can provide this information. Your realtor can also provide a comparative market analysis (CMA or "comps") listing the recent sales of properties in the neighborhood where you want to buy a home. This provides insight into the fair price of the house and provides an important clue about the value of your property from the perspective of an appraiser.

If several similar raised ranches in the area have sold for $87,000 to $90,000 within the previous six months and the raised ranch you are considering has a listing price of $97,000, you can be fairly confident that this house is overpriced and will probably not sell for the asking price. Another consideration is the fact that this house probably would not be appraised for the asking price. Based on the recent history of other similar houses selling for less, the house would be appraised for the same amount as these other houses (i.e., $87,000 to $90,000). If the house appraised for less than the selling price, you may have difficulty getting a loan. Therefore, you need to make a fair offer that will be acceptable to your lender.

If you have secured the services of a buyer's broker, the broker should be able to provide advice regarding the amount to be offered as well as any other terms and conditions that would be beneficial to you for inclusion in the offer. For example, you could include the stipulation that the home seller pay half of your points or provide additional money up front for the replacement of the carpet. An inexperienced homebuyer may not be aware that such contingency clauses can be added to the offer.

All negotiating must be in writing for it to be legally binding. Therefore, you can only submit a written offer to buy a house. This offer to purchase may also be called a contract-to-purchase, an offer, a binder, or earnest money agreement. Regardless of the nomenclature used, once signed by both parties, you are legally bound to the terms of the offer. A well-written offer protects the buyer and should be written with particular attention to detail. The preprinted offer to purchase contracts used by many real estate agents are written to protect the seller, not the buyer. Although you can use a preprinted form as a starting point, you should amend it as necessary to include all of your requested special contingencies. Everything with regard to the sale of a house (not just the price) is negotiable, so use this to your advantage and modify your offer accordingly. Each clause that makes the entire offer subject to or contingent upon its fulfillment is referred to as a "contingency." For example, the offer should be contingent upon your obtaining financing for the home, and the offer should have a specific time frame within which it must be accepted or rejected. It would be money well spent to have your attorney review and make any necessary modifications to the offer to ensure that your needs are addressed before the offer is submitted to the seller for his or her consideration.

Once your offer is prepared and properly signed, it is usually presented by the real estate agent to the seller. However, you, your attorney, or your buyer's broker can also present it personally. The buyer is usually expected to provide earnest money as an indication of the sincerity of their offer. Your realtor, attorney, or buyer's broker will recommend the amount customarily given as earnest money in your region. The earnest money is deposited in an interest bearing trust account or with a neutral third party (such as a title company, escrow service, or attorney acting as an escrow agent). Do not make the check out to the seller. If your offer is not accepted, the money will be returned to you. If your offer is accepted, the earnest money will become part of your down payment.

The seller now has the following options:

- Accept the offer as written, sign it, and make it a firm contract.
- Reject the offer. Upon the rejection of an offer, the seller cannot later change his or her mind and hold you to the terms of the offer.
- Provide a written counter offer with written modifications made to the offer. You are free to accept or reject this counter offer. You can even make your own counter offer.

With each change in terms, the other side is free to accept or reject the offer or counter it again. The offer only becomes a binding contract when both sides have signed the same document indicating their unconditional acceptance of the written terms as they appear on the document.

The party who pays for the items in the following list is frequently determined by local custom. However, you are free to negotiate this through your offer to purchase. By having the seller pay for as many of these items as possible, you can save even more money.

- Termite inspection
- Home inspection
- Survey
- Buyer's closing costs
- Points to the buyer's lender
- Repairs required by the lender
- Home protection policy (optional)

With a signed contract in hand, you must then get to work arranging for the financing of your mortgage.

FINANCING THE AMERICAN DREAM

Too often, the process of finding a mortgage is undertaken lightly with only a minimal effort made to find the lowest mortgage rate or best terms. Comparison shopping for the best mortgage will yield dramatic savings over the course of the mortgage. Paying only one-half of 1 percent more in the annual percentage rate results in spending thousands of extra dollars over the course of the loan for interest and a higher monthly mortgage payment. When looking for a mortgage, shop for the best loan, do not shop for the lender. Today, many lenders do not even retain the loans they make. They sell the loans on the secondary market to other lenders or quasi-governmental agencies, such as Ginnie Mae, Fannie Mae, and Freddie Mac. Therefore, if you are thinking about taking out a mortgage with your local bank because you like the bank, think twice. You may not have this bank as your mortgage holder for very long because your mortgage will probably be sold to another lender. The terms of the mortgage will impact your finances for years to come. Spending extra time now searching for the best loan will allow you to save thousands of dollars.

Your first step in shopping for the best mortgage is to become acquainted with the various types of mortgages and the terms that are used by lenders. This knowledge will enable you to shop with ease for the specific type of loan that will best meet your needs.

Lenders are becoming increasingly creative in the types of mortgages they offer. Homebuyers most frequently choose either a fixed rate mortgage or an adjustable rate mortgage because they provide the most economical way to buy a house. There are advantages and disadvantages to each of these loans. When determining which loan will be the most beneficial to you financially, carefully evaluate various factors including the interest rate, the length of time you plan to live in the house, the points paid to the lender, and the rate of inflation.

30-Year Fixed Rate

This mortgage spreads out the total amount borrowed (principal) over a 30 year period of time, so the monthly payments are lower than if they were spread out over a shorter period of time. The interest rate remains unchanged throughout the length of the loan. Because the loan is spread out over such a long period of time, you pay significantly more interest than compared to a shorter loan. However, the total amount of interest paid is deductible on your federal income tax.

15-Year Fixed Rate

This mortgage spreads the amount borrowed (principal) over 15 years. In exchange for a lower interest rate, the borrower pays a larger monthly payment. The interest rate is typically one-quarter to one-half percent lower than compared to a 30-year mortgage and remains unchanged throughout the life of the loan. Because a smaller portion of the monthly payment goes toward interest, the tax deduction is reduced. The main advantage to a 15-year mortgage is the dramatic savings in interest that will be realized during the life of the loan. When a $100,000 30-year 8 percent fixed mortgage is compared with a $100,000 15-year 7.75 percent fixed rate mortgage, the monthly payment for the 30-year mortgage is $242 less. However, you would save $94,726 in interest and pay off the mortgage 15 years earlier with the 15-year mortgage.

Biweekly Fixed Rate Mortgage

A biweekly mortgage is paid every other week instead of monthly. Consequently, 26 payments are made during the course of a year. This results in paying less interest and shortens the term of the loan from 30 years to 18 or 20 years. This payment schedule may be easier if you are paid biweekly. However, for some people it could cause difficulty in managing their money if they are paid monthly. The same objective can be met with a 30-year fixed rate loan by simply paying extra money toward the principal occasionally, so that at the end of the year this amount is equivalent to one extra mortgage payment.

Adjustable-Rate Mortgages (ARM)

An adjustable-rate mortgage differs from a fixed-rate mortgage in that the interest rate is not predetermined for the length of the loan. Consequently, the homebuyer must be willing to accept a degree of uncertainty regarding the exact amount of their monthly loan payment over the course of the loan. The interest rate for an ARM is tied to a designated index that is used to calculate the loan rate at the end of each adjustment period. This figure is usually determined by adding two to four percentage points to the index. The most common indexes used for ARMs are the one, three, and five year U.S. Treasury securities. Many people sign up for an ARM because the initial interest rate is generally lower than the traditional 15- or 30-year fixed mortgage rates. The interval between the rate changes is called the adjustment interval. Typically, the rate is adjusted every one, three, or six years depending on the index that is used. Others have an initial fixed rate for a period of three, five, seven, or even 10 years, after which the rate adjusts on an annual basis. The more short term the index that is tied to your ARM, the more volatile your payments. This can be advantageous if interest rates fall, but could require your monthly mortgage payments to increase dramatically if interest rates rise. It is frequently recommended that if you plan to be in your house for less than five years, you would probably benefit the most by paying the lower interest rate offered by an ARM when compared to a fixed-rate mortgage. If interest rates for fixed-rate mortgages are high, you may also benefit by getting an ARM, and then refinancing to a fixed rate when mortgage rates go below your ARM rate. However, if the interest rate of fixed-rate mortgages is low, an adjustable ARM is probably not the best option even if you are only going to be in your home for less than five years. When negotiating the original mortgage, ask if the ARM can be converted to a fixed-rate mortgage. This will allow you the option of locking into a lower rate when the rates of fixed-rate mortgages become favorable. Most ARMs provide limits or caps on large rate increases or decreases. During a time of escalating interest rates, caps protect the borrower from extreme increases in their monthly payments.

Do not agree to an ARM without payment cap limits and lifetime caps on interest rates.

- A lifetime cap limits how much the interest rate can rise during the term of the loan.
- A periodic rate cap limits the amount your payments can rise from one adjustment period to the next.
- A payment cap limits the amount a payment can rise over the life of the loan. Even if the underlying index rises substantially, your payment can only increase to the payment cap limit.

Beware, some ARMs come with a prepayment penalty. If you sell your home before the mortgage is paid off or refinanced your home, you would be required to pay this additional fee if your ARM includes a prepayment penalty.

Determine the Annual Percentage Rate (APR)

Compare interest rates between mortgages by using the true annual percentage rate (APR) of the loans you are considering. Although lenders may use a variety of methods to state the interest rate, by law they are required to give you this standard figure.

Points

Points are charged by the lender to originate the mortgage. They are paid at the time of closing to the lender. One point is equal to 1 percent of your loan amount. Some lenders will charge more points but a lower interest rate, whereas others will charge no points and a higher interest rate. The payment (or nonpayment) of points must be factored into any comparison of mortgages. To compare mortgages with varying points and interest rates, consider the payment of one point as being equivalent to an additional one-eighth of 1 percent of the stated APR interest rate of the mortgage over a 30-year loan. Therefore, a 9 percent 30-year fixed-rate mortgage with no points is equivalent to an 8.5 percent fixed rate loan with four points. Some lenders will allow the payment of discount points by the borrower to reduce the interest rate of the loan. Discount points are 1 percent of the amount borrowed. Within limits set by the IRS, points are usually tax deductible in the year the house was purchased. At the Frugality Network, you will find links to free calculators for your use in comparing mortgages with varying points and interest rates, *www.frugalitynetwork.com/calculators.html*.

Fixed Versus Adjustable Rate Mortgage (ARM)

To determine whether a fixed or adjustable rate mortgage is best for you, perform a side-by-side comparison of the features of the best fixed-rate loan you can find and the best ARM loan. For each loan to be considered, write down the following information.

- Interest rate
- Annual percentage rate (APR)
- Length of the loan
- Points
- Discount points
- Index rate*
- Initial adjustment period*
- Years before the first adjustment*
- Interval between subsequent adjustments*
- Maximum increase per adjustment period*
- Lifetime cap on the interest rate increase*

(* = for ARMs only)

To make this comparison more accurate and less time consuming, use one of the online calculators at The Frugality Network Web site, *www.frugalitynetwork.com/calculators.html*. Here you will find various free calculators to compare fixed- and adjustable-rate mortgages. These calculators compute the total amount you would pay for the house over the course of the fixed-rate loan as well as the best and worst case scenario for the ARM. They will also determine your total interest payments, your first month's payment, and your last month's payment.

Assumable Mortgage

When the homebuyer assumes the payment of the seller's mortgage, it is called an assumed mortgage. Not all mortgages can be assumed. Lenders commonly write a clause into the mortgage contract indicating that it is not assumable. The buyer benefits financially because there are minimal closing costs associated with assuming a mortgage when compared to obtaining a new mortgage. This type of financial transaction is especially attractive to a buyer when the interest rate on the assumable mortgage is lower than the current market rate. However, the buyer must pay the seller the difference between the remaining balance of the mortgage and the selling price of the house (i.e., the equity in the home) at the closing.

Partial or Full Financing by the Seller

On occasion, the seller of the home is willing to provide financing to the buyer. The seller and the buyer draw up a formal written contract regarding the interest payment, length, and other terms. The homebuyer makes monthly payments to the seller instead of the bank. The loan is secured by the property. Sellers occasionally offer this type of financing when they have an assumable mortgage.

Finding the Best Mortgage

After you have determined the type of loan that will be the most beneficial to your financial situation, it is time to begin your search in earnest for the best mortgage. Various institutions provide money for private home mortgages: savings and loans, savings banks, commercial banks, credit unions, mortgage bankers, and mortgage brokers. Many newspapers publish a list of the interest rates for mortgage lenders in the area. Remember, when looking for a mortgage, shop for the best loan, not the lender. The lender does not have to reside in the same city or county or state. Many lenders will loan money to homebuyers in another state. Therefore, you would be astute to shop for a lender online because you just might get a better rate. The Web site provided by Intelligent Life Corporation, *www.bankrate.com*, posts the most recent mortgage interest rates from over three thousand five hundred lending institutions.

Lenders not only offer traditional loans but also provide loans guaranteed by the FHA (Federal Housing Administration) or the VA

(Veterans Administration). Through an FHA or VA loan, a low-income or medium-income family can obtain a low interest mortgage with little or no money down. If you or your spouse is a veteran, consider a Veterans Administration (VA) loan, which requires no down payment and a fixed-rate with a long repayment period.

Look for Less Publicized Sources of Mortgages

You may be surprised at the various sources of mortgages that you will find if you simply do a little extra research. For example, the USDA (United States Department of Agriculture) Rural Housing Service has various programs available to help low-income and moderate-income rural residents purchase a home. Your state may also sponsor programs with below market mortgages. Keep your eyes open for these little known sources. Sometimes, you will find a source that is only available for a brief period of time or on a first-come, first-served basis.

FHA guaranteed loan:
Housing Counseling Clearinghouse
P.O. Box 10423
McLean, VA 22102-8423
Phone: (800) 217-6970
www.hud.gov

VA Loan
Veterans Affairs Home Loan Program
Contact your local VA regional office
www.homeloans.va.gov

The USDA Rural Housing Service
Contact your local USDA Rural Development office for more information
Call the Loan Administration (314) 206-2700, 7:00 A.M. to 5:00 P.M. central time, Monday through Friday
www.rurdev.usda.gov

State sponsored loans:
Call your state department of consumer affairs to determine if any loans are currently available.

Once you have determined the type of loan, (15-year fixed, 30-year fixed, or ARM), that would best meet your needs, it is time to contact the lenders offering the best mortgage rates and terms. The intent of this phone conversation or meeting is to begin to refine your choice of lenders and ultimately find the one to which you will submit an application for a loan. Discuss with the lender the details of the mortgage, confirm that your understanding of the advertised offer is correct, and ask about anything in your situation that might cause your loan to be rejected. (For example, the loan you're considering may require a 20 percent down payment and you only have a 10 percent down payment). Confirm how long the currently advertised rate is guaranteed after the application is submitted. The following list contains specific information you should obtain regarding each mortgage:

- Name, address, and phone number of lending institution
- Date contacted
- Period of time interest rate is guaranteed while the loan is processed
- Type of mortgage: Fixed-rate or ARM
- Length of loan
- Interest rate
- Annual Percentage Rate
- Required down payment
- What are the qualifying guidelines?
- Estimate of closing costs
- Is there a prepayment penalty?
- Discount points
- Origination points
- Range (the minimum and maximum amount loaned)
- Is the loan application fee refundable if you change your mind?
- ARM: Index rate
- ARM: Initial adjustment period
- ARM: Years before first adjustment
- ARM: Interval between subsequent adjustments
- ARM: Maximum increase per period
- ARM: Lifetime cap on interest rate increase

Comparing Apples to Apples

The easiest way to compare mortgages is to use the APR. The APR is the actual cost of your mortgage for a one-year period of time. The APR reflects the impact of the origination fees, points, and mortgage insurance by including them in the loan rate as though these charges were spread out over the length of the loan. Therefore, comparing the APR for two 15-year or 30-year mortgages will give you a fairly accurate side-by-side comparison.

At the Frugality Network Web site, *www.frugalitynetwork.com/*, you will find a variety of free calculators to use in comparing mortgages. Compare fixed rate with adjustable rate mortgages. Compare mortgages with different points and interest rates.

Filling Out a Loan Application

Once you find the best mortgage, contact the chosen lender to make an appointment for the completion of the formal loan application. The lending agency will provide a detailed list of the documents you should bring with you to the interview.

When submitting your loan application, the lender will most likely collect specific fees. The following list contains some of the commonly required fees:

- Appraisal fee: Approximately $350
- Credit report fee: Approximately $50
- Flood determination fee: Approximately $20

The lender will require that various inspections and surveys be performed on the house. As the potential homeowner, you should take an active part in this process because it provides a great deal of information about the house that you are about to buy. The home inspection and appraisal can have an additional, more dramatic implication. If the house does not meet your guidelines when it is inspected and appraised, (this stipulation should have been included in the offer contract) you can back out of the contract and not be legally obligated to purchase the home.

Ask the loan originator for a written "good faith estimate" of closing costs. Review this list with him or her to determine if you can "opt out" of any of the services. For example, if you are not in a hurry, you may be able to opt out of having your documents sent via overnight carrier. Your costs will be less if they are sent by regular mail. Be alert to any unusual or vague charges. Many mortgage programs include "junk fees." An alert homebuyer can spot them and should be able to get them eliminated or reduced. Review the "preparing for the closing" section for a complete list of customary closing costs.

Home Inspection

Unless you are skilled in the evaluation of a home, having your home inspected by a qualified home inspector is money well spent. It may also be a requirement of the lender. Omission of a home inspection is comparable to buying a used car without driving it and having it checked out by a good mechanic. A complete inspection includes a visual examination of the building from top to bottom. The inspector evaluates and reports on the condition of the structure, roof, foundation, drainage, plumbing, heating system, central air-conditioning system, visible insulation, walls, windows, and doors. The inspector does not "pass" or "fail" a building, he or she simply describes the condition of the building and any major repairs or replacements that he or she feels are necessary. You must carefully review the written inspection report. If the inspection reveals that previously unnoticed repairs are needed, depending upon the terms of the offer to purchase contract, you may be able to have the seller repair them at his or her expense. If your budget is tight, or you don't want to pay for the necessary repair work that will be required at some future date, you may decide to forego the purchase of the house. Provided the contract was written with an "escape clause" if the property did not meet with your expectations upon completion of the inspection, you will not be obligated to purchase the house.

If possible, try to be at the house when the inspection is performed and personally talk with the inspector regarding his or her findings. You can learn a great deal of helpful information about the house from the inspector. For example, the inspector may tell you that the heating system is in good condition and should not need to be replaced for five to eight years. However, the shingles may appear to be those that were originally placed on the house when it was built 25 years ago and should be replaced within the next one or two years. Depending on the size of the house and type of shingles, re-roofing a house can cost thousands of dollars. This unbiased information can be invaluable in planning for upcoming home repairs.

Homebuyers frequently ask a realtor to recommend a home inspector. However, this may not be the best referral source because the realtor has a vested interest in having the house pass the inspection. Consequently, he or she may suggest someone who does not perform a thorough inspection. You need to have a high-quality inspection performed by a competent, trained person. Ask for a referral from friends, coworkers, and relatives. Contact the home inspectors in your area to inquire about their experience, training, and credentials. Lastly, contact your local Better Business Bureau to learn if they have had any complaints filed against any of the home inspectors you are considering.

Property Survey

A survey is performed to verify the boundary lines of the property and determine if there are any encroachments onto your property by your neighbor's buildings and the location of any easements. Knowledge of your property lines may come in handy at some future date if you want to put up a fence or build an addition onto your home. Try to be present for the survey or inquire regarding the method of marking the property lines, so you can quickly identify them, if needed, in the future. The surveyor can also tell you about any easements that are placed on your property by the city, town, county, or state.

The Appraisal

An appraisal is required by the lender to determine the current value of a property. The appraisal of the property you desire to purchase is as important as your credit history in obtaining a mortgage. It is also a critical factor in determining how much of a mortgage the lender will approve. The lender usually chooses the appraiser, but the buyer pays for the appraisal. If the appraisal indicates that the value of the property is less than the amount of the mortgage, you will be refused a mortgage or offered a smaller mortgage. This would require that you come up with a larger down payment if you still want to buy the house. Of course, buying a house for more than its value could be compared to paying more than the sticker price for a new car.

Title Insurance

Title insurance guarantees against errors in the title search and ensures that there are no defects, liens, or encumbrances on the property that may affect your rights of ownership, possession, or use of the property. It also insures against forgery, fraud, missing heirs, or divorce actions. If the previous owner did not own the home very long, you may be able to get a lower rate on your title insurance if the insurer agrees to reissue the previous insurance, and if there have been no claims against the title since the previous title search was performed. Contact the seller to determine the name of their title insurance company, and then contact the company directly to inquire about this option. Frequently, both the seller and buyer obtain title insurance. You can save money if you use the same title insurance firm as the seller. Because the insurer will need to research the property for both you and the seller, be sure to ask for a discount.

Private Mortgage Insurance

The amount of mortgage insurance required by a lender is based on the amount of down payment as it relates to the appraised value of the house. If you pay 15 percent of the appraised value of the house as a down payment, you will pay less for mortgage insurance than if you pay only 10 percent down. The fee charged for mortgage insurance is a percentage of the amount borrowed. However, frequently the percentage rises as the amount of the down payment decreases. For example, you may be required to pay .078 of 1 percent of the amount borrowed if you had only a 10 percent down payment. If you put 15 percent down, you will only have to pay one-half of 1 percent.

Note, if you are seeking an FHA loan, VA loan, or other governmental loan, you will be required to get mortgage insurance if your down payment is less than 30 percent of the appraised value of the loan.

Do not take out mortgage insurance unless the lender requires it. This insurance benefits only the lender. Therefore, the lender has an expressed interest in its purchase and maintenance. If you are paying more than 25 percent down and a private lender continues to insist that you carry it, perhaps it is time to shop around for a better mortgage from another lender.

Homebuyers are able to avoid this expense by paying the minimum required down payment at the time of purchase.

Attorney Fees

Most lenders require that an attorney review the closing papers prior to the closing and be present at the closing. The expense for the lender's attorney is included in the closing costs. Many states require that an attorney represent a homebuyer in the purchase of a house. You can save hundreds of dollars by choosing an attorney to represent you who is also acceptable to the lender, negating the need for two attorneys. Ask the lender to provide a list of acceptable local attorneys. Contact these attorneys to discuss their usual and customary fee for a real estate transaction. This information is usually given over the phone and will allow you to comparison shop for the best price. Talk to friends, relatives, and coworkers to inquire about any personal experiences they have had with any of the attorneys on the list. This too will assist in making your final decision. Meet with the attorneys you are considering to discuss any concerns or problems you anticipate and obtain a clear understanding of their role in the pending real estate transaction. Discuss with the attorneys what you expect of them and come to a clear mutual understanding regarding fees before you agree to have a specific attorney represent you.

CHOOSING A CLOSING DATE

Because mortgage loans are due on the first of the month, you will be required to pay interest from the day you close on the loan until the end of the month. By closing the loan on the last day of the month or near the end of the month, you will reduce closing costs because you can avoid or greatly reduce the amount of prepaid interest you will be required to pay.

The closing date must be prior to the expiration of your loan commitment. Allow ample time for the completion of any inspections, repairs, and the processing of the loan.

Preparing for the Closing

At the closing, you will sign legal documents and pay the balance of your down payment, closing costs, and escrow fees.

The documents you will sign fall into two basic categories: the agreement between the lender and the buyer and the agreement between the seller and the buyer. The lender agreement includes the terms and conditions of the mortgage, whereas the seller agreement formally transfers the ownership of the property.

Contact the closing agent for your mortgage and ask to review the settlement form *before* the closing. They should have this information available for you to review one business day before the closing. Carefully review all closing costs on the settlement form that will require payment. Compare this final list of closing costs with the "good faith estimate" you received from the lender when the original application was made. Question any changes or additions. Recalculate all figures to confirm that no computation errors were made. Confirm that you are not being double charged for some items that you already paid. If, for example, you already paid the loan origination fees, bring the receipt or other documentation to the closing so this amount can be deducted from your closing costs.

Closing costs include numerous fees associated with obtaining a mortgage and transferring the ownership of the property. These fees are paid at the time of closing. The seller may pay some of these fees based on the final agreement negotiated in the sales contract. Closing costs are usually 3 to 6 percent of the sales price of the house. For a $100,000 house, expect to pay closing costs of $3,000 to $6,000.

The following list contains some of the fees traditionally included in the closing costs:

- Balance of down payment
- Credit report
- Insurance fees
- Inspections
- Recording fees
- Lender's attorney fees
- Documentary stamps on new note
- Loan application fees
- Title search
- Property appraisal
- Survey
- Transfer taxes
- Buyer's attorney fees
- Origination fees on mortgage
- Escrow account balances and prepaids (taxes, insurance, etc.)

Frequently, these fees are paid with a personal check. Contact the closing attorney to confirm if a certified or cashier's check is required and to whom the check should be made payable. Plan to pay for discount points and the loan origination fees with one check. Other closing costs should be paid in a separate check. This will clearly segregate these prepaid interest expenses from the other nondeductible closing costs to facilitate their exclusion from your taxable income when you complete your taxes.

Escrow

Your lender may require that you put aside money at the time of closing to prepay a portion of your insurance and taxes. This money will be placed in a special escrow account until it is needed for the payment of these fees. Lenders frequently collect one-twelfth of the annual premiums along with the mortgage principal and interest each month. When the payment is due, the lender forwards the money that has been held in escrow to the appropriate payment address.

The Closing

At the closing, you sign the papers, pay the closing costs, escrow, and remaining down payment. If you have used the information contained in this chapter of the book wisely, you will walk away with a house you can comfortably afford for many years to come. Congratulations on a job well done!

8

Stretching Your Grocery Dollars

In this chapter you will learn how to stretch your dollars and slim down your grocery budget. By using a few basic techniques, you will not only spend less money, but also less time shopping and preparing healthy, appetizing meals for your family. You will be amazed how easily you can reduce the amount of money you spend for groceries without making your family feel deprived.

MEAL PLANNING

The most effective way to dramatically reduce the amount of money spent on groceries is also the easiest and most efficient use of your time. Plan your meals in advance and purchase those items needed to prepare those meals. Sound simple? It is. Too often, the evening meal is planned immediately after work while walking the aisle of the grocery store or while standing before the counter at the local pizzeria. Invariably, you do not leave the store or restaurant without spending at least $20. This process is frequently repeated several times a week. Sound familiar?

By planning my menus using the technique I call the Frugal Meal Planning Method, I was able to reduce our grocery bill by 50 percent. I developed this technique more than 16 years ago, and it has consistently worked well in keeping down our food expenses.

Planning your meals in advance does not take more time. Calculate the time you spend on unplanned trips to the grocery store each week. Include in this figure the amount of time spent going to fast food restaurants or delis (because you had nothing to eat in the refrigerator). I believe you will find that your disorganization is costing you a great deal of time. I would imagine that you are losing one or two hours each week on these activities. Planning my meals takes only 20 to 30 minutes per month. In fact, in this time, I can plan four weeks worth of meals using the Frugal Meal Planning Method. In one hour, I purchase all of the required food. Therefore, in one hour and twenty minutes, I plan all of our meals and purchase all of the food needed for the entire month.

Menu Cards

The main component of the Frugal Meal Planning Method is the menu card. Although you can successfully plan your meals without menu cards, I have found that they make the process of choosing meals more efficient. They also facilitate my ability to provide a more diverse diet for my family.

Make a menu card for each main dish recipe using a 3 × 5 inch file card. Print the name of the dish on the top of the card. Ingredients and quantities are listed next. (Do not rewrite the recipe—the ingredients are listed so you can develop a shopping list.) Include only those items you do not normally keep on hand. For example, I always have flour, sugar, ketchup, mustard, oil, margarine, milk, salt, pepper, and various herbs and spices. Therefore, I do not include these ingredients on my menu cards. Next, write the name of the cookbook and page number where the recipe can be found for the given dish. In the top-left corner, indicate the main protein source of the recipe (poultry, fish, pork, meat, vegetarian, bean, eggs, etc.). In the upper-right corner indicate if the dish freezes well. When preparing a dish that freezes well, I frequently double the recipe. The second dish is frozen for a night when I am too tired to cook. Refer to the sample menu card in Figure 8-1 for Turkey Tetrazzini.

File the menu cards in a 3 × 5 inch file card box with dividers for each protein source. For example, chicken and turkey menu cards are filed behind the poultry tab.

It *does* take time initially to set up your menu cards. In return, however, you will spend less time at the grocery store. Review cookbooks to write up a card for each recipe your family enjoys. You can rewrite an entire recipe on the menu card, but I find this to be too time consuming. Referencing the

> **FIGURE 8-1**
>
> **Sample Menu Card**
>
> Poultry   Freezes well
>
> *Turkey Tetrazzini*
>
> 1 pound of turkey (2 turkey legs)   8 oz. spaghetti
> 1 cup chicken/turkey broth   ¾ cup parmesan cheese
> 1 can mushrooms or 5 fresh mushrooms
> celery salt, paprika, nutmeg
>
> The Frugal Gazette, Volume 1, Issue 2

cookbook and page number takes less time. Recipes from newspapers or magazines can be cut out and pasted onto a 3 × 5 inch menu card. Once set up, it takes only a few minutes to plan a two week menu.

To reduce food expenses, plan your meals by choosing main dishes using the following suggestions.

- Choose only inexpensive main dish recipes for your menu card file.
- Plan more than one dish from a single poultry item, roast, ham, and so on. If you are planning to make Turkey Tetrazzini using turkey legs, use the bones to prepare Turkey Noodle Soup later in your menu cycle.
- Plan your menus based on grocery store sale items as well as what you currently have on hand.
- Prepare dishes with meat used in the dish, not as the main course. For example, you would need two and a half pounds of ground beef to prepare hamburgers for a family of four. With two and a half pounds of ground beef, you could make one lasagna, one cheeseburger casserole, and one taco casserole using three quarters of a pound of beef in each dish.

The Seven Steps of The Frugal Meal Planning Method

1. Review the items in your refrigerator, freezer, and kitchen cabinets to determine what you currently have available to use in preparing meals. Do you have any fresh fruits, vegetables, unfrozen meat, fish, or poultry that will spoil?

2. Review the weekly grocery store advertisements to determine what is on sale.
3. Go through your menu cards and choose meals for the next 7, 14, 21, or 28 days. Make your choice of meals based on the weekly specials at the grocery store as well as what you currently have available in your cabinets, refrigerator, and freezer. Maximize the use of previously purchased food when planning your menus.
4. Develop a shopping list based on your menu needs. Review the ingredients and quantities listed on each of your chosen menu cards. Add needed items to your shopping list. Do not forget to include vegetables, fruits, and bread to your list to ensure that you will be serving well-balanced meals. Be frugal and very specific when preparing your shopping list. For example, when reviewing her menu cards, Alyssa found that she only needed one potato for the next two weeks. At the store, she found that she could buy a single potato for 29¢ (if purchased by the pound for 69¢ per pound). However, she was tempted to buy a five-pound bag of potatoes for $1.59 because the price per pound was significantly less. However, only one potato was needed and the remaining four and a half pounds of potatoes would have gone to waste. She would have spent $1.30 too much. Her most frugal option was to buy the single potato for 29¢.
5. Go grocery shopping for the items on your list.
6. Daily, review the preselected menu cards to choose the main dish for the evening meal. Prepare dishes made with fresh foods first to prevent them from becoming spoiled. Refile the menu card in the menu card file box after the dish has been prepared.
7. When planning meals for the next menu cycle, carry over any remaining, unused cards. After all, you still have the food that was purchased to prepare the dish. For example, if 14 menu cards were selected two weeks ago, but your family ate leftovers one night and ate out on another night, you would have two cards left over. These two cards should be added to the menu for the next two weeks. Therefore, you will only need to choose 12 more menu cards to make the following two week (a total of 14 meals) menu complete.

When I double a recipe in chain cooking, (chain cooking is discussed below) the extra dish is frozen for future use. To be certain this dish isn't forgotten, I make a separate menu card indicating the name of the dish, the date it was initially prepared, and the location. This menu card is placed in the menu card file under the "Frozen Prepared Foods" tab, so I can use it in a future menu cycle.

The Frugal Meal Planning Method can easily be modified to meet your specific dietary needs. For example, because my kids take their lunches to school, I purchase lunch supplies to last the menu cycle. Cookies are baked every two weeks and then frozen for inclusion in their lunches. I freeze a two-week supply of lunchmeat and bread. Even milk can be frozen for up to 6 months. Every Sunday morning, we eat a large family breakfast, so I include breakfast menu cards to plan this meal as part of my menu cycle as well.

CHAIN COOKING

Chain cooking is a term given to a cooking method practiced by many home cooks. When chain cooking, extra food is prepared to use in another dish or extra dishes are prepared for future meals. Most often, it is the main dish that is prepared in advance and frozen, but side dishes and desserts can also be prepared using this method. Chain cooking can dramatically reduce the time, energy, and money spent on groceries and food preparation.

Chain cooking can be practiced in several ways:

- Double a recipe and serve half for supper the night it is prepared. Freeze the extra dish for another night's meal. Double the recipes nightly for the first two weeks of the month, and eat the frozen dishes the last two weeks of the month. It takes very little extra time to double a recipe.
- Prepare multiple recipes with similar ingredients. For example, chain cook several Italian dishes that contain spaghetti sauce as a basic ingredient.
- Prepare a variety of dishes at one time and freeze them for future meals. An entire month's worth of meals can be prepared on a single day. This is also called once-a-month cooking.

CHAIN COOKING TIPS

- Freeze family-tested recipes. It's a waste of time and money to double or triple a recipe that your family finds unappealing.
- Prepare recipes that freeze well.
- Wrap food properly for storage in the freezer. Improper wrapping can result in a dish that tastes like cardboard. Carefully adhere to the freezing guidelines for the recipe.
- Label the outside of each dish with the name of the dish, the date it was frozen, and the reheating instructions.
- Try to vary the dishes served from one night to the next to prevent "casserole overload."

Once-a-Month Chain Cooking Tips

- Do not undertake chain cooking on a large scale unless you are well rested. Preparing an entire month's worth of meals in a single day can be a lot of work. You will be required to stand at the stove or counter for long periods of time, cutting, cooking, blending, and stirring multiple dishes at various stages of preparation.
- Do not plan to prepare the food on the same day it is purchased. Grocery shopping can be very tiring.
- Plan each dish carefully. This includes the storage methods and containers to be used. Do you have adequate room in the freezer? Do you have an ample supply of containers, plastic wrap, and so on? Take into consideration the reheating method you will use when planning the freezer container for the dish. For example, if a dish will be reheated in the microwave, freeze it in a microwave safe dish.
- Prepare dishes with like ingredients starting with the protein source: meat, hamburger, chicken, fish, and so on. Then consider the filler ingredients: vegetables, pasta, rice, and so on. It is easier and more efficient to prepare dishes that use the same protein and filler ingredients, but differ in spices. This allows you to take advantage of sales and buying in bulk.
- If you are preparing multiple dishes, chop all like vegetables at the same time to streamline the preparation and clean up. For example, chop all onions at once, and cook all rice needed for the various dishes in one large pot. A food processor comes in handy, but is not mandatory.

Figure 8-2

Food	Storage length in freezer
Cooked meat and poultry slices	1 month
Meat and poultry in gravy or sauce	2-6 months
Casseroles and combination dishes	3-6 months

- Plan to use all ingredients purchased for the chain cooking recipes to avoid leftovers.

The most challenging part of chain cooking may be to find recipes that retain their flavor and quality after freezing. The taste and texture of some spices and foods change dramatically in the freezer. As a result, dishes to be frozen are sometimes prepared differently than if they are served immediately.

Refer to Figure 8-2 for the recommended storage length for dishes prepared using once-a-month cooking methods.

GROCERY COMPARISON SHOPPING MADE EASY WITH PRICE CARDS

Comparison shopping will consistently result in saving money. Unfortunately, most people only comparison shop when making a large purchase, such as a car. When this strategy is employed for purchasing groceries, it becomes an extremely effective method to pay less for your groceries. The secret to the efficient and effective implementation of comparison shopping for groceries is the prerecording of prices for quick reference when needed. Using price cards to record and track the price of groceries you purchase regularly simplifies this process.

Index cards, usually 3 × 5 inch cards, are convenient to use as price cards. Make a price card for all staples you use in the preparation of meals, such as flour, sugar, salt, ground black pepper, and so on. Include price cards for pet food, cleaning products, baby formula, disposable diapers, paper products, and automotive products, such as motor oil. You can always add more price cards as you begin to use them on a regular basis to compare prices.

The cards can be stored in a recipe type file box and removed when needed for a shopping trip. They fit comfortably into a purse or coat pocket and are easy to flip through when needed to compare a specific price. Update your price cards yearly or whenever you become aware of a price change.

Make a price card for each item you routinely purchase. On each card indicate the following information for a given store. Refer to Figure 8-3.

1) Indicate the name of the food.
2) Write the name of the store.
3) Fill-in the brand name of the least expensive product at the store that will meet your needs.
4) Record the regular price for the given item.
5) Indicate the size of the product.
6) Compute the price per unit.
7) Write the sale price of the product.
8) List the sale price per unit.

You may not want to put this much detail on your cards. Modify the information on your price cards to meet your own needs. Many shoppers have told me that it took them several years to determine the least expensive places to shop after moving to a new community. However, the use of price cards will enable you to have this information after only one shopping trip to each grocery store in your new community.

When making up price cards for the first time, you can expect to spend about one hour in each store recording the price for the items on your cards. With price cards in hand, visit your local grocery store to indicate their lowest price for each item on your price card. Carefully evaluate the price of all brands for the given product, not just those you normally buy. Many times, the

---

FIGURE 8-3

1) Canned Green Beans

2) Your Wholesale Club   3) ABC Brand   4) 49¢/   5) 15 oz can
6) 3.27¢/oz   7) SALE PRICE 3/$1   or   8) 2¢/oz

Save More On Food Store-Save More Brand, 45¢/15 oz can or 3¢/oz, SALE 4/$1 or 1.5¢/oz

IGB Food Store-Generic Brand 69¢/14 oz, or 5¢/oz, SALE 45¢/can or 3¢/oz

least expensive generic or store brand is hidden on the bottom shelf. Only include those products on your price card that are acceptable for your use. In other words, if you will only serve your family ABC brand of canned green beans, there is no need to include the price of any other brand on your price card. Brand loyalty can significantly increase your food costs. Is one brand really better than another brand?

Some people have told me that they use the newspaper sale advertisements as the only source of prices on their price cards. I would not recommend this method. The sale price listed in the newspaper does not provide all of the required information necessary to meet the objective of knowing the absolute lowest price at the store for each item on your card. Using the sale price from the newspaper is not very efficient because it can take several weeks to collect only a small percentage of the total number of prices on your cards.

I try to be inconspicuous in the store as I record the prices. I have heard of frugal shoppers going to the grocery store with laptop computers to use when documenting the lowest prices. Apparently, this is not an acceptable practice as far as some store managers are concerned because these computer savvy shoppers were asked to leave.

When planning your meals, use your price cards to determine the best place to shop for maximum savings on your needed items. Record the sale prices on your price cards to develop price points for those items you purchase most often. Use your price cards to evaluate the current sales prices and determine if any are at your price point so you can stock up when you come across a genuinely low price. Always look for new shopping locations and additional ways to pay less for groceries. Does your community have a food co-op? Natural health food stores are usually good places to purchase herbs and yeast at reduced prices. Does your local service station or convenience store sell milk for less per gallon than your grocery store?

Yes, it does take a little extra time initially to make up the price cards, go to the store, and write down the prices charged for each item. Consider this effort to be an investment of your time. You will feel empowered as you walk the aisles of the grocery store with your price cards and shopping list based on your planned menus. Instead of feeling helpless and dependent, you will feel powerful and competent in your ability to control your grocery budget.

Price Points

Based on the information listed on your price cards, develop your own "price points" for those products you buy frequently. Track the grocery store's weekly sales by reviewing their advertisements, and you will become aware of those items that go on sale periodically as well as learn the lowest price for each of these items. The lowest price represents the price point. Price points can only be determined by monitoring the sale prices at your local grocery stores over a period of time.

From my own experience, I know that when a local store advertises canned vegetables at four cans for $1, I should stock up! I have noted that one of the stores in my area will usually put canned vegetables on sale for this low price about every three or four months. Therefore, when I see this sale price (i.e., my price point of 25¢ per can), I buy a four-month supply of canned vegetables.

CLIPPING COUPONS

Clipping and using coupons reduces the cost of products for which they are issued. However, they must be used cautiously or they can actually cause you to spend more money.

Coupon Facts

A coupon is generally issued by one of two sources: a specific store or a manufacturer. If a coupon is store issued, it can only be redeemed in the identified store on the dates indicated. A manufacturer issued coupon can, theoretically, be redeemed at any store that sells the product provided it is used before the expiration date.

Stores have the legal right to develop their own policies regarding the acceptance of coupons. Therefore, a store is not required to accept manufacturer issued coupons. Some warehouse type stores, for example, accept only store issued coupons. Because store policies vary greatly, contact the store directly to inquire about their coupon acceptance policy. In some parts of the country, grocery stores issue coupons that can be used to triple the listed discount of a manufacturer issued coupon. These are called triple coupons. A coupon with a face value below a specified amount (usually 99¢ or less) is tripled when a triple coupon is presented. Some stores accept a competitor's store issued coupon or routinely double the face value of all manufacturer issued coupons. Grocery stores frequently base their coupon redemption policies on their competitor's policy in the immediate area. Therefore, you will probably find that most stores in your local area have similar coupon redemption policies. If one store changes its policy to be more beneficial to the consumer, you would be wise to quickly notify the managers of other grocery stores in your area. These stores will probably change their policies to be in line with the competition, and you can then take advantage of additional savings.

Manufacturers issue coupons to encourage sales of their product. They hope that once you try their product, you will buy it again and again. Coupons are frequently issued as a part of the marketing and advertising campaign in the introduction of a new product. Unfortunately, these marketing campaigns are expensive and serve to drive up the price of the product. Therefore, you will frequently find products with manufacturer issued coupons to be more expensive than those without coupons. Coupons are rarely issued for generic products or store brands, so they can be sold for less to the consumer.

Use Coupons Cautiously

Let's look at a typical way coupons are used. Alyssa has a manufacturer issued coupon for 25¢ off Happy Homemaker brand window cleaner. The selling price for this product is $2.75 for a 24-ounce spray bottle, or 11¢ per ounce. (To determine the price per ounce, divide the price by the volume, or $2.75 ÷ 24 ounces = $.11 per ounce.) To determine the after-coupon discount, Alyssa deducts the 25¢ coupon from the $2.75 retail price and finds that she would pay $2.50 for the window cleaner. If Alyssa had a triple coupon, she would be able to triple the 25¢ coupon and deduct 75¢ from the original price. The final price using the tripled coupon would be $2.00, or 8¢ per ounce, ($2.00 ÷ 24 ounces = $.08). A careful review of the other products on the shelf reveals that a 26-ounce bottle of generic window cleaner sells for only 99¢, or 4¢ per ounce, ($.99 ÷ 26 ounces = $.04). Even if she uses the triple coupon to purchase the Happy Homemaker window cleaner, Alyssa would still pay $1.01 more than if she purchased the generic window cleaner. By using the coupon, she would not save any money—she would actually spend $1.01 more.

To determine if you are saving money by using a coupon:

- Compare the price of similar products with the price of the item after the coupon is deducted.
- If the total volume or weight differs between the products, compare the price per unit for a true side-by-side comparison.

Locating Coupons

Coupons are readily available at no charge from many sources.

- Clip coupons from newspapers, magazines, and from advertisements received in the mail.
- Trade coupons with friends, relatives, and coworkers.
- Coupon exchange tables in grocery stores, libraries, community centers, churches, or food banks are a good way to trade coupons with other shoppers. If your community does not have a coupon exchange table, discuss this option with the local library or other interested group.
- Coupons are occasionally printed inside a product's box or label.
- Call or write the manufacturer and offer your comments or praise about their product. Manufacturers frequently send coupons or free samples as a result of such contact. Call the 800 directory at (800) 555-1212 or look on the label for the manufacturer's 800 number.
- Coupons for immediate use are sometimes located on the product label. Simply peel off the coupon and turn it in like any other coupon at the cash register.
- Some grocery stores place store issued coupons in special shelf displays near the product. These coupons frequently state "not subject to doubling or tripling."

Time Considerations

Yes, using coupons can be very time consuming. Some people spend two or more hours each week locating, clipping, organizing, and updating coupons. They then take the additional time required in the store aisle to carefully consider the actual savings for each coupon. If you have the time to devote to this effort and are cautious when using coupons, then by all means use coupons. You can save money.

Unfortunately, many people consider the use of coupons to be too time consuming and simply don't use them. Throwing good coupons away is like tossing money in the trash. As Ben Franklin said, "A penny saved is a penny earned." (Today, if you're in the 25 percent tax bracket, a dollar saved is $1.33 earned!) For those people with only limited time, I suggest using Guerrilla Couponing Tactics. This method allows you to obtain maximum savings in a minimum amount of time

Guerrilla Couponing Tactics

This method was developed out of my desire to reduce our grocery budget with only limited time to devote to the effort. I found that going to the store with a shoe box filled with coupons required that I spend about one and a half to two hours in the grocery store. I simply do not have that amount of time to devote to grocery shopping. I also found that this effort does not consistently result in buying products at their lowest price. Often, I find a similar product for less money on the shelf even after I deduct the coupon's discount from the regular price of the item. Yet, there were times when I saved a significant amount of money for products my family uses. I carefully evaluated when it was beneficial to use a coupon and when the rewards seemed to be too few and far between to make it worth the expenditure of time. As a result, I developed some general rules about using coupons. In following these tactics, I save money and time using coupons.

1. Clip all coupons for products you would be willing to use. Do not discard the coupon because it is not a product you normally buy. Ask yourself, "Would I use this product if I got it free?" If the answer is yes, clip the coupon.
2. Develop a simple way to keep coupons organized so they can be quickly reviewed and selected. Small accordion-shaped files are available to use in organizing coupons. However, recycled shoeboxes or an old recipe box work equally well and cost less.
3. Take full advantage of the coupon policies at stores where you shop. Many stores, other than grocery stores, frequently accept

coupons: pharmacies, discount stores, and even convenience shops. If a store doubles or triples coupons only on one specific day each week, shop on those dates. For example, ABC Grocery store's policy is to triple a coupon with a face value up to 99¢ cents. Therefore, if you have a 99¢ off coupon and a store issued triple coupon, this store will discount the given item $2.97, (99¢ × 3). Although most stores only discount the item up to its retail price, some stores will refund the difference if the price of the item is less than the tripled amount. If the sale price of a product is $.96, and your coupons total $1.50, you will receive 54¢ back or have 54¢ deducted from your total grocery bill. Not only do you walk out of the store with a free product, but the store pays you 54¢! Refer to Figure 8-4.

4. Use coupons for items on sale. If you have limited time to devote to the use of coupons, focus your use of coupons on sale items only. If you are willing to use generic products, you will almost always find a generic or store brand for less than a name brand item that is not on sale and is only discounted through your use of a coupon. However, you probably will save money by using a coupon to purchase a name brand item that is on sale. Read sales circulars from stores that accept coupons. Review your clipped coupon file to determine if you have any coupons for these sale items. A guerrilla coupon clipper's primary goal is to purchase the product for the least amount possible, preferably free.

5. Coupons are not finite resources. If a coupon is redeemed, invariably, you will find another coupon for the same product or a similar acceptable product within the next few days or weeks. Therefore, always compare the after-coupon cost per unit of the smallest size with a larger size of the product. This seems contrary to most savings methods when buying in large quantities is frequently cheaper. However, your goal is to spend as little money as possible on the product. For example, the coupon for $1.50 off a bottle of Sudsy Shampoo indicates "any size bottle." The after-coupon price for the 36-ounce bottle of shampoo is $3.50 (or 10¢ per ounce). However, the after-coupon price for the 12-ounce bottle is only 4¢ (or less than 1¢ per ounce). Determining the unit price affords the opportunity to compare the price of two dissimilar sized products with the discount factored into the cost of each product.

6. Always compare the after-coupon price with the generic equivalent and other brands on the shelf to confirm that you are paying the lowest price by using the coupon.

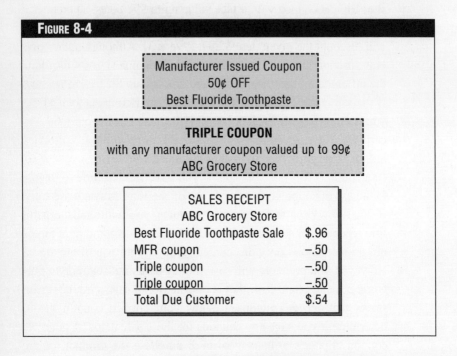

Figure 8-4

GROCERY SHOPPING IN A WHOLESALE CLUB

I have shopped in wholesale clubs for over 14 years. Some people call them warehouse stores or warehouse clubs because they look like a big warehouse. I have shopped in several different stores including the largest chain of wholesale clubs in the United States. Although it is true that you can save money shopping in one of these stores, you must shop in a prudent manner, or you may spend more, not less, on groceries.

I frequently hear people give general recommendations regarding specific things you should always buy at a wholesale club to save money. I have never found these generalized statements to be true. For example, although dog food is cheaper per pound at my local warehouse club, the local discount store frequently has it on sale for even less. The regular price of the store brand dog food in a grocery store where I shop is less per pound than the price of the name brand dog food at the wholesale club. Paper products are frequently on sale in a grocery store at much lower prices than those of the wholesale club, and I do not have to buy a four year's supply to get the price reduction.

You must pay a membership fee for the privilege to shop at a wholesale club. The average annual membership fee is $25 to $50. Before joining, carefully consider how much you expect to purchase at the wholesale club over the next year. To determine if you will be able to recover the cost of the membership fee and realize additional savings, compare the prices at the wholesale club with those charged at local grocery stores. Be certain to consider the price per unit for an accurate side-by-side comparison. Most wholesale clubs offer a free one-day pass that allows you the opportunity to look around and compare prices before joining. Your price cards will make this comparison shopping easy. Review your price cards and consider which items can be purchased at the wholesale club for less. Then consider if these items can be purchased on sale somewhere else for even less. Try to determine how much money you will save each year if these select items were purchased at the wholesale club. If you find that only one or two items represent genuine savings at the wholesale club, you probably won't save any money by joining a wholesale club. Instead, it may cost you more money to shop at the wholesale club when you factor in the price of the annual membership fee. For example, let's say you can buy milk for 50¢ less per gallon at the wholesale club (and this is the only item that you could buy for less at the wholesale club). Your family drinks one gallon of milk per week. This reflects a total annual savings of $26 (52 weeks × 50¢ = $26). However, you must pay a $50 annual membership fee. Therefore, you didn't save $26. When you factor in the membership fee you have to pay for the privilege of buying the milk at the wholesale club, you actually spend $24 more on milk than if you had purchased it at the local grocery store ($50 membership fee minus $26 money saved = $24).

Note: In many parts of the country, gas stations sell milk for less than the local grocery stores as a way to get you to stop and purchase gasoline My local gas station sells it for $1.99 per gallon, whereas the wholesale club price is $2.49 per gallon.

The following list contains factors to consider when contemplating joining a wholesale club.

- Frequently, wholesale clubs sell only large, institutional sizes. Carefully consider whether you will be able to use the entire product

before it spoils. You are not saving money if part of your purchase ends up in the trash. Learn ways to properly store food so it will last longer. Do you have enough room to store a case of bath tissue or 50 pounds of all-purpose flour? Find creative ways to expand your storage space.
- Wholesale clubs offer only limited selections of a few food products. They do not carry all of the items stocked in a grocery store. Therefore, even if you do join a wholesale club, you will still have to shop in a traditional grocery store.
- Are you really saving money driving several miles out of your way to buy only one or two items at a wholesale club?
- Unlike a grocery store, wholesale clubs offer only a limited selection of generic products. This only serves to further limit your opportunity to pay less for groceries. For example, the only ketchup sold at the ABC Warehouse Club is Vine Fresh brand, and it is only available in one gallon cans. XYZ Grocer, on the other hand, carries six different name brands of ketchup plus three generic brands in four different sizes. This provides the consumer with the opportunity to compare prices and perhaps pay less. This option does not exist at a wholesale club. The name brand ketchup sold at the wholesale club may sell for less per unit than the same brand ketchup sold at the traditional grocery store. However, upon examining the other options on the grocery store shelf, you will probably find a generic brand ketchup that is even cheaper
- Name brand products sell for less at the wholesale club. If you buy only specific name brands of food and household items, you will pay less per unit for the same brand than if it was purchased in a grocery store at the regular price. However, I frequently find name brand items on sale at local grocery stores for a price that is less per unit than that charged at a wholesale club.
- Wholesale clubs seldom have sales. These restrictions further limit your ability to pay less for groceries.
- Shop in a wholesale club cautiously. Do not assume that you are always paying the lowest price. I can frequently buy food or other household products on sale at a grocery store, discount store, and so on for less than at the wholesale club.

- Most wholesale clubs do not accept manufacturer's coupons. Because grocery stores accept coupons (and most in my area will triple them), I use triple coupons for sale items. This technique further reduces the price. Use the price per unit on your price cards to compare prices. For example, bath tissue at the warehouse club sells for $9.99 for 24 rolls or 42¢ per 1000 sheet roll. However, by purchasing bath tissue when it was on sale at the local grocery store and using a triple coupon, I pay 10¢ per 1000 sheet roll. The local discount pharmacy frequently has 1000 sheet rolls of bath tissue on sale at three rolls for $1, or 33¢ per roll.
- Because wholesale clubs sell only large, institutional sizes, you will spend more money at the wholesale club. If you're on a limited budget or fixed income, you may find yourself spending an entire month's food budget to purchase only six items. This certainly doesn't allow for much variety in your diet.

9
The Road to Lower Transportation Costs

Navigate the road to lower transportation costs with skill and confidence. This road need not be fraught with anxiety and fear around every corner. By becoming educated about the basic rules of the road, you can successfully navigate the path to buying a car. Hop in and buckle your seat belt for an enjoyable ride!

NEW OR USED CAR?

One of the primary reasons most people buy a new (as opposed to used) car is the increased status associated with its ownership. Some believe a new car provides more reliable transportation that results in fewer repairs. However, this belief completely ignores the additional costs associated with owning a new car and the loss of money due to depreciation. The average car depreciates in value by about 50 percent every four years with its maximum depreciation occurring in the first four years.

Refer to Figure 9-1 for a comparison of the projected expenses associated with owning four different Ford Taurus SHO four-door sedans. The first, a 1999 model, was purchased when it was new; the 1997 model was two years old at the time of purchase. The 1995 model was four years old when purchased, and the 1993 model was six years old when acquired. The difference in the costs associated with owning the 1999 model and the 1993 model is $19,352. Repair costs were not estimated because there are too many variables that can influence this expense. Repairs on the 1993 Taurus would be far less than $19,352 over a five year period of time. In fact, for $19,352, you could buy two more 1993 models and still have $1,952 left over.

Figure 9-1
Ford Taurus SHO 4-door sedan
5-Year Ownership Cost: 1999–2003

Year of car	1999	1997	1995	1993
Purchase price	$29,115	$17,500	$11,750	$8,700
Original price	29,115	26,460	25,140	24,829
20 percent down payment	5,823	3,500	2,350	1,740
Monthly payment x 5 years	489.18	294.03	197.42	146.17
Depreciation	18,545	10,100	6,350	5,350
Financing*	6,059	3,642	2,445	1,810
Insurance**	4,530	3,810	3,655	3,505
State fees***	1,200	636	442	317
Fuel****	4,346	4,346	4,346	4,346
Maintenance*****	2,690	2,690	2,690	2,690
Repairs	Unable to estimate	Unable to estimate	Unable to estimate	Unable to estimate
Total 5 year ownership cost	**$47,940**	**$32,624**	**$25,328**	**$21,368**

*Financing is determined using an annual interest rate of 9.5 percent for a 60 month loan with a 20 percent down payment.

**Insurance costs for over 5 years are based on the rate for a 44-year-old single female homeowner in CT with a good driving record and a $500 deductible.

***State Fees are calculated by using 1 percent of the current retail value for each of the five years. The residual value is projected based on historical data for this make and model of car.

****Fuel costs are based on an average 14,000 miles per year with a driving pattern of 60 percent highway and 40 percent city.

*****Maintenance costs are based on the manufacturer's recommended maintenance schedule.

Consider also the increased monthly payment that is required to buy a new car. The 1999 model requires a $489.18 monthly payment, whereas the 1993 model's payment is $146.17. The difference between these two payments ($343.01) could be placed in a money management account and used to pay for any required repairs to the 1993 model. If you placed $343.01 into an account every month for the length of the loan (five years), you would have a total of $20,580.60 at the end of that period of time. (Note: The $20,580.60 does not take into consideration any accrued interest that would be earned on this money.) Even if you spent $1,000 per year on repairs to your 1993 car, you would still have over $15,000 in your money management account after five years. This $15,000 could be used to pay cash for the car that will replace your 1993 model in the year 2004, after owning it for five years. If you maintained the 1993 Taurus properly, did not put excessive miles on the car, and kept your maintenance records, you should be able to sell it for as much as $4,000.

The quality of cars has steadily increased. CNW Marketing/Research reports that the quality of used vehicles from one to eight years of age consistently increased from 1990–1998. In fact, during this eight-year period of time, used vehicle purchasers reported a 37.4 percent increase in the overall quality of their pre-owned cars.

How to Buy a Used Vehicle

Knowledge gives power to those who possess it. Knowledge will increase your confidence and provide the determination necessary to enter into this unknown and perhaps uncomfortable situation. By arming yourself with the knowledge contained in this chapter, you will have the weapons necessary to become empowered and capable of purchasing a high-quality used vehicle.

STEP 1 Evaluate Your Finances and Determine How Much You Can Afford to Spend on a Vehicle

The evaluation of your finances is an essential step in buying a vehicle. After completing the first five chapters of this book, you will have a clear picture of your personal finances. At this point, you must determine the total amount you can spend on a car. If you placed money aside on a regular basis in preparation for this major purchase, this is the amount you dedicated to this expense. If you did not plan for this expense, you must determine the amount you have available for a down payment as well as how much of a monthly payment you can afford. At the Frugality Network Web site, *www.frugalitynetwork.com/calculators.html*, you will find a variety of calculators to determine the monthly payment based on the total amount to be borrowed. If you must take out a loan, try to keep the total amount borrowed to a minimum by carefully evaluating how the monthly payment may impact your ability to attain your goals and personal mission. (Financial institutions recommend that the monthly payment be no more than 15 percent of your take-home monthly income.)

There are a variety of ways to finance your vehicle: a home equity loan, a loan from a financial institution, a loan against a retirement plan, etc. Contact the financial institution directly to discuss the details of their used car loans. One Web site, *www.bankrate.com*, sponsored by Intelligent Life Corporation, makes shopping for a low interest rate used car loan easy because it lists interest rates of more than 3,500 financial institutions. After you have completed the next three steps to determine the vehicle of your needs, contact the financial institution with the best rate and terms to obtain pre-approval for the amount of money you will require. Having your financing in place before you shop for a vehicle dramatically increases your bargaining power when negotiating the best price for a used vehicle.

STEP 2 Determine the Type of Vehicle by Making a List of Your Needs

Base your choice of vehicle on these needs. How will you use the vehicle? How many miles will you drive it each year? How large is your family? Do you need air conditioning? Do you live in an area that gets a great deal of snow? Carefully evaluate your needs in a vehicle based on the costs associated with these needs, not your wants. Even though you may occasionally offer to car pool a few times per year, does this justify spending several thousand dollars more to purchase a sports utility vehicle or minivan? A small or midsize economy car will comfortably transport your two children to all of their activities (and get better gas mileage, so you will spend less for gasoline). If you drive more than 14,000 miles a year, your vehicle will depreciate at a faster rate, so your most practical choice would be a fuel saving economy car instead of a large luxury vehicle. If you live in a part of the country that receives a significant amount of snowfall, a vehicle with front-wheel drive or four-wheel drive should be considered. The bodies of some cars, vans, or trucks are more prone to rust, so these specific models should be avoided in a cold, snowy climate. Be conservative in determining your list of needs because each need can potentially raise the price of the vehicle. The added luxuries (sunroof, heated seats, electric windows, etc.) do not increase the quality or durability of the vehicle.

STEP 3   Narrow Down Your Choice of Vehicles to Determine the Specific Make(s), Model(s) and Year(s) That Will Fit in Your Price Range and Meet Your Needs

As you identify vehicles that seem to meet your stated objectives, add them to your "preliminary list." Find out everything you can about the vehicles on your preliminary list.

Review the *Consumer Reports Buying Guide,* which is published and updated annually, and research the vehicles' reliability records. In this book, you will find recommendations from the Consumers Union for the most reliable vehicles plus the rating of potential trouble spots on cars, trucks, vans, and sports utility vehicles. Most public libraries have this book available for your use in the reference section. The Consumers Union can be trusted as a respected, unbiased source of information about the quality of vehicles. Its information is obtained as a result of surveying thousands of vehicle owners every year. You may find that one model and year of a vehicle was prone to major problems. However, the problem was not reported in subsequent years because the manufacturer took corrective action. Add any viable vehicles to your preliminary list. Remove any that do not meet your need for reliable, inexpensive transportation, or make note of which years to avoid.

Another source of detailed information regarding a vehicle is the Web site sponsored by Edmund Publications Corporation at *www.edmunds.com.* There you will find the current suggested retail price and trade-in value for all makes, models, and years of cars, trucks, vans, and sports utility vehicles. Edmunds.com also lists the equipment that was originally standard for each model plus the optional equipment that could have been added when the vehicle was new. For example, a search for "1995 Ford Taurus" reveals that Ford made six Taurus models that year: 4-Dr GL Sedan, 4-Dr GL Wagon, 4-Dr LX Sedan, 4-Dr LX Wagon, 4-Dr SE Sedan, and the 4-Dr SHO Sedan. It further indicates that the SHO Sedan came with a 5-speed transmission as part of the standard equipment package. An automatic transmission was available as an option. An automatic transmission was standard equipment on the GL Sedan and a 5-speed transmission was not available. Therefore, you would be wasting your time trying to find a Taurus GL Sedan with a 5-speed transmission. This information can prove to be very valuable in negotiating the best price for a vehicle. Also included are ratings (scale of 1–10) for the safety, reliability, performance, comfort, and value for each model.

Using the information you gleaned from the Edmund's Web site, further refine your preliminary list to include the exact make(s), model(s), year(s), and features that you need. You may find that you must remove some of the vehicles from your list because they do not come with the needed features.

Most people prefer a used vehicle that is less than five years old with less than 50,000 miles on the odometer. Excessive mileage causes wear and tear on a vehicle. However, some vehicles have a record of excellent reliability. The odometer of these vehicles may indicate 70,000 miles, and the owners can still be assured of reliable transportation for many years to come, if they are properly maintained and serviced. Contact a service technician who is Automotive Service Excellence (ASE) certified for the type of vehicle(s) you are considering and obtain his or her opinion and experience regarding the longevity of the vehicle. You can also predict the durability of a particular model by simply looking at the vehicles around you on the road. You certainly don't see too many Ford Pintos on the road. However, the old Volkswagen Beetles of the late 1960s and early 1970s are still on the road. The general guideline used to evaluate a vehicle's mileage is as follows: An average of 10,000 miles a year indicates a prime vehicle, 15,000 miles a year is average, and vehicles with an average of more than 15,000 miles a year should be avoided. Determine the maximum number of miles that are acceptable for the make, model, and year of vehicles on your list. Add this information to each vehicle listed on your preliminary list.

To evaluate the safety of a given model of vehicle, visit the Web site of the Insurance Institute for Highway Safety at *www.hwysafety.org*. Listed at this site are the crash test and vehicle evaluation reports that have been performed on a number of vehicles. Remove any vehicles from your preliminary list that do not ensure the safety of you and your family.

To learn about any recalls or manufacturing defects that have been found in the vehicles on your list, visit the Web site of the National Highway and Traffic Safety Administration (NHTSA) at *www.nhtsa.dot.gov*. Here, you can review a complete list of all recalls and Technical Service Bulletins (TSB) issued for the make, model, and year of vehicle(s) you are considering. A TSB is issued by the manufacturer and is commonly referred to as a "secret warranty." When a manufacturer's defect is found in a vehicle and does not require a recall, a TSB is issued by the manufacturer instructing its authorized repair centers to repair the defect at no charge (if the repair is necessary to resolve the customer's complaint). Unfortunately, most consumers are unaware of this option and simply take their vehicles to a mechanic and pay to have the repair performed. Hence, the name "secret warranty." Other TSBs deal with the notification of the availability of new parts, installation instructions, or new repair techniques. The NHTSA Web site also provides information about the safety of specific vehicles based on their crash test results. Review the TSBs, recalls, and crash test results for all vehicles on your list. These provide a window to the future in evaluating the need for future repairs. The NHTSA Web site should be consulted if you have problems with your vehicle. You just might not have to pay for the repair because it may be covered under the secret warranty. Use this information to further modify your preliminary list as necessary.

Determine the current market value for all vehicles on your list. There are three sources for this information:

NADA Official Used Car Guide: www.nada.org
The Kelly Blue Book: www.kbb.com
Edmunds: www.edmunds.com

There is no charge to obtain the current retail and trade-in value for vehicles at these Web sites. However, the Kelly Blue Book and NADA Official Used Car Guide are available in print. Many public libraries have them available for your use. The value of a used vehicle is based on many factors including mileage, condition, and options. This information will help in negotiating a fair price and in determining the amount of money that is required to purchase the vehicle of your needs.

STEP 4   Consider the Annual Insurance Rate in the Overall Cost of the Vehicle

The cost of insurance varies depending upon the make and model of the vehicle. To keep your costs down, remove those vehicles from your preliminary list that might result in excessive insurance premiums.

STEP 5   Locate Used Vehicles for Sale

Review your preliminary list, and develop another list that contains only those vehicles that meet the needs you identified and confirmed after completing Steps 1 through 4. This new list is your "search list." Include detailed information about each vehicle on your search list to ensure that you can quickly identify the best and most qualified vehicles for your consideration. For example, your search list should not only include the make, model, and year of the vehicle, but also the number of acceptable miles, options that are desired, and special considerations about the vehicle that must be evaluated before the purchase. Using your search list, locate actual used vehicles for sale.

Used vehicles are purchased from a variety of sources: auctions, new car dealerships, independent used car lots, private sellers, or rental car companies. To save time and gasoline, call the dealers to determine if they have the make, model, and year of vehicle(s) on your list. Review the classified advertisements and any specific publications listing used vehicles for sale to find one for sale by a private seller in your area. Many newspapers or other more specialized publications list classified advertisements on the Internet. Contact the publication to determine if it has a Web site. Using a publication's Web site makes shopping for a vehicle much easier because it frequently includes a search engine that eliminates the need to read through all of the ads. Instead, you can search for a specific make, model, and year of vehicle in just seconds. You will find links to many Web sites that list millions of used vehicles for sale on the Frugality Network Web site, *www.frugalitynetwork.com/automobiles.html.* Listed below are the most common sources of used vehicles.

New Car Dealerships and Independent Used Car lots

New car dealerships sell used vehicles that are traded-in when the owner buys a new vehicle. Used car dealers also sell demonstrators and program vehicles. Demonstrators are new cars that have never been owned, leased, or used as rentals. These cars are usually driven by salespeople or are test-driven by customers. Program vehicles are current year models with low-mileage that are returned from short-term leases or rentals. Because independent used car dealerships sell only used vehicles, they have a much larger selection. Both dealerships frequently offer some type of warranty regarding the mechanical condition of a used vehicle. However, their prices are almost always higher than the market value of the vehicle as reported in the Kelly Blue Book or other sources listed in this chapter. Salespeople at a dealership have a reputation for using tough, high-pressure, and intimidating negotiating tactics. These methods can intimidate many unprepared car buyers.

Buyer Beware

Dealers are not required to give a refund to used car buyers and can develop their own return policy. If desired, a dealer may choose to have a no-refund policy. Of course, if they do have a refund policy, they must adhere to it. Some dealers describe their refund policy as a "cooling-off" period, a "no questions asked" return policy or a money-back guarantee. Always inquire about a dealer's refund policy before purchasing a vehicle, and request a written copy. Read it very carefully to make certain you are in agreement with the terms of the policy before buying a vehicle from the dealer.

The Used Car Rule of the Federal Trade Commission requires a dealer to post a "Buyers Guide" in all used cars, vans, and trucks. This guide must clearly state if the vehicle is being sold "as is" or with a warranty. It must also state the percentage of repair costs that the dealer will agree to pay under the warranty. Anytime you buy a used vehicle from a dealer, keep the Buyers Guide that was posted in the vehicle. If changes in the warranty coverage were negotiated at the time of purchase, to be enforceable, these changes must be reflected in writing on the vehicle's Buyers Guide. This Guide is therefore a part of the sales contract and takes precedence over the written contract. If the vehicle is sold "as is," the box next to the "As Is—No warranty" disclosure on the Buyers Guide must be checked. Some states do not allow used car dealerships to sell vehicles "as is." Several states require a disclosure other than the Buyers Guide. Regardless of the specific disclosure used in your state, if the dealer fails to provide the proper disclosure, the sale is not "as is." Contact your state's attorney general to determine the disclosure requirements in your state.

Auctions

Buying a vehicle at an auction can be very risky and is not advisable for the average buyer because you cannot test-drive the vehicle or have it inspected prior to the sale.

Private Sellers

Purchasing a vehicle from a private seller usually results in the best quality vehicle for the lowest price. By dealing directly with the owner, you can obtain firsthand information regarding the mechanical, maintenance, and repair history of a vehicle. Most state laws require that a vehicle from a private seller be purchased "as is" unless a written contract is drawn up between the seller and the buyer stating the contrary. If the vehicle is purchased without a written contract from a private seller (i.e., "as is") and the vehicle is later found to have a serious defect, the seller is under no obligation to provide a refund or repair the problem. Some used car dealers advertise a vehicle in the classifieds listing their home phone number and address. An unsuspecting buyer is lead to believe that the vehicle is for sale by a private seller. To confirm the genuine owner of the vehicle, ask to see the original title. You can also confirm the name of the legal owner by contacting your state department of motor vehicles.

Rental Car Companies

Rental car companies sell their cars when they accrue excess miles. Although rental companies maintain service records for your review, the car may have been subject to abuse from the many people who drove the car. Some rental car companies sell their cars directly to the public, others sell them to used and new car dealerships.

The Internet

The Internet can be used not only to locate a used car, but it represents the largest source of information about used vehicles. Message boards abound on the Internet where owners post their experiences regarding a specific model of vehicle. Web sites dedicated to the pricing of new and used vehicles provide detailed information about the various models of cars, trucks, minivans, and sports utility vehicles. You may be able to find the vehicle of your needs online by visiting one of the many Web sites that list used vehicles for sale. Since used-car prices tend to fluctuate based on the geographic region, local trends, or popularity, you may be able to save hundreds of dollars by driving a few extra miles to buy a used vehicle. Internet shopping also allows you to comparison shop in the privacy of your home with no pressure from a salesperson. Many used car dealers as well as private individuals now list their vehicles online. To save time, you would be wise to use the Internet first when trying to locate a used vehicle. The remaining steps in the process remain the same, regardless of whether you located a car online or in the classified section of your local newspaper. I would not recommend that you buy a car unseen. The Internet is simply one more method now available to locate a used vehicle. The Frugality Network, www.frugalitynetwork.com/automobiles.html, has listed hundreds of Web sites that you will find invaluable in researching and locating the used vehicle of your needs.

STEP 6 Inspect and Evaluate Every Aspect of the Vehicle

Your inspection begins with the first contact made with the dealer or owner of the vehicle. To be more efficient and to save time, contact dealers and individual owners over the phone to narrow down your search. Most of your questions can be answered over the phone. Write down the response to each question. This information will prove helpful if you later decide to test-drive this vehicle or further pursue the purchase. Dealers can sometimes provide the name and phone number of the previous owner of a used vehicle, so you can interview the previous owner regarding the history of the vehicle. The following list contains a number of questions you should ask in the interview:

- What is your asking price? Is this price negotiable? (Consider how firm the owner is on this price or would he or she be willing to negotiate.)
- Can you describe the vehicle including make, model, year, interior and exterior colors, transmission type, size of engine, and so on? (Use the list of standard equipment and options that were available for your model as a guide. This information is available at www.edmunds.com.)
- What is the condition of the exterior, interior, and mechanics? (Write down the owner's comments. If you do go to see the vehicle and there are discrepancies between the owner's description of the vehicle and your opinion of the vehicle, you will be able to use these discrepancies to further reduce your offer.)
- For an individual seller: Why are you selling the vehicle? How long have you owned the vehicle? Where did you buy the vehicle?
- How long has the vehicle been for sale?
- For an individual seller: Have you had any problems with the vehicle?
- How old are the tires? Battery?

- Has the vehicle ever been involved in an accident?
- Do you have maintenance and repair records for the vehicle?
- For an individual seller: Are you the owner of this vehicle? Are you a used car dealer? Do you work for a car dealership?

If the vehicle seems to meet your needs and is priced within your range, make arrangements to see the vehicle in person. Of course, the depth of your inspection is limited to your personal expertise and experiences. An untrained eye can overlook major problems or hidden defects. However, using a little common sense can secure valuable information about the vehicle. Review every part of the vehicle that is supposed to perform a function. Turn on the headlights. Confirm that the brake lights work. Turn on the radio, wipers, heater, air conditioner, mirror controls, electric windows, and so on. Is the interior clean and in a state of good repair? Does it smell moldy in the interior? (A sure sign that the vehicle was in a flood and should be avoided.) Make a note of anything that does not function as it was intended. (This information can be used to justify offering a lower price on the vehicle when negotiating the price.)

After you have checked out every "gadget" to determine whether it is working, take the vehicle for a test-drive. Because you are an experienced driver, you can use your common sense to arrive at some conclusions about the vehicle. Do not turn on the radio. Instead, listen carefully to the engine. If possible, try to drive it for at least 15 minutes so the vehicle has ample time to warm up. Does the vehicle change gears smoothly? Do the breaks make any noise? Drive the vehicle on varied road conditions including the highway, up hills, and stop-and-go traffic. Does it "bog-down" going up hills? Does the steering wheel vibrate at certain speeds? Does the cruise control work? Do you feel comfortable when driving the vehicle? Do you have adequate headroom and legroom? Trust your instincts about the vehicle. If the vehicle runs rough, emits smoke from the tail pipe, and is priced $2,000 below the market value, common sense tells you to walk away from the vehicle.

Ask to see the vehicle's maintenance record. Compare the intervals between the servicing of the vehicle with those recommended by the manufacturer in the service manual. This information can also be obtained by contacting a factory authorized repair shop for the type of vehicle you are considering. The repair shop may provide this information over the phone. If dealing directly with the owner and he or she does not have repair records, inquire regarding the name of the facility that provided these services. Later, you can contact the facility to determine any repairs and the maintenance history. If the owner does not have records and cannot tell you where the vehicle was serviced, you will probably be accurate in assuming that the vehicle was not properly maintained and/or that it has a serious defect the owner is trying to hide.

Do not become overly concerned if your inspection and test-drive do not reveal any problems. If the vehicle appears to be in good condition, is priced right, and meets your needs, before you even consider negotiating a price, you should have the vehicle thoroughly inspected by a mechanic. This inspection will determine if there are any problems and reduce the risk that you are buying someone else's lemon. Never omit having the vehicle inspected regardless of how much you like lemonade.

Odometer Fraud

It is not uncommon for a used car dealership or individual seller to roll back an odometer in an effort to increase the value of a vehicle. To avoid becoming a victim of odometer fraud, check with your motor vehicle department to determine the current and past owners of a given vehicle. Look for any irregularities in the mileage reported each time the title changed hands. Does your state require emissions testing? Contact the emission controls department to determine the mileage recorded each time emissions testing was performed on the vehicle. The state will require the VIN of the vehicle to provide this information. Some states may not be able to provide much information regarding the title. Via the Internet, you can obtain a vehicle history report from the Carfax Web page at *www.carfax.com*. For a fee, Carfax will issue a report detailing, among other things, the odometer history and if the vehicle was ever issued a salvaged title or reported as a total loss by an insurance company. As a free service at this site, you can enter the VIN and find out if the vehicle was ever listed as a "lemon" according to the state lemon laws. If the reported mileage on the title is more than what is currently showing on the odometer, report the owner or dealer immediately to the police for odometer fraud.

Manufacturer's Warranty and Previously Purchased Service Contracts

A manufacturer's warranty or a separately purchased service contract may be transferable to the new owner of a used vehicle. Not all warranties and service contracts are transferable. On occasion they are only transferable after an additional fee is paid or when certain conditions exist. Always inquire about any existing service contracts and warranties on any vehicle that you are considering. Ask to review the actual written warranty or service contract for a clear understanding of what is covered and whether it can be transferred.

Implied Warranties

In most states when a vehicle is purchased from a dealer, it is covered by an implied warranty. An implied warranty is a legal term referring to the general understanding that when a dealer sells a vehicle, the buyer believes it to be in working order. An implied warranty generally exists for the first 30 days after a vehicle changes hands. Therefore, a reputable dealer would repair or replace a vehicle that suffered from a major mechanical problem rendering it inoperable within 30 days after it was purchased—even if it was not purchased with any extra warranty or service contract. Of course, this is assuming that the vehicle was not mistreated or abused by the buyer. An implied warranty is not a written warranty. However, if the dealer has written into the contract that you are purchasing the vehicle "as is" and/or they indicate "as is" on the Buyer's Guide, this makes the implied warranty null and void.

The Decision to Buy a Service Contract or Extended Warranty

Too often the salesperson at the dealership offers a service contract or extended warranty option as he or she is totaling the miscellaneous charges immediately before you pay for the vehicle and take possession. This tactic does not allow ample time for you to seriously consider this expense. Instead, ask the salesperson to provide a written copy of the service contract or extended warranty before you have the vehicle inspected. Determine the company that is issuing the warranty or service contract. Contact the Better Business Bureau and your state attorney general's office to inquire if they have had any complaints about the issuing company. Review the list of covered repairs on the service contract or warranty and compare them with the mechanics inspection report. Take advantage of the experience and skill of the mechanic to inquire about the chances that the vehicle you are considering will need to have any of the covered repairs performed. Determine what is covered on the extended warranty (parts, labor, or both). How long is the warranty—30 days, 60 days?

What percentage of the repair work is covered? For example, in a 50/50 warranty, the dealer pays half, and you are responsible for the other half. Are there any exceptions or repairs that are not covered? You do not have to buy an extended warranty from the dealership where the vehicle was purchased. Contact other used car dealers in your area to inquire if you can buy an extended warranty contract through them. The prices are sometimes negotiable. The terms and benefits for different service contracts or extended warranties also vary.

Evaluate the financial benefit of the service contract or warranty by comparing its cost and your out-of-pocket expense for the required deductibles with the estimated repair costs quoted by your mechanic. More often than not, the service contract or extended warranty only represents a needless expense. A more financially sound decision would be to take the money you would have spent on the service contract and put it in your money management account for future repairs to the vehicle.

Inspection by a Qualified Mechanic

Never buy a used vehicle without having it inspected by an independent qualified mechanic. Never trust an inspection performed by a mechanic hired by the dealership. The inspection you pay to have performed on the vehicle you are considering will provide a good indication of its overall reliability and mechanical condition.

Be certain that the mechanic is skilled in repairing the make, model, and year of vehicle you are considering. This is especially important if the vehicle was imported from another country. Ask friends, coworkers, and relatives for a recommendation of a reliable mechanic. Review the Yellow Pages for mechanics capable of providing "Automotive Diagnostic Service" and ensure that they are certified to perform an inspection from the manufacturer or have received independent certification, such as the ASE. Contact the Better Business Bureau, your state attorney general's office, or the consumer protection agency to inquire about any complaints that have been filed against the facility you are considering to do the inspection of your vehicle. If you have identified several possible mechanics who can provide this service, contact all of them by phone to compare the cost and any differences in the type of inspection they will perform. Make certain that the mechanic understands that no one other than you should be provided with the results of the inspection, so the seller cannot use this information to their advantage in selling the vehicle to another person or against you in the negotiations.

The chosen service station or automotive repair shop should perform a complete bumper-to-bumper inspection of the vehicle and include the body of the vehicle as well as the mechanics. Ask for a written list of deficiencies and cost estimates for any recommended repairs. Review this list carefully, and make certain that you understand all of the recommendations. Ask to speak directly to the mechanic. This list will serve as a valuable tool in negotiating a fair price and help you to further evaluate your future repair costs if you choose to buy the vehicle. Can you or a friend/spouse perform any of the repairs for less? The final decision to buy or pass on the vehicle is yours, not the mechanic's. The mechanic only provides an objective evaluation of the vehicle.

STEP 7 The Negotiation Process

Once you have found a vehicle that meets your needs, has been thoroughly examined by a mechanic of your choice, and is found to be in good condition, you are ready to begin to negotiate the price. Of course, most people acknowledge that negotiating with an individual seller is much easier than negotiating with a car salesperson.

Never let the seller know that you like the vehicle. Always maintain an impartial, unemotional attitude about the vehicle anytime you are dealing with the seller. This allows you to be taken more seriously if you threaten to walk away from the deal. Try not to be defensive or argumentative, but by all means remain fair in your offers and expectations. Always bring your own calculator to the negotiations along with all notes and information you have collected about the vehicle.

Allow the seller to make the first offer by asking, "Is this your best price for this vehicle?" After the seller has responded to your question, discuss what you perceive to be the true value of the vehicle based on the required repairs, age of the vehicle, mileage, and options. (Use the figures from the www.edmunds.com Web site as confirmation of your offer.) Remember that knowledge is power, and this information enables you to have the upper hand over the seller.

It is not recommended that you make your final offer first. Instead, make an offer that is lower than you would be willing to pay. You should be able to justify this offer based on the repairs recommended by your mechanic and the suggested selling price from the Kelly Blue Book, Edmunds Web site, and/or NADA. If necessary, reduce your first offer to an amount below the fair market value. If the seller objects to this offer (which you should expect), ask him or her to counter the offer. Do not offer any more money until he or she makes a counter offer. The negotiations will go back and forth in this manner until a price is agreed upon. If the seller does not come down to a price that you believe to be reasonable, walk away from the deal. You can continue your search at another dealership or with another individual owner. There are plenty of used vehicles available for your consideration; recognize that this vehicle just wasn't for you.

During negotiations, inquire about any additional charges that may be added to the final price of the vehicle. Dealers add preparation charges, transportation fees, licensing fees, and many other charges. These fees add up quickly. The primary purpose of these fees is to serve as another means to make a profit for the dealer. By acknowledging the fact that you anticipate that the salesperson will add these fees, you level the playing field. Make it clear to the salesperson that the price you are negotiating is the final price after all dealer fees and charges have been included. Refuse to pay one cent more than the price you are negotiating.

STEP 8 The Purchase

You have made it to the final step in your journey. Remain vigilant in this last step to ensure that the appropriate paperwork is completed so you become the legal owner of the vehicle and that it accurately records your negotiated agreement.

If you are buying a used vehicle from an individual, check with your department of motor vehicles to determine the specific paperwork that is required for you to title and register it in your name. Inquire about the need to have any of the documents notarized by the seller. Draw up a bill-of-sale that includes the owner's name and address, your name and address, the make, model, and year of the vehicle, the total purchase price, and the VIN. Both the seller and buyer should sign the bill-of-sale. Buying a vehicle from an individual is usually only a matter of exchanging the money, the title, bill-of-sale, and any other documents required by your state.

The dealership will have its unique documents along with the title, Buyer's Guide, and bill-of-sale. Review all calculations and fine print on the paperwork that is presented for your signature. Always confirm that the correct VIN is on the paperwork. Question anything and everything that does not reflect the negotiated deal you made with the salesperson. This is your last opportunity to walk away from the purchase of the vehicle. Do not let the dealer make you feel pressured or obligated—remember, there are plenty of other used vehicles out there for you to find and purchase. It is your money and every extra dollar that is paid to the dealer is one less dollar in your bank account.

As you drive away in your new used vehicle, you will feel a great sense of self-pride and accomplishment. By following these eight steps, you can rest comfortably in the knowledge that you purchased a car that will provide reliable, inexpensive transportation for years to come. Congratulations, you did it!

PAY LESS FOR AUTOMOBILE INSURANCE

Most vehicle owners consider automobile insurance an essential living expense. It ensures that you will be able to pay for vehicle repairs or hospital bills if you are involved in an accident. Automobile insurance also protects you against the claims of others who sustain damage or injury from your vehicle. Various factors should be carefully evaluated to ensure that you are getting adequate coverage and paying a fair price.

Auto Insurance: The Basics

Automobile insurance policies usually include the following coverage:

- Bodily injury liability: Many states require that a vehicle owner maintain a minimum level of bodily injury liability insurance. This insurance protects other people when damage is caused as a result of your own driving. There are two parts to liability insurance: bodily injury and property damage. Bodily injury covers losses resulting from death or injury when you are the one at fault. Insurance "limits" refer to the maximum amount that is paid per accident or per person. States with mandatory vehicle insurance require minimum levels of liability coverage. These limits are typically abbreviated by indicating the maximum paid to each person injured, followed by the maximum to be paid for everyone injured and the total amount that will be paid for property damage. The term 25/50/10 means that the insurance company will pay up to $25,000 to each person injured, no more than $50,000 for all injuries, and up to $10,000 to repair any property damage. Carefully evaluate how much liability insurance you need. Carrying only the amount required in your state is placing your personal assets at risk. If you are sued and the judgment against you exceeds your insurance limits, you will be held personally responsible to pay the difference. Most states also require a certain level of property damage insurance. This insurance pays for any damage to property caused as a result of your driving. Your state's minimum requirement may be too low to adequately protect you, especially when you consider the fact that most newer cars cost well over $20,000.

- Umbrella coverage: An umbrella policy covers liability expenses that exceed the dollar limits of both your automobile and homeowners insurance policies. Other situations may also be covered, such as a lawsuit against you for libel, slander, mental anguish, and so on. To qualify for an umbrella policy, your insurer may require that you have both automobile and homeowners insurance. You may also have to carry a specific amount of automobile liability coverage to be eligible for an umbrella policy. This option could be a very cost-effective strategy in lieu of raising the limits of your automobile liability insurance. Compare the cost of increasing your property damage liability to the level that will be provided by an umbrella policy with the cost of the umbrella policy to determine the most cost-effective solution for you.
- Uninsured motorist coverage: This insurance covers your medical bills should you be involved in an accident with someone who does not have automobile insurance. Most states that require uninsured motorist coverage set minimum requirement amounts. This protection can also pay the balance of your damages if they exceed the limits of the other driver's insurance policy.
- Personal injury protection (PIP): States with no-fault laws require personal injury protection insurance. This insurance pays for medical costs along with other accident related expenses regardless of

who was at fault in the accident. PIP also reimburses the insured for lost income.
- Medical payment insurance: This insurance is especially relevant if you live in a state that does not have no-fault laws. This type of insurance will pay for your medical injuries regardless of who was at fault in the accident.
- Collision insurance: Damages are covered if you have this insurance regardless of who was at fault. Collision coverage always carries a deductible (or the amount that you must pay out-of-pocket after the accident before the insurance company begins to pay). Deductibles range from $100 to $2000. Some lenders require collision coverage until the loan is repaid. It is recommended to carry collision coverage for vehicles less than three years old. If your vehicle is three to seven years old, your decision will depend on how much risk you are willing to assume. Generally, it is not recommended to carry collision coverage for a vehicle older than seven years. A vehicle with a low resale value should not have collision coverage because the additional cost of paying for this coverage would pay for the replacement of the vehicle within a short time. The resale value represents the maximum amount an insurer would pay for the vehicle if it were severely damaged in an accident. For example, if a vehicle has a resale value of $500 and it is damaged so severely that it is determined to be irreparable by the insurance company, the most it will pay you is $500. However, depending on the make, model, and year of the vehicle as well as where you live, you may have to pay $500 or more per year for this coverage. Note: The amount of money you paid for the vehicle or the amount that is still due on the loan does not affect the insurance rate. Vehicles made in the United States rapidly depreciate in value. After five years, a domestic vehicle is typically worth only 30% of its original cost.
- Comprehensive insurance: Comprehensive insurance covers those damages to your automobile that are not covered by collision insurance. The cost of comprehensive insurance is based on the kind of vehicle you own and where you live. Comprehensive policies always have deductibles, which can range from $50 to $500. As a general rule, the higher the deductible on your insurance policy, the lower the insurance premium.

YOUR STATE'S REQUIREMENTS

The Federal Consumer Information Center Web site, *www.pueblo.gsa.gov/crh/insurance.htm*, lists the addresses, phone numbers, and Web sites for the insurance regulators of every state. This will provide you with the appropriate contact to answer any questions you have specific to the insurance requirements in your state.

Choosing an Insurance Company

The following list contains the various types of insurance companies from which you have to choose:

- Stock insurers: Stockholders own this type of insurance company.
- Mutual companies: This type of insurance company is owned by its policyholders. Some mutual companies require a onetime "membership fee."
- Direct writers: These companies deal directly with consumers and do not have agents. In theory, their rates are lower because commissions are not paid to an insurance agent.
- State sponsored insurance systems: Some states have established insurance systems primarily to insure drivers that are rejected by private insurance companies. They are also known as assigned-risk plans or pools because private insurers in the state are required to take on a certain number of these high-risk motorists.

Auto Insurance Comparison Shopping

The same coverage can vary by hundreds of dollars when comparing the premiums charged by various insurance companies. Studies show that two-thirds of us contact only one or two companies or agents prior to purchasing insurance. To be assured the best rate, you must contact as many insurance companies as time allows. Your state's insurance department can provide a list of companies licensed to sell insurance in your state.

This list will facilitate your search to find an insurance company that can provide low-cost insurance to meet your needs. Your state's insurance department may be able to provide other useful data as well. Many states publish a consumer guide listing the premiums charged by various insurance companies for a basic insurance policy. This information can help to narrow down your list of companies to contact for a specific quote. Why contact those with the highest rates?

Of course, price alone should not be your main consideration in choosing an insurance company. First and foremost, you need a company that has the financial assets to pay for any submitted claims. An easy way to evaluate the financial stability of an insurance company is to consider its Standard and Poor's Insurer Financial Strength Rating. Since 1916, the Standard and Poor's company has evaluated the financial security characteristics of insurance organizations with respect to their ability to pay insurance policies and contracts in accordance with their terms. To determine a specific insurance company's Standard and Poor's Insurer Financial Strength Rating, visit its Web page at *www.ratings.standardpoor.com/ratings/insurance/index.htm*.

Contact your state's insurance department to inquire if they have any complaints filed against a specific insurance company. This information is available for public review.

The type of service you receive may be important to you when choosing an insurance company. Ask the insurance company you are considering how claims are handled. Will you be required to obtain estimates if you have a claim for damage done to your vehicle or does the insurance company have a drive-in claims service department? If you have the time to obtain written estimates after an accident, this may be an acceptable option. However, if your schedule does not allow you to take a day off to obtain estimates, you might be better off considering only those insurers that offer more service to their insured. Do you prefer the personalized service of working with the same agent any time you have questions or concerns? Or, is contacting an 800 number acceptable? Inquire among friends regarding their personal claims experiences with their insurance companies.

Once you have narrowed down your list of insurance companies, you are ready to begin comparison shopping. Comparison shopping takes time. The traditional way to comparison shop is to contact the insurance companies on the phone or in person. To streamline this laborious task, try this simple yet efficient technique. Using the following two-step method, you could send out the quote-seeking information to dozens of insurance companies in less than two hours! When the agents or representatives begin to call with the information, tell them to send a written estimate for your review. Contact only those with the lowest acceptable estimate for more detailed information.

1. Send a form letter to the various insurance companies from which you are seeking a quote. The cover letter should state simply that you are requesting a quote on your automobile insurance coverage.
2. Attach the additional information that is required by the prospective insurance company so you will receive an accurate quote.

The following list contains information that you should include to prospective insurance companies:

- Your name.
- Your address.
- The make, model, and year of your vehicle(s).
- Age and gender of all drivers.
- How the vehicle will be used (i.e., personal use only, driven to and from work, etc.).
- The driving record of all drivers to be insured under the policy including at-fault accidents and moving violations. Contact the Department of Motor Vehicles (DMV) in the state where you live to receive a copy of your DMV report.
- The estimated number of miles the vehicle will be driven per year.

Include any other information that may be necessary to obtain discounts. (Refer to the "Seven Ways to Reduce Insurance Costs" section for more information on discounts.)

Determine specifically what types of insurance coverage you need and the amount of each. Include a complete detailed listing of the amount of coverage you are seeking in the letter to the insurance company, and include a list of any discounts that you feel you may be eligible to receive. Simply copy the form in Figure 9-2, and fill in the amount of coverage for each type of insurance you have determined to be appropriate to meet your needs. You can complete the "total premium" section upon receipt of the estimate.

Figure 9-2

Type of insurance	Amount of coverage
Bodily injury liability	_____
Property damage liability	_____
Umbrella coverage	_____
Uninsured motorist	_____
Under insured motorist	_____
Personal injury protection	_____
Medical payment	_____
Collision w/_____deductible	_____
Comprehensive w/____deductible	_____
Other charges:	_____

Total premium_____

Six Ways to Reduce Insurance Costs

Take control of your money by taking steps to reduce your auto insurance. Included are seven factors that you may not have considered in your battle to reduce your living expenses.

ASK FOR DISCOUNTS

Companies offer a variety of discounts on insurance premiums. Do not assume that the company or agent will automatically give you any discounts that you are eligible to receive. Be sure to ask about any of the following discounts that may apply to your situation and inquire about any other discount the company may have. It is impossible to include every possible discount offered by every insurance company. However, the following list contains the most common discounts offered by insurance companies.

- Multiple vehicles: If more than one vehicle is covered on a policy, many insurance companies discount all or part of the policy by 10 to 25 percent.
- Defensive driving course: Receive a 5 to 10 percent discount by completing a state approved course. This frequently applies only to people age 55 and over.

- Automobile/homeowners package: Receive 5 to 15 percent off both automobile and homeowners insurance policies when both are with the same company.
- Good driver discount: Insurance companies discount a premium of 5 to 10 percent if you have maintained a good driving record for at least two years. Sometimes, you must be with the same insurer for several years to qualify.
- Mature driver discount: For drivers over age 50, 5 to 15 percent discounts are common.
- Automatic safety belt and air bags: Receive 10 to 30 percent off the medical payments for the personal injury protection portion of the premium and as much as 60 percent off the same coverage if you have air bags in your vehicle.
- Anti-theft devices: The installation of an alarm system or other anti-theft device can save 5 to 50 percent off comprehensive insurance.
- Anti-lock brakes: Discounts of 5 to 10 percent from medical, liability, and collision coverage are given if the insured vehicle has anti-lock brakes. Some states require insurance companies to make this discount available.
- Student driver training: This discount is available only to high school students and provides 10 percent off the total premium.
- Good student discount: High school or college students demonstrating proof of at least a B average or better are eligible for a 5 to 25 percent discount off most coverage.
- Student away at school: When a student resides more than 100 miles from the family home without access to the family vehicle, the premium may be discounted by 10 to 40 percent.
- Car-pool: With the certification that the insured vehicle is used in a car pool for commuting, the driver may receive 5 to 25 percent off the total premiums.
- Low mileage: Driving a given vehicle less than 30 miles each week to and from work can earn a 15 percent discount off the rate charged to drivers who commute more than 100 miles a week. Driving a vehicle a total of less than 7,500 miles a year may entitle you to a 15 percent discount.

BUY A "LOW PROFILE" VEHICLE

Before buying a new or used vehicle, contact your insurance company and inquire about which vehicles are less expensive to insure. Vehicles with high repair costs or those that are more frequently stolen carry increased insurance rates. Write to the Insurance Institute for Highway Safety to obtain the Injury, Collision, and Theft Losses Report. This report can also be found on the Car Safety Web site at *www.carsafety.org*. This report provides the collision, theft, and injury losses of most vehicles. These losses are assigned numerical values. The higher the value, the greater the loss and higher the risk. Insurance companies use these numeric values to assign their rates. Your insurance company can also provide information regarding its rates as they apply to a given vehicle rating. This report provides a good starting point in finding an acceptable low profile vehicle.

Contact:

The Insurance Institute for Highway Safety
1005 North Glebe Road, Suite 800
Arlington, VA 22201
Phone: (703) 247-1500

DROP COLLISION AND/OR COMPREHENSIVE COVERAGE ON OLDER VEHICLES

If your vehicle has a resale value of less than $1,000, it is probably not cost-effective to have collision or comprehensive coverage. Any claim you make would not exceed the annual cost of the insurance and deductible amounts. Review the Edmunds Web site at *www.edmunds.com* or the Kelly Blue Book Web site at *www.kbb.com* to determine the current value of your vehicle.

RAISE YOUR DEDUCTIBLES ON COLLISION AND COMPREHENSIVE COVERAGE

Deductibles represent the amount of money you pay out-of-pocket before the insurance company begins to pay for the damages. By increasing the deductible, you can substantially lower your insurance premiums. For example, increasing your deductible from $200 to $500 can reduce your collision and comprehensive premiums by 15 to 30 percent.

CONTACT BOTH INDEPENDENT AND "CAPTIVE" AGENTS TO OBTAIN AN INSURANCE ESTIMATE

Independents represent several companies. Frequently, they can obtain competitive price quotes. Captives, or "exclusive" agents, on the other hand, represent only one company.

GO WITH A GROUP

Some insurance companies do not use agents at all. Instead, they sell directly to certain groups. For example, GEICO sells directly to government employees. Look into group auto insurance offered through your employer, professional societies, or other membership. (Caution: Do not automatically assume their rates are less than ones you can get on your own. Always compare their rates with those offered by other companies.)

10

The Emperor's New Clothes

Do you recall the fairy tale about the Emperor who had very special garments made by two weavers? These two crafty men claimed to make the most beautiful garments ever created. However, the clothing had the peculiar quality of becoming invisible to those unfit for the office they held or those that were impossibly dull. In reality, these weavers were only skilled at swindling money, not creating unique garments. No one dared admit that he or she could not see anything as the cloth was woven and then sewn into the Emperor's garments. To admit this would be an affirmation that you were unfit for your post. Everyone pretended they saw the Emperor garbed in beautiful new clothing as he walked in a procession through the streets of his kingdom. It was not until a young innocent child stated the obvious that everyone admitted the truth about the Emperor's new garments. "The Emperor has no clothes!"

Do you buy clothing from trendy stores with the most popular labels? The Emperor found out in the most embarrassing way that people do not notice labels or a store's reputation when they make note of your clothing. Instead, they notice only the most obvious features. Within a few seconds of meeting you, a new acquaintance will size up your appearance by noting if your garments are clean, neatly pressed, in a state of good repair, reasonably stylish, appropriate for the season, and color coordinated. He or she will also make note of your posture and how you present yourself. Unless you are wearing clothing with the name of the manufacturer imprinted in an obvious location, the people around you are unaware of the brand of clothing you are wearing.

Although I will primarily address clothing in terms of a woman's wardrobe, this wardrobe planning technique works for all family members. Your daughter's wardrobe scheme could be pink, white, and light green with primary colors used for your son. This common sense approach not only decreases the cost of a wardrobe, but makes shopping more efficient and easier.

THE FIVE RULES TO REDUCE CLOTHING COSTS

When purchasing clothing (and shoes) for yourself or your family, develop a battle plan and stick to it. The rules of engagement are contained in the following list for your convenience and ease in implementation.

RULE #1
Never Pay Retail

There are many ways to purchase clothing and shoes at a discount. Shop at wholesale clubs, consignment shops, yard sales, discount stores, thrift stores, factory outlets, off-price stores, department store clearance centers, catalog outlet stores, and designer outlets. Traditionally, the large department stores have their end-of-season clothing sales in January, April, June, and November. Most discount stores, including thrift and consignment shops, also have end-of-season sales.

YOUR DOLLARS BUY MORE AT A CONSIGNMENT STORE

Consignment stores have become very popular within the past few years and can now be found all over the United States. Consignment shops vary greatly from one another in price, selection, cleanliness, and quality of clothing. Some consignment shops look like expensive boutiques, whereas others have the appearance of an inner-city thrift shop.

It is a safe assumption that the better consignment shops are in the nicer parts of your community. You may have to visit several consignment shops before you find one that meets your needs and standards. Yet, persistence will pay off in big savings. Name brand clothing and shoes, in good condition (sometimes with the original price tags), can be purchased at a consignment shop. Garments are generally "gently worn" and have the appearance of new clothes that were washed once or twice. Most stores accept only garments in immaculate condition. The store's owner/manager usually determines prices, so they vary from one store to another. Clothes are frequently priced at less than 50% of their original selling price.

The inventory of these stores can turn over fairly quickly because consignors bring new items almost daily. Therefore, you may want to stop by your favorite consignment shop on a regular basis for the best selection. Some stores routinely discount a garment after it has been in the store for more than 30 days. Don't forget to inspect the garment very carefully to ensure that you don't overlook a flaw or any other damage. Inquire about the return policy prior to the purchase because many stores do not accept returns, give refunds, or allow exchanges.

SELLING CLOTHES AT A CONSIGNMENT SHOP

Consignment stores also offer you the opportunity to sell your outgrown or unneeded clothing. This provides another opportunity to further reduce your clothing costs. Contact local consignment shops to determine the conditions under which they operate. Some charge a yearly fee and others do not. Frequently, the consignor receives 50 percent of the selling price. Some people actually make money buying used clothing and reselling them at consignment stores. For example, if you purchase a $20 sweater at a yard sale for $1 and sell it at a consignment store, it might sell for 50 percent of the retail price or $10. You would then receive 50 percent of the selling price, or $5! You would make $4 in profit.

BUYING CLOTHES AT A DISCOUNT STORE OR OFF-PRICE STORE

The majority of clothing is now purchased at discount stores. However, discount stores have a reputation for selling clothing of inferior quality. You will not save any money if the garment falls apart or shrinks dramatically after two or three washings. Always examine a garment before purchasing to ensure it will wear well. Discount stores frequently have return policies that allow the return of a defective garment. Inquire about the store's return policy and always keep your receipts. Off-price stores purchase excess inventories from manufacturers and department stores. They often sell clothing with designer labels at incredibly low prices. Occasionally the garments are irregulars, seconds, or defective—so inspect them carefully. Several large off-price chain stores have locations nationwide.

The following list contains three off-price chain stores that sell clothing for the entire family. Their toll free number is provided for your convenience in locating a store near you.

- T.J. Maxx: (800) 926-6299
- Marshall's: (888) 627-7425
- Burlington Coat Factory: (800) 444-COAT

WHOLESALE CLUBS OFFER DISCOUNTS TO MEMBERS ONLY

To belong to a wholesale club, you must pay a yearly membership fee. Before joining one, carefully consider how much you will buy during the next year. Always compare prices to determine if, in fact, you will save money. Most wholesale clubs offer free one day passes so you can evaluate their merchandise and compare prices before you join. Wholesale clubs offer a limited selection of products that can vary from week to week. Just because they sell your favorite brand of jeans today does not mean they will carry them tomorrow. Although clothing is discounted below the regular price of department stores, they seldom have sales.

YARD SALES, TAG SALES, GARAGE SALES, AND FLEA MARKETS

These nonretail options represent the greatest opportunity to save money. Clothing is priced at only a fraction of its original cost. Sweaters typically sell for $1 or less and jeans sell for as little as 50¢. Do not be put off by the poor quality clothing you may occasionally find for sale. Keep looking for clothing that meets your standards, and you will be surprised and pleased at what you will find. Of course, selection is limited, quality varies, and items are sold "as is" with no refunds.

BARGAIN HUNTING IN THRIFT STORES

Thrift stores are owned and operated by various charitable organizations including churches, women's clubs, Goodwill, and the Salvation Army. You can find a fairly wide selection of clothing at a thrift store. The clothing quality varies greatly, so garments must be carefully evaluated. The colors of some of the garments may be a bit faded from being washed. Yet, if you were to look at the clothes your family is currently wearing, you would find that many of them have faded colors. Volunteers usually staff these stores. Therefore, you may want to consider volunteering your time to work at a thrift store as a service to your community. Volunteers can also choose from the donated items before they are put out for general sale.

FACTORY OUTLET SHOPPING

A genuine factory outlet store is owned by the manufacturer and serves as a way for the company to sell excess inventory and defective merchandise including seconds, irregulars, and damaged goods. Prices in a real factory outlet can be quite reasonable. Nevertheless, you must be prepared with the knowledge of regular retail prices so you do not pay too much for an item. Never assume that because you are shopping in an outlet store, you are automatically paying less for a given garment than if it was purchased in a traditional retail store. Retailers count on shoppers making this assumption and frequently price their clothing and shoes accordingly. Always be cautious when buying defective items because they frequently cannot be returned. Carefully examine the garment to determine if the defect could affect its durability or appearance.

Some manufacturers produce clothing lines specifically for their outlet stores. Therefore, if you are of the opinion that you can purchase a garment for $45 at an outlet that would have sold at a manufacturer's retail store for a "suggested retail price of $90," you may be wrong. In fact, the garment you purchase may be available for sale only at the outlet store and the real retail price is $45 because it is not the same quality and material as that sold in their retail store at the mall. Before going to an outlet, you should have an idea of the genuine retail price for the clothing. You will then know if the clothing is, in fact, reduced.

CLEARANCE OR SALVAGE STORES OFFER A UNIQUE ASSORTMENT OF GOODS

These businesses purchase a store's remaining inventory as a result of bankruptcy or excess seasonal stock. They frequently sell a variety of items, not just clothing. Selection and quality changes from week to week. An astute shopper will haunt these locations for bargains.

DEPARTMENT STORE CLEARANCE CENTERS AND CATALOG OUTLET STORES

Several well-known department stores and catalog companies sell damaged, returned, and end-of-season clothing at their own clearance centers. Prices are dramatically reduced from their main stores. These stores may be a bit hard to find because they're not usually located in large shopping malls, but they're more than worth the effort to seek out.

SHOP SMART

It is not uncommon to purchase an item in the boy's/men's department for less than it is in the girl's/women's department. For example, a size 6x turtleneck sweater in the girl's department of a discount store may sell for $10. Yet, in the boy's department, you would find the same sweater for $8.50. Many pregnant mothers-to-be have already found that they can simply wear a large-size man's shirt instead of buying a maternity smock. White shirts or sweaters can be worn with every color or print. Colored socks are usually more expensive than white socks. The price per pair is cheaper when you buy them in packages of 6 to 12 pairs. (You will also find that matching socks is easier when you have multiple pairs of the same color sock.)

RULE #2
Purchase Clothing and Shoes Based on Quality, Durability, Longevity, and Fit, Not by the Brand Name

Too often, paying more for brand-name garments or shoes does not result in a better quality item. Instead, it only provides higher profit margins for the manufacturers and funds their expensive advertising campaigns.

Because you can no longer rely on the manufacturer (i.e., the brand name) to consistently ensure a quality garment or pair of shoes, it is up to the consumer to carefully inspect the item.

To respect the life force that was given to earn your money, you must act responsibly with your money. When purchasing clothing and shoes, failure to act in a responsible way can result in buying an item that does not wear or launder well and ends up in the garbage. You end up wasting the time (i.e., your life force) spent to earn the money, wasting the time spent to locate and purchase the item, and then wasting more money and time to replace the item.

ALWAYS INSPECT CLOTHING CAREFULLY BEFORE PURCHASING

Look for signs of quality construction and material. Refer to the Clothing Quality Checklist in Figure 10-1 for use in evaluating the quality of a garment. Hold the item up to the light and carefully inspect it. Occasionally, an item is dramatically reduced because it has a ripped seam, missing button, or some other minor flaw. In these instances, a little repair on your part can pay off at the checkout. Simply take the item home and sew up the seam, replace the button, and so on. If, however, you notice a flaw and the item is not reduced, ask the clerk to reduce the garment due to the defect. Purchasing a stained garment is risky unless you know what made the stain and how to get it out. Items may have imperfections marked with small stickers. "Irregular" clothing means the item does not meet the manufacturer's quality control standards. They may have flaws in the color, a stain on the fabric, or may fit improperly. Garments marked as a "second" or "third" often have serious flaws and must be examined carefully to determine if the defect is acceptable.

Sometimes the reason an item of clothing is in an off-price store or outlet store is because it is incorrectly sized. Do not trust the size printed on the label. Try on the article of clothing to ensure a proper fit. Is it comfortable? Can you sit, stand, bend, move, and reach with ease? Look at yourself from all sides. Does the garment "hang" well? Does the color flatter you? Do you already own something that will coordinate with the item? What does the overall appearance say about the garment? If your first impression says "poor quality" that's what others may also say. If it does not fit properly, it is no bargain.

> **FIGURE 10-1**
>
> **Clothing Quality Checklist**
>
> - Look for stains and signs of wear on the clothing.
> - Look for close, unbroken, even length stitches (about 10–12 stitches per inch).
> - Facing and interfacing should be smooth and unnoticeable.
> - Plaids, stripes, and cross seams should match evenly.
> - Look for evenly spaced gathers and pleats.
> - Hems should be securely sewn in place, uniform in width, and invisible on the outside.
> - Quality fabric should be evenly woven without flaws.
> - Flat pockets should have reinforced corners with no bunching or tucks.
> - Look for flat seams that are pinked or overcast on the inside.
> - Zippers, snaps, buckles, buttons, and other trim should be sewn securely.
> - Fabric with plaid or striped design should match at the side seams.
> - The length of both sleeves and pant legs should be symmetrical.
> - Knits should have even circular loops in the fabric with no snags.
> - Look for symmetrical darts and collars.
> - When buttoned, the front of the garment should be flat.

CHOOSE CLOTHING BASED ON THE FIBER CONTENT INFORMATION LISTED ON THE GARMENT LABEL

Clothes made with 100 percent cotton usually shrink one to two sizes when washed, wrinkle easily, and fade. Polyester-cotton blends shrink very little, if any, and retain their colors. Nylon and polyester fabrics are strong and do not shrink or wrinkle. However, they are prone to pilling and grease stains. Acetate is a fairly weak, fragile fabric that wrinkles easily and can be damaged by perspiration, but it is resistant to shrinking and pilling. Clothes made with acrylic fabric do not wrinkle or shrink, but can be damaged by perspiration and are prone to pilling and grease stains. Rayon should be avoided in children's clothes because it shrinks when washed, stretches, wrinkles easily, and is damaged by perspiration.

Dry cleaning clothes can be expensive. Therefore, do not purchase clothes that need to be dry cleaned if you are trying to keep clothing costs to a minimum. Also, few busy parents have the time to hand launder clothes. Read the garment care label to know what you may be getting into before you purchase the any garment.

RETURN DEFECTIVE CLOTHES AND SHOES, IF STORE POLICY ALLOWS IT

Sometimes, even with careful consideration and inspection, the item does not wear or launder well. When this happens, promptly return it! You purchased the garment or shoes in good faith, expecting it to get a reasonable amount of wear. Always keep receipts because most stores require that you show proof of purchase. Many people are under the false assumption that stores are required by law to issue refunds. In reality, stores can determine their own refund policy. Some simply do not offer this option. As a smart shopper, you should find out the store's return policy before the time of purchase. When returning an item, do not feel intimidated by the salesperson or manager—it is your money and they were at fault, not you. Unfortunately, too often, we do not take the item back, but instead just toss it out. Once again, this is not respecting the life force that was given to earn the money that was used to buy the item.

KEEP AWAY FROM FADS, INSTEAD CHOOSE ENDURING STYLES

Some styles come and go in a matter of months, whereas others endure for years. To remain stylish and spend less money, choose garments and shoes that represent conservative styles that have remained popular over the course of time. You and your family can be well dressed without wearing this week's latest fad. For example, regardless of the color scheme of a woman's business wardrobe, three pairs of dress shoes in three colors (bone, navy, and black) are all that is needed to coordinate with any color scheme wardrobe. Instead of buying 10 or more pairs of shoes, a businesswoman need only buy three.

RULE #3
Plan Your Wardrobe

One of the easiest and most important ways to contain clothing costs is through careful wardrobe planning. This should be done twice each year with children because they outgrow their clothes so quickly. Once or twice a year (in the spring and fall) is sufficient for an adult.

The first step is to go through closets and drawers to determine articles of clothing that you have available to use in your wardrobe. Set aside garments that need to be mended. Try on clothing to evaluate the fit and style. Set aside clothing that no longer fits or is hopelessly out of style. Can the clothing be altered for a better fit or updated in some manner? Outgrown or unwanted clothing can be given to a younger sibling, friend, or relative, taken to a consignment shop, sold at a yard sale, or donated to charity.

Review the remaining acceptable clothing to determine the number of bottoms (pants and skirts) and tops (shirts, blouses, sweaters, and T-shirts). By combining tops and bottoms, determine the total number of outfits you or your family member has to wear. The total number of outfits (an outfit is a clothing combination consisting of one top and one bottom) that you need is a personal decision. However, 10 outfits is a conservative, yet acceptable number. Ten outfits will allow you to wear a different outfit every day of the week (Monday through Friday) for two weeks. One pair of shoes may be all that is needed to coordinate with these 10 outfits. By purchasing three bottoms and four tops, you can coordinate a total of 12 different outfits by using the technique demonstrated in Figure 10-2.

FIGURE 10-2

Wardrobe

Pant A	Skirt D	Shirt G
Pant B	Shirt E	Shirt H
Pant C	Shirt F	Jacket I

Outfit combinations

Pant A + Shirt E	Pant C + Shirt E
Pant A + Shirt F	Pant C + Shirt F
Pant A + Shirt G	Pant C + Shirt G
Pant A + Shirt H	Pant C + Shirt H
Pant A + Shirt E + Jacket I	Pant C + Shirt E + Jacket I
Pant A + Shirt F + Jacket I	Pant C + Shirt F + Jacket I
Pant A + Shirt G + Jacket I	Pant C + Shirt G + Jacket I
Pant A + Shirt H + Jacket I	Pant C + Shirt H + Jacket I
Pant B + Shirt E	Skirt D + Shirt E
Pant B + Shirt F	Skirt D + Shirt F
Pant B + Shirt G	Skirt D + Shirt G
Pant B + Shirt H	Skirt D + Shirt H
Pant B + Shirt E + Jacket I	Skirt D + Shirt E + Jacket I
Pant B + Shirt F + Jacket I	Skirt D + Shirt F + Jacket I
Pant B + Shirt G + Jacket I	Skirt D + Shirt G + Jacket I
Pant B + Shirt H + Jacket I	Skirt D + Shirt H + Jacket I

FIGURE 10-3
Family Member Measurements and Sizes

Waist measurement: _____

Inseam: _____
(distance from the ankle to the crotch)

Arm length: _____
(distance from wrist to top of shoulder)

Shoulder measurement: _____
(across the back—measure the distance from one shoulder seam to the opposite shoulder seam)

Chest measurement: _____

Hip measurement: _____

Shirt size: _____

Pant size: _____

Shoe size: _____
(including width)

Make a list of only those specific items needed to complete the number of outfits you deem to be an acceptable size wardrobe for you or your family member. Bring small swatches of material from current garments when you shop to easily match colors. Cut the swatch from the facing, seam allowance, or hem, where it will not be noticed or cause damage to the garment. Tape these swatches to one 3 × 5 inch card for each person in your family. Write the family member's measurements and sizes on the back of the swatch card. Refer to Figure 10-3 for the required measurements. Indicate the date the sizes were taken because kids can grow rather quickly. If you are shopping for someone who is not with you, bring a cloth tape measure so you can easily measure the garment to ensure a proper fit.

A child does not need an extensive wardrobe. Refer to Figures 10-4 and 10-5 for the components of a satisfactory wardrobe for a child at various ages. Children experience dramatic growth spurts. If your child outgrows his or her jeans/pants before the end of the season, your budget will not be thrown into a tailspin if you have maintained his or her wardrobe within the listed recommendations and did not buy excessive clothing at the beginning of the season. Spend the extra money left from your clothing budget to buy one or two more pairs of jeans/pants to wear until the change of seasons.

The key to having a wardrobe that enhances your appearance is quite simple: A good wardrobe is not collected, it is built. The best way to implement this strategy is to choose a color scheme for your clothing based on two or three interchangeable colors. In other words, colors that coordinate with each other. For example, one color scheme is red, black and white; a second is tan, cream, and navy; and a third is tan, hunter green, and cream.

Figure 10-4
Fall and Winter Wardrobe

AGE	SEX	CLOTHING NEEDS
Infant	Boy	5–7 sleepers, 1 winter coat, 1 dressy outfit
Infant	Girl	5–7 sleepers, 1 winter coat, 1 dress
Preschool	Boy	3–5 pairs pants or jeans, 4–6 shirts, sweaters or sweatshirts, 1 winter coat, 1 dressy outfit
Preschool	Girl	3–5 pairs jeans/pants, 4–6 shirts/sweaters/sweatshirts, 1 winter coat, 1 dress
School-aged	Boy	3–5 pairs jeans/pants, 4–6 shirts/sweaters/sweatshirts, 1 winter coat, 1 dressy outfit
School-aged	Girl	3–5 pairs jeans/pants/skirts, 4–6 coordinated shirts/sweaters/sweatshirts, 1 winter coat, 1 dress

Figure 10-5
Spring and Summer Wardrobe

AGE	SEX	CLOTHING NEEDS
Infant	Boy	5–7 sleepers/onesies, 1 sweater, 1 dressy outfit
Infant	Girl	5–7 sleepers/onesies, 1 sweater, 1 dress
Preschool	Boy	3–5 pairs shorts, 4–6 T-shirts/sleeveless shirts, 1 waterproof jacket/raincoat, 1 dressy outfit
Preschool	Girl	3–5 pairs shorts, 4–6 T-shirts, 1 waterproof jacket/raincoat, 1 dress
School-aged	Boy	3–5 pairs shorts, 4–6 T-shirts/sleeveless shirts, 1 waterproof jacket/raincoat, 1 dressy outfit
School-aged	Girl	3–5 pairs shorts/skirts, 4–6 T-shirts/sleeveless shirts, 1 waterproof jacket/raincoat, 1 dress

Because people tend to choose the colors of their clothing based on their preferences, you probably already have some prominent color schemes in your wardrobe, which you can further build upon.

A wardrobe based on a color scheme facilitates the interchange of clothing. For example, using only eight items of clothing, you can put together a total of 32 different outfits. Refer to Figure 10-2. To minimize problems associated with matching clothing consisting of a plaid or print design, all of the items in Figure 10-2 are solid colored garments. However, one pair of pants, one shirt, a skirt or a jacket could be a print, stripe, or plaid and 32 different outfits can still be achieved.

The next time you think you need to buy a new outfit, look at your current wardrobe and use your creativity to coordinate a "new" outfit. Take the jacket from a two piece suit and add it to a different skirt and blouse. Play with your wardrobe and try new combinations. Add a belt or scarf to update an old suit. Raise or lower a hem. Layer clothes. You will be surprised at the many new "outfits" you have in your own closet. Best of all, it's free!

RULE #4
Make Clothes Last As Long As Possible

Launder clothing properly to extend the life of garments. Follow the instructions printed on the garment label or you may end up with a shrunken garment. Refer to Figure 10-6 for the basic steps to launder clothes.

The pilling that occurs from frequent washing can ruin sweaters. Small inexpensive fabric shavers work very well at removing these pills and restoring the sweater to looking new again.

T-shirts with company and team logos continue to be very popular and fairly expensive. Because most are made of 100 percent cotton, they frequently shrink and fade with repeated washing and drying. To prolong the life of a T-shirt or any lightweight cotton knit shirt, hang it on a plastic or coated hanger immediately after removing it from the washing machine. Hang the shirt to dry in an area with good air circulation. When dry, you may notice that it is not as soft and is more wrinkled than one dried in a dryer. If this is unacceptable, toss the dry T-shirt(s) in the dryer and turn it on for only one or two minutes. It will come out soft and almost wrinkle free. Of course, placing only one dry T-shirt in the dryer at a time is not as energy efficient as drying several. Save up your dry T-shirts until you have a full dryer load for maximum savings. If desired, toss in a dryer sheet to reduce static cling, which further improves softness and gives them a fresh smell.

FIGURE 10-6

Clothes Laundering Basics

1. Inspect clothes carefully for spots and stains.
2. Pretreat spots and stains.
3. Sort clothes according to color, the type and amount of soil, and the type of fabric.
4. Before washing a garment that is permanent press, knitted, napped, or has a great deal of texture, turn it inside out to prevent it from looking worn or faded and prevent pilling.
5. Use the correct water temperature for the color and type of fabric.
6. Use the appropriate type and amount of detergent.
7. Select the proper setting on your washing machine.
8. Dry clothes at the proper setting.

CHILDREN'S CLOTHING

Buy garments one size larger than the child currently wears so he or she can wear them twice as long. Do not let children wear good "school clothes" to play in after school. Rough play can tear clothes and/or cause them to become excessively worn. Most often, the knees of pants wear out first. Knee patches ironed onto the inside of pants will prevent them from being torn or worn through and make them last twice as long.

RULE #5
Buy Only Sure Things—When in Doubt, Don't Buy It!

Before purchasing a garment, take the following points into consideration to determine if the purchase represents a legitimate expenditure of your money or a potential waste of your money and the life force given to earn the money.

- Will the item be worn often? Once a week or only twice a year?
- Can it be worn more than one season?
- Is it well made?
- How is it laundered? (Dry cleaning is expensive.)
- Will it coordinate with at least two other items currently owned?
- Does it duplicate something you already have?
- Is it really needed?
- Do you genuinely like the item or do you just like the low price?
- Are you falling into the "I can't go wrong at this price" trap? (You can go wrong if it is not something you will wear and enjoy.)
- Can it be exchanged or returned?
- How much trouble will it be to exchange and/or return?
- Is it the correct size? Does it fit well and look flattering on you? Never buy something that is too small with the intent of losing weight so you can fit into the garment.

BECOME KNOWLEDGEABLE REGARDING PRICES AND STYLES

Do your homework. To reduce the costs associated with clothing your family, you must enhance your ability to spot a genuine bargain when you see it. Visit retail department and specialty clothing stores to become familiar with the current styles and regular prices. This research shopping will educate you to recognize a genuine bargain. Comparison shop to ensure that you are purchasing an item for the best price.

Frequently, discount stores sell similar styles for less. Your research shopping will allow you to identify the less expensive generic clones of styles seen in the expensive stores. You may be able to buy a clone of a $75 sweater for only $15 at a discount store. Only your bank account would know for certain where it was purchased.

Be alert and look for bargains. All too often, consumers go into one of the stores listed in this chapter and claim they are unable to find any bargains. Astute, price savvy shoppers know that clothes with incredible prices do not jump off the rack and bite them on the arm. Successful shoppers dig through the racks to find the garments with the best prices. They hunt for good prices and garments to enhance their wardrobe. Happy hunting!

11

Dieting Tips for Utility and Maintenance Bills

Put your utility bills on a waste reduction diet by limiting their intake of energy. The money spent on utility bills represents a significant portion of most families' living expenses. The average family spends about $1,300 each year on heating, cooling, and other utility bills in the home. By simply implementing a few energy efficient techniques, the average homeowner can reduce energy bills up to 50 percent.

The most efficient way to determine where you should first focus your attention is via a home energy audit. With a little knowledge, you can perform the audit yourself. Many utility companies provide this service for a nominal fee or at no charge. A professional contractor can perform a detailed energy audit using specialized equipment to find inefficiencies that are not detectable by a visual inspection. The utility company and professional contractor will provide a list of recommended improvements to make your home more energy efficient. However, many homeowners can employ common sense and basic knowledge regarding what is required to improve the energy efficiency of their homes. The money saved by those homeowners who perform this assessment themselves can be used to pay for those repairs and upgrades that will increase the energy efficiency of their home.

ENERGY AUDIT

Perform an energy audit by carefully examining the interior and exterior structure of your house.

- Evaluate the location and thickness of insulation in your walls, ceilings, attic, floors, and crawl spaces. Are all exterior walls insulated? Measure the thickness of the current insulation to determine the insulation's R-value. Note: Insulation must not be compressed because this decreases its R-value.
- Examine the interior of your home. Look at exterior walls, doors, windows, and ceilings for holes and cracks through which air can leak from your house. Continue inspecting for air leak sources by walking around the outside of your home to evaluate the windows, doors, and places where any wiring or pipe penetrates through an exterior wall.
- Is the fireplace damper open? Do you have tempered glass doors on the fireplace?
- Are your appliances and heating/cooling systems properly maintained as recommended by the manufacturer?
- Evaluate the type of lights being used throughout your home. Is the use of daylight being maximized?

The first area to focus your attention on is your home's insulation and weatherization. By investing a few hundred dollars for the purchase and installation of proper insulation and weatherization products, you can reduce your heating and cooling bills by as much as 30 percent.

Insulation

Look at the current amount of insulation in your attic, crawl spaces, and other places where insulation or the framing of your home is visible to determine the type and thickness of your insulation.

The degree of insulation provided by a specific type of insulation is measured in R-values. The higher the R-value, the more resistant the area is to the transfer of heat. The U.S. Department of Energy (DOE) recommends ranges of R-values for different areas of the country. However, some states have codes recommending lower R-values than those recommended by the DOE. Unlike the DOE, state and local codes usually factor in the cost-effectiveness of increasing the R-value. Contact your local building department to determine your municipality's recommendation for the insulation of homes in your part of the country.

There are four main types of insulation. Each type of insulation is made for a specific use and purpose.

- Batts are used between the studs of the walls or between ceiling and floor joists. They are made of fiberglass or rock wool.
- Rolls or blankets of insulation are laid on top of the attic floor. They are made of fiberglass.
- Loose-fill insulation is blown into the attic or walls of an existing house. It is made from fiberglass, rock wool, or cellulose.
- Rigid foam boards are made to use in a confined space, such as exterior walls, basements, foundation walls, concrete slabs, and cathedral ceilings. They are made of polyisocyanurate, extruded polystyrene (XPS or blueboard), expanded polystyrene (EPS or beadboard), or other materials.

The easiest and most effective way to increase the energy efficiency of your home is to ensure that you have enough attic insulation. Installing more insulation in the attic is a simple process, which just about any homeowner can do without the assistance of a professional. Consult your municipality's building department to determine the recommended R-value of insulation for attics in your region. Add additional insulation to your attic to ensure that the R-value in your attic meets or exceeds this recommendation.

Ventilation in the attic is important to evaluate and consider when adding insulation. A properly vented attic reduces cooling bills in the summer and ensures that there is no moisture buildup. Excess moisture reduces the life of a roof and shingles. Depending on the architectural style of your home, your current attic vents may be located under the soffit or eaves, on the roof, or cut into the side of the house. Ensure that any current attic vents are not blocked with insulation or any other objects. Insulation should be at least three inches away from recessed lighting fixtures or any other heat producing equipment unless it is specially designed for direct insulation contact. Look for the indication "I.C." on the fixture label to confirm that it is rated for direct contact with insulation. If no indication is found, keep the insulation a proper distance away from the object.

Evaluate the insulation of crawl spaces. Are the walls insulated? Is the ceiling of the crawl space insulated? Measure the thickness of any insulation that is present. Determine the local recommendations regarding the

R-value for the insulation of the ceiling and walls of crawl spaces and adhere to these standards by adding more insulation.

Add additional insulation to meet the R-value recommendation to any other area of your house detected as deficient during your inspection.

Weatherization and Air Leaks

Next, consider other ways that you lose heat from your home in the winter and cool air in the summer. Any homeowner can perform this simple and inexpensive test to evaluate whether air is leaking from the house. Light an incense stick and hold it near the sources of air leaks listed in Figure 11-1 or any other location that represents an opening to the outside. This test is best performed on a windy day. Watch the smoke from the incense to determine if it is being influenced by air leaking around or through one of these sources. Depending upon where the air leak is found, you can easily fix it by caulking, sealing, or weather stripping.

- On the exterior of your house, caulk around the perimeter of all doors and windows that are found to be leaking air.
- Place weather stripping on all doors and windows to ensure a tight seal when they are closed.
- Use caulk to eliminate any air leaks where pipes, wiring, or ducts penetrate an exterior wall, floor, ceiling, or soffit over a cabinet.
- Place specially designed gaskets behind electrical outlet and light switch plates on all exterior walls.
- For single-pane windows, install storm windows or place a heavy-duty, clear plastic sheet over the window to seal out any infiltration of air.

Figure 11-1
Air Leak Sources

Recessed lights	All ducts
Attic hatches	Fireplace and chimney penetration
Electrical outlets	Warm air register
Electrical switches	Window sashes and frames
Electric wires	Baseboards and trim
Dropped ceilings	Plumbing access panel
Door sashes and frames	Light fixtures

Ensure that the storm windows you install have weather stripping on all moveable parts with interlocking or overlapping joints. Evaluate additional products that are available commercially for this purpose.
- Inspect your current storm windows and repair or weatherize if needed.
- Keep the fireplace flue damper tightly closed when not in use.

Heating and Cooling

A typical family spends 44 percent of its utility costs on heating and cooling the home. To reduce your costs, maintain the equipment properly and upgrade it as needed.

KEEPING WARM IN THE WINTER

The following list contains additional ways to reduce your energy costs associated with heating your home:

- Close off unoccupied or unnecessary rooms that can be isolated from the rest of the house. Turn down the thermostat or turn off the heat to the rooms. If you have a heat pump, however, do not close the vents because this adversely affects the effectiveness of the heat pump.
- For a forced air furnace, clean or replace the filter at the recommended interval.
- Set your furnace thermostat as low as is comfortable.
- At least once per season, bleed the trapped air from each hot water radiator.
- Use kitchen or bath ventilating fans sparingly in the winter because they remove warm air from the room.
- Ensure that all warm air registers, baseboard heaters, and radiators are clean and free from obstructions.
- During the daylight hours, open the drapes and window shades of windows with a southern exposure to allow for solar heat gain.
- Place insulating curtains and/or window shades on all windows. Close all shades and curtains at night to minimize the chilling of the room from the cold windows.

- If you are in a position to purchase new heating equipment, always look for the Energy Star label. The Energy Star program is a service provided by the U.S. Department of Energy (DOE) and the Environmental Protection Agency (EPA). It is designed to help consumers identify energy efficient appliances and products.

KEEPING COOL IN THE SUMMER

If the temperature is comfortable outside, keeping cool inside may be as simple as moving the cooler air through your home. Open windows to allow movement of air through your home or through specific rooms. Cross ventilation is important to the movement of air.

FANS

Window fans are less expensive to operate than air conditioners and work well to bring in cool air. Place one fan in a window blowing cool air into the room and a second fan in another window blowing the hot air from the room to the outside. Ceiling fans are also useful in improving air circulation. They are fairly easy to install and relatively inexpensive. However, portable fans are cheaper and provide more flexibility because they can readily be moved from one room to the next and directed toward a specific location. Attic fans help to remove hot air from the inside of the house and vent it out through the attic. They can dramatically improve the movement of air within a home. However, they are more difficult to install than ceiling fans. Visit a home improvement center to view the various types of attic fans available. They may offer free classes regarding the installation of attic fans.

AIR CONDITIONERS

All air conditioners require routine maintenance to run efficiently and effectively. Ignoring routine maintenance can result in expensive repairs. Check the owner's manual of your unit for the maintenance schedule.

Set the thermostat of a central air conditioner to the highest comfortable setting. For every degree the thermostat is raised, cooling costs are cut by 5 to 7 percent. Over the course of a hot summer, this represents significant savings.

When leaving your home or apartment for more than a few hours, turn up the air conditioner, or turn it off all together. Conserve the cool air and minimize heat gain by pulling down shades, closing windows, and drawing curtains. Upon returning, re-adjust the temperature to a comfortable level. There is no need to keep the house at its optimal cooling temperature if no one is home.

Close off rooms (and their air conditioning vents) that are not being used to minimize the total area being cooled and further lower utility bills. Do not close the vents if you use a heat pump for cooling your home.

Central air conditioning units are designed to reduce the temperature in your home to about 20 degrees below the outside temperature. If the thermostat is set to a temperature of more than 20 degrees below the outside temperature, you are overworking your central air conditioning unit and wasting energy. This can be very damaging to the unit and should be avoided.

INTERNAL HEAT GAIN

Heat is generated within your home as you cook, bathe, dry clothes, and use various appliances. The following list contains some methods to reduce this internal heat gain:

- Take shorter showers. Use the exhaust fan in the bathroom to vent this steam to the outside.
- Use the clothes dryer only at night when it is cooler. Take advantage of the summer heat by hanging clothes outside to dry.
- Do not bake anything in the oven because it generates a significant amount of heat in a home.
- Restrict the use of the stove. Serve cold salads and sandwiches or barbecue outside to keep cooking heat within your house to a minimum.
- Use the stove's exhaust fan to vent cooking heat to the outside.
- Prepare food at night when it is cooler and re-heat it the next day prior to serving.
- Use a Crock-Pot or an electric skillet to cook food. They generate less heat than the burner on a range.
- Use the microwave oven for baking and cooking because it produces minimal heat gain.

- Place lids on all pots when cooking to minimize cooking time and reduce heat gain.
- Place pans of hot water outside to cool. (Pour boiling water on weeds to kill them without poison.)
- Minimize the use of heat generating small appliances, like a curling iron or clothes iron. Turn them off when not in use, and do not let them "heat up" for a long time.
- Insulate hot water pipes and the hot water heater to reduce heat released into your home. Insulation reduces the year round cost to heat hot water. Several types of insulation are available to cover exposed hot water pipes. This insulation is easy to install and pays for itself within a month or two in savings on your heating and cooling bills. Hot water heater "blankets" and pipe insulation are available in home improvement centers and discount stores.
- Incandescent lights generate heat, so turn off all unnecessary lights. Use low watt light bulbs. Fluorescent light bulbs emit the least amount of heat.

SOLAR GAIN

When the hot sun enters a window, it also heats up the room. This solar heat gain can make your home not only uncomfortably warm but more difficult to cool. By simply keeping out the sun, the amount of heat gained can be reduced by up to 40 percent. The hot sun coming through a window in the summer can be compared to turning on your oven and leaving the door open.

Various measures can be taken to reduce solar heat gain. The best methods keep out not only the sun but also the heat. Try this test on a closed window shade; place your hand on the shade when the sun is shining on it. Does it feel hot? Any heat you feel on the shade is also entering the room. The less heat you feel when touching the shade, the better because you are keeping the heat out of the room. The following list contains some methods to reduce solar heat gain in your home:

- Close the curtains. The most effective curtains have an insulated lining.
- Close the window blinds or shades. Insulated window shades work best.

- Tinted window film allows light to enter the room without heat gain. Tinted film can be purchased at home improvement centers or lumberyards. Check the Yellow Pages for names of companies that tint car windows. You may be able to buy the film at a reduced price from this source.
- Use white paper to cover windows and keep the sun out. Because white paper absorbs little heat from the sun, it does not contribute to the heat gain in a room like some other materials. Simply tape white paper to the window. Some people use aluminum foil to cover windows. Although this method does block out the sun, the foil heats up and allows a great deal of heat to enter the room.

DUCTS

If you have a forced air furnace or air conditioner, within the walls and floors of your home is an intricate branching system of tubes that carry the warm air and/or cool air from your home's furnace/air conditioner to each room. This system is made up of ducts that consist primarily of sheet metal or fiberglass. Examine the ducts in your home to determine if they are properly insulated. Look for sections that have separated or for obvious holes in the ductwork. Uninsulated or poorly insulated ducts leak heated/cooled air into spaces where it is not needed. Therefore, you may be paying hundreds of dollars every year in higher heating and cooling bills because of these leaks. Pay particular attention to ducts in the attic and crawl space to ensure that they are sealed and insulated properly. If duct tape is used to repair and seal a duct, confirm that the Underwriters Laboratories (UL) has approved the tape. If the UL logo is printed on the label, you can rest assured that the tape will function as intended.

HEAT PUMPS

Heat pumps can save up to 40 percent off the cost of a traditional electric furnace or air conditioner if installed in a house in a part of the country with a moderate climate. If you have a heat pump in your home, do not adjust the heat pump's thermostat manually to make the electric resistance heating (or backup heat) come on. This type of heating is more expensive. Maintenance of the system according to the manufacturer's instructions is important. Change the air filter monthly or when recommended by the manufacturer.

THERMOSTATS

A thermostat is a temperature sensitive switch that controls a furnace or air conditioning system or both. When the indoor temperature reaches a level above or below the predetermined thermostat setting, the furnace or air conditioner begins to heat or cool your home until the temperature setting is attained.

Your energy consumption and heating bills can be decreased in the winter by setting the thermostat to 68°F when you are awake and lowering the setting when you are asleep or away from home. This requires the manual adjustment of the thermostat at the appropriate time. It is estimated that an average home will realize a 1 percent savings on their heating bill for each degree if the setback is done daily and the period that it is set back is at least eight hours in length. For example, if the thermostat is turned back 10° to 15°F for eight hours every night during the winter months, you could save up to 15 percent a year on your heating bill.

A heat pump is not designed to be set back when it is warming a home. Maintaining a moderate setting is the most efficient way to use a heat pump. However, there are now specially designed programmable thermostats for use with a heat pump that will provide an added measure of energy efficiency. When cooling a home, heat pumps function like other types of air conditioners, so you can manually increase the temperature for added savings.

A very common misconception held by many is that a furnace must work harder than normal to warm the space back to a comfortable temperature after a thermostat has been set back, resulting in little or no savings. Years of research have proven this to be incorrect. The fuel used to reheat a house to the desired level is equal to the same amount of fuel saved as a result of lowering the thermostat while you are away. Fuel is saved from the time the temperature stabilizes at the lower level until the house is reheated. Therefore, the longer your house remains at the lower temperature, the more energy (and money) you save.

Another misconception is that increasing the thermostat setting to a very high temperature allows the house to warm up faster. Regardless of how high the thermostat is set, the furnace will emit the same amount of heat. Raising the temperature to a higher degree will simply require the furnace to run longer.

PROGRAMMABLE THERMOSTATS

A programmable thermostat adjusts the temperature levels in a home according to a preset schedule. This eliminates the need to remember to reset the thermostat several times a day and can be preset, making the house warm when family members rise in the morning.

A homeowner can easily install most styles of programmable thermostats. However, carefully evaluate the programmable thermostat before purchasing it to ensure that the chosen model does not have to be installed by an electrician. Consider the various options for the different models to determine the one that will meet your needs.

FIREPLACES

Unfortunately, a fireplace is one of the most inefficient heat sources you can possibly use. A significant amount of warm air from the room goes up the chimney along with the smoke from the fire, forcing your furnace to work overtime.

During the winter months, when the furnace is heating your home, use the following suggestions to reduce your energy loss due to your fireplace:

- Install tempered glass doors along with a hot air exchange system that blows warmed air back into the room. The glass doors minimize the loss of room air up the chimney and the air exchange system will add more hot air to the room.
- Seal the chimney flue of any fireplace that is no longer used.
- Unless a fire is burning in the fireplace, keep the damper closed.
- When the fireplace is in use, open the damper in the bottom of the firebox. If your fireplace does not have a damper, open the nearest window a small crack and close the doors to the room. Lower the thermostat setting in the room to 55°F.
- Confirm a tight fitting seal on the flue damper and repair it as needed.

Water Heating

Heating water represents the third largest energy expense for most families. An average family of four uses 700 gallons of water in one week simply by showering every day for five minutes. This amount of water would provide drinking water to one person for three years.

Cut your water heating bills in the following ways:

- Reduce the amount of hot water used.
- Insulate your water heater.
- Turn down your hot water heater's thermostat.
- Purchase a more energy efficient water heater.

The following are additional ways to reduce your consumption of hot water:

- Install low flow showerheads.
- Install aerators on all faucets.
- Repair a leaky faucet promptly.
- Insulate your electric hot water storage tank (do not cover the thermostat) and all pipes.
- If your water is heated with natural gas or oil, insulate the water storage tank and pipes. Use caution not to cover the water heater's base, top, thermostat, or burner compartment. Consult your furnace technician the next time the unit is cleaned for specific instructions regarding the insulation of your storage tank.
- When you need to purchase a new water heater, look for one with a thick, insulating shell. The energy and money saved by this extra insulation will continue throughout the life of the appliance.
- Turn down the thermostat on your water heater to 115°F.
- Built-up sediment impedes the proper functioning of a water heater and encourages corrosion. Follow the manufacturer's guidelines regarding the periodic draining of your hot water heater tank.
- Consider replacing your water heater with a solar water heater.
- Take showers instead of baths and limit the time spent in the shower to no more than five minutes. If necessary, set a timer.

Lighting

The fastest way to reduce your lighting energy bills is to replace your incandescent light bulbs in high use areas with fluorescent bulbs. Incandescent light bulbs continue to be used most frequently in many homes today. However, they represent the most inefficient and most expensive method to light a room. Fluorescent bulbs last six to 10 times longer and more than pay for themselves in energy savings over their lifetime. By replacing only 25 percent of your incandescent light bulbs with fluorescent bulbs, you can save 50 percent on your lighting bill.

The following are additional ways to reduce the amount of electricity required to light up your life:

- Turn off the lights in any unoccupied room. Install timers, photo cells, or occupancy sensors to reduce the amount of time the lights are on in a specific room.
- Instead of illuminating the entire room, use task lighting so light is available where it is needed.
- Install three-way lamps, and use the lowest lighting level necessary.
- In the workroom, garage, and laundry areas, install four-foot fluorescent fixtures with reflective backing and electronic ballasts.
- Use compact fluorescent bulbs where you normally use incandescent bulbs. They are four times more energy efficient and provide the same amount and quality of light.
- Take advantage of free light through the use of light-colored, loose-weave curtains on your windows that allow daylight to penetrate the room. Decorate with light colors that reflect daylight into the room and make it appear brighter.

Laundry

The majority of energy expended in the laundering of clothes is used to heat the water. Therefore, you will dramatically reduce the energy and associated costs by washing clothes with cool or cold water (use cold water detergents) and the appropriate water level setting necessary to clean the given load of clothes. By simply changing the temperature setting from hot to cold, you reduce the amount of energy required to clean the load by 50 percent.

The most energy efficient washing machines are front loading (horizontal-axis) machines. Their initial cost is more than the traditional top loading models. However, the additional cost is quickly recovered because they use about one-third less energy and less water to clean the same size load of laundry washed in a top loading machine. You will save even more because a front loading machine removes more water from clothing during the spin cycle, thereby reducing the time necessary to dry them in the clothes dryer.

PURCHASING A MAJOR APPLIANCE

Household appliances use about 20 percent of a family's energy consumption. Refrigerators and clothes dryers use the most energy. When buying a new appliance, the operating costs as well as the purchase price should be carefully considered. Refer to Figure 11-2 for the average life span of major household appliances.

Figure 11-2

Household Appliances	Life Span
Refrigerators	15 years
Freezers	15 years
Room air conditioners	10 years
Dishwashers	10 years
Clothes washers	14 years
Electric/gas range	15 years
Microwave	7 years
Electric/gas clothes dryer	12 years
Water heater	15 years

Look for the Energy Star label to find the most energy efficient appliance in its class. The U.S. EPA and DOE award the Energy Star rating. To be awarded this rating, the appliance must substantially exceed the minimum federal standards. To help in determining the annual operating costs and annual energy consumption of a product, the federal government requires that most appliances display the bright yellow and black EnergyGuide label.

The EnergyGuide label provides two important pieces of information about the appliance you are considering. This information is useful for comparing different brands and models of a particular kind of appliance.

1. The estimated amount of energy consumed on a scale comparing similar models.
2. The estimated annual operating cost based on the national average price charged for electricity.

To compare two similar appliances, factor the price as well as the annual operating cost by the average lifetime. This method provides you with the opportunity to factor the operating costs into your purchase decision. The actual equation is annual operating expense × (multiplied by) average lifetime (in years) + (plus) retail price = (equals) lifetime operating expense. In Figure 11-3, two dishwashers are compared. In this hypothetical purchasing situation, the most economical dishwasher is the one with the retail price of $340. Because the annual operating expense is $30 per year less, even with the higher price factored into the equation, you would save $230 over the lifetime of the appliance by purchasing the more expensive dishwasher.

Figure 11-3
Dishwasher Comparison

	Annual operating expense	Average lifetime	Retail price	Lifetime operating expense
ABC dishwasher model #123	$130	10 years	$340	$1,640
XYZ dishwasher Model #789	$160	10 years	$270	$1,870

Appliance Repairs

Two major appliance manufacturers have technician hotlines available to the consumer. Their technicians will answer questions regarding the repair of your appliance so you can perform the repair yourself, saving you the cost of a service call. General Electric (GE) and Maytag are the only major manufacturers of appliances that continue to provide this service for the products they make. GE does have a fee for this service, whereas Maytag provides it at no charge. However, if you are unable to repair the appliance and are required to have a GE service technician come to your home to perform the repair, GE will refund the amount charged for the initial phone consultation with the technician.

GE Answer Center
Phone: (800) 626-2000
Cost: $14.99
Hours: 8:00 A.M. to 9:00 P.M. EST, Monday–Saturday
Major appliance brands: GE, RCA, Monogram, Hotpoint
Note: Technicians cannot provide technical assistance over the telephone for microwaves, hot water heaters, gas appliances, or the "smart boards."

Maytag Customer Care Center
Phone: (800) 688-9900
Cost: Free
Hours: 8:00 A.M. to 5:00 P.M. EST, Monday–Friday
Appliance brands: Maytag
Note: Technicians cannot provide technical assistance for microwave ovens.

Dishwashers

Dishwashers use the majority of their energy for heating water. Read the owner's manual to determine if your water heater must be set at a specific temperature to accommodate the dishwasher. Some dishwashers contain internal heating elements that heat the water needed to wash the dishes to the required temperature. Therefore, you do not need to raise the thermostat on your water heater. It can be lowered to an energy saving 115°F.

The following are additional ways to reduce your energy costs associated with using a dishwasher:

- Only run the dishwasher when it is full, but not overloaded.
- Use the energy saver feature (if available) and do not use the "heat dry" options. Instead, open the dishwasher and allow the dishes to air dry at the end of the cycle.

- Do not use the "rinse hold" option because it uses three to seven gallons of hot water.
- Dishwashers use less water than most people do when washing dishes by hand. Therefore, by using a dishwasher you are conserving your use of water.

Refrigerators

Refrigerators with top loading freezers are more energy efficient than those with freezers on the side.

The following are additional ways to reduce your energy costs associated with using a refrigerator and freezer:

- Monitor the internal temperature so it is not kept overly cold. The recommended temperature for the fresh food compartment is 37°–40°F and 5°F for the freezer section. A separate freezer should be kept at 0°F.
- To determine the temperature in the refrigerator, place an appliance thermometer in a glass of water in the center of the refrigerator. Read it after 24 hours. For the freezer, place the thermometer between frozen packages. Read it after 24 hours.
- Keep all liquids covered and food wrapped because uncovered foods release moisture and make the compressor work harder.
- Clean the condenser coils and maintain the refrigerator and freezer according to the manufacturer's recommendation.

Ranges

When purchasing a gas oven or range, look for one with an automatic, electric ignition system. An electric ignition uses up to 53 percent less gas because the pilot light does not burn continuously.

The following are additional ways to reduce your energy costs associated with using a range:

- Confirm that your gas range has a blue flame when the burner is on. A yellow flame is an indication that the gas is burning inefficiently and an adjustment may be needed.

- Keep the burner and reflectors clean for range top burners. This allows them to reflect heat better back onto the food being cooked.
- Cover all pans when heating food on the range. A lid makes the food heat up faster so it uses less energy. Use the appropriate size pan for the burner.
- When cooking with electricity, turn the stovetop burners off several minutes before the allotted cooking time. The heating element frequently remains hot long enough to complete the cooking without using more electricity. This same principle applies when baking in the oven.
- Use a toaster oven for small meals rather than your stovetop burner or oven. A toaster oven uses about half as much energy as a full-size oven.
- Pressure cookers and microwave ovens save energy because they require less cooking time.

12

Reducing the High Cost of College Tuition

Have you put aside $20,000 to $100,000 for your child's college tuition? If not, take heart because with a little research and diligence, you can send your child to college without going into serious debt. A step-by-step plan is provided for your use in evaluating the many opportunities available to secure a college education. Scholarships and grant sources are now more accessible than ever before due to the Internet. In fact, a student willing to commit time to researching the options provided could very likely secure enough funding to go to college at no cost. Postal addresses and Internet Web site addresses are listed in the next few sections for your convenience

Submit an FAFSA

The first step in getting money for college is to complete the Free Application for Federal Student Aid (FAFSA) and submit it to the U.S. Department of Education. Based on your income, your child may qualify for grants to completely fund his college tuition. For help in completing the FAFSA (or to obtain a copy of the blank form), call (800) 801-0576. Your child's high school guidance counselor or the financial aid office of the college of your choice may also have the FAFSA forms.

The FAFSA can also be completed over the Internet on the FAFSA Web site at *www.fafsa.ed.gov.*

FAFSA information can be entered online and transmitted directly to the Central Processing System.

It is important that this form be completed and on file even if you do not think your child will qualify for aid due to financial need. Being rejected for federal aid is sometimes a prerequisite for private awards.

When to Apply

Begin searching for scholarships in your child's junior year of high school. Apply within the specific deadlines for each scholarship; usually before January 1 of the student's senior year. The early bird gets the worm and sometimes the scholarship.

Federal Money

The federal government provides $35 billion dollars every year for education after high school. Of course, some of this is in the form of loans. Yet, much of this money is given in the form of grants that do not need to be repaid.

The Pell Grant and the Supplemental Education Opportunity Grant (SEOG) are two such programs that give several thousand dollars to each qualifying student.

To find out about federal grants for which your child is eligible, call (800) 4-FED-AID.

State Grants

All states provide programs that give qualifying students money for college tuition. The types of grants available vary from state to state. The State Student Incentive Grant (SSIG) and the Paul Douglas Teacher Scholarship are two such programs offered in some states. To find out who to contact in your state about free money for college, call (800) 4-FED-AID.

Scholarships

It is estimated that more than $50 billion dollars is awarded in scholarships each year. Although many scholarships are awarded based on scholastic aptitude, 76 percent of all scholarships are awarded based on criteria other than grades. These merit-based scholarships are given to students based on criteria not related to financial need. Does your child have a physical aptitude for sports? Does he or she play a musical instrument? Is he or she involved in community service projects and volunteering? Even students with average grades and no special interests are eligible for scholarships. What is the student's ethnicity? Religion? These criteria could also make him or her eligible for a scholarship. Today, there are more scholarships than ever before. The trick is to be diligent in your search and apply to all sources that are appropriate. Because scholarship amounts vary, your child may have to apply and receive several scholarships to completely finance his or her education.

INSTITUTIONAL SCHOLARSHIPS

All colleges have money donated to them specifically for scholarships and grants. When your child applies for admission, contact the financial aid office of the school and request information about the availability of institutional scholarships and grants. Learn all you can about the college financial aid process. Meet personally with your child's financial aid administrator to discuss scholarship and grant options.

PRIVATE SOURCES

Investigate private sources of scholarships or grants in your community. Funds may be available based on your child's academic achievement, athletic ability, artistic or musical talent, religious affiliation, ethnicity, memberships, hobbies, or other special talents. Contact employers to see if they, their unions, or professional associations sponsor any aid programs.

Investigate foundations, religious organizations, civic groups, fraternities or sororities, and patriotic or fraternal associations like the American Legion, YMCA, 4-H Club, Elks, Kiwanis, Jaycees, Chamber of Commerce, and Boy or Girl Scouts. Also explore organizations associated with your child's field of interest, such as the American Medical Association, Society of Automotive Engineers, or the American Bar Association.

If your child is an eligible dependent of a veteran, contact the local Veterans Administration to determine if educational benefits are available.

HOW TO FIND PRIVATE SCHOLARSHIPS, GRANTS, AND MORE

To investigate scholarships, go to the nearest public library with a good reference section and look for directories containing lists of scholarships, grants, and monetary awards for education. College admissions offices and high school guidance counselors should also be able to provide information about scholarships.

The Internet offers the most comprehensive and perhaps most current source of information about scholarships and grants. One such site, fastWEB, provides information about 400,000 scholarships, grants, and loans for both undergraduate and graduate students. While online, you can complete a student profile about your child's major area of interest, his or her grade-point average, special interests, and ethnic origin. The site will link the student profile to specific grants and scholarships for which your child may be eligible. In less than five minutes you will receive a detailed list of scholarships. The URL for fastWEB is *www.fastweb.com*.

Similar online free search services are the CollegeNet Scholarship Search at *www.collegenet.com/mach25* and Fastaid at *www.fastaid.com*.

Many libraries and schools provide free Internet access. Use the Internet in your search for free college money. It's time well spent.

SCHOLARSHIP SCAMS

Today, there are over 2,500 scholarship search companies. They charge an average of $180 to give you a list of scholarships to which your child may apply. However, according to the National Association of Student Financial Aid Administrators, more than 300,000 people are cheated out of more than $5 million by scholarship scams each year. To keep from being taken in, the Federal Trade Commission suggests you run the other way if you hear any of the following statements from a scholarship company.

- "The scholarship is guaranteed or your money back."
- "You can't get this information anywhere else."
- "I just need your credit card or bank account number to hold this scholarship."
- "We'll do all the work."
- "The scholarship will cost money."
- "You've been selected by a national foundation to receive a scholarship."
- "You're a finalist," in a contest you never entered.

Many scholarship scams are based on the "$6 billion dollar myth." This myth is based on the belief that there are large sums of hidden or unclaimed scholarship money. In fact, very little scholarship money goes unused. However, scammers promise to secure some of this money for your child. Yet, they do not have any sources that are not just as readily available to you via the traditional methods previously listed.

If you feel the need to use one of these companies, always read the fine print on all contracts or applications. If a company has not followed through on its promises, take a copy of all literature and correspondence to the Better Business Bureau, your state Consumer Protection Office, or your state Attorney General's Office.

MILITARY OPTIONS

Join the Army, Navy, Marines, or any other of the armed forces to get a free college education. The armed forces provide many programs to pay for college tuition. The following list contains some related opportunities.

- If accepted to attend a military academy, tuition is free. Upon graduation, students are granted a commission and are required to serve in the military.
- The Reserve Officer Training Corps (ROTC) scholarship program covers most of the cost of tuition, fees, and textbooks and provides a monthly allowance.
- The Montgomery GI Bill provides money after active service to attend college.
- Most branches of the military offer some kind of tuition assistance for military personnel to take college courses at civilian colleges during their off-duty hours.

To learn more about these educational opportunities in the military, contact your local armed forces recruiter.

Reduce College Tuition

Reducing tuition costs or reducing the number of required credit hours means that your child will need to find less money to pay for college.

Depending upon a child's scholastic ability, he may be able to earn college credits by taking college courses or advanced placement (AP) exams while still in high school. Students with high grades on AP exams in many different subjects are sometimes granted a full year of course credit. These savings can be significant if a student is able to enter college as a second year student. The student would be able to save the cost of tuition and fees for an entire year of college. Inquire of the admissions offices of the colleges of your choice to determine if they give credit for AP exams.

First and second year college students can also take College Level Examination Program tests for course credit. The price of taking the exam is only a fraction of the price to take a college course. Discuss this option with your college advisor or admissions office.

Another cost savings possibility is for your child to attend a community college for the first year or two, then transfer to a more expensive four-year college to complete a degree. This can be a more affordable approach to receiving a degree from a prestigious institution that you are unable to afford for the entire four years.

Work Study

Work-study programs allow students to go to school while earning money toward their education. These jobs are usually 10 to 15 hours a week on campus. Wages are based on federal minimum wage guidelines, but are not taxable so no withholding tax is deducted.

Community Service

High school graduates can earn education awards through the National and Community Service or AmeriCorps programs. By working before, during, or after college, students can fund their education or repay student loans. For more information about these and other community service programs of the Federal Government, refer to the following list.

- The Federal Consumer Information Center (CIC) in Pueblo, Colorado offers several publications that are helpful in learning more about free sources of money for college. These booklets are available at no charge from the CIC Web site at *www.pueblo.gsa.gov.*

You can also write or call CIC at:
Consumer Information Center
P.O. Box 100
Pueblo, Colorado 81002
Phone: (800) 688-9889

- Paying for College. A Guide for Parents and their Children. This free, 24-page booklet from the Consumer Information Center explains how to estimate college expenses and put together a financial plan.
- Preparing Your Child for College, A Resource Book for Parents. This free, 54-page booklet from the Consumer Information Center helps both parents and their children to understand the process of selecting and paying for college.
- The U.S. Department of Education offers a free guide for parents called The Student Guide, Financial Aid. This guide provides an overview of financial aid sources for undergraduates. To request a copy of this guide, write or call:
U.S. Department of Education
Student Financial Assistance Programs Federal Student Aid
    Information Center
P.O. Box 84
Washington, D.C. 20044-0084
Phone: (800) 4-FED-AID

- To obtain information about the "School-to-Career" or the "School-to-Work" programs, write or call:
School-To-Work Opportunities Information Center
400 Virginia Avenue, SW
Washington, D.C. 20024
Phone: (800) 251-7236
www.stw.ed.gov

- For information about the "Tech-Prep" and "2+2" programs, write or call:
National Tech Prep Network
P.O. Box 21689
Waco, TX 76702-1689
Phone: (800) 972-2766

- For information about AmeriCorps, call (800) 942-2677, or visit its Web site at *www.cns.gov.*

- To learn about opportunities in the U.S. Armed Forces call
  - Army: 800-USA-ARMY
  - Air Force: 800-423-USAF
  - Navy: 800-USA-NAVY
  - Marines: 800-MARINES
  - Coast Guard: 800-424-8883
  - Army Reserve: 800-USA-ARMY
  - Navy Reserve: 800-USA-USNR
  - Air Force Reserve: 800-257-1212
  - Army National Guard: 800-638-7600
  - ROTC: 800-USA-ROTC

13

Cleaning Cents

Use common household products as well as common sense to save cents! In this chapter, you will find a variety of techniques and recipes to make cleaning easier and much more economical.

MAKE YOUR OWN CLEANING PRODUCTS

Keep your home and clothing clean with products made from basic, readily available supplies. These homemade products cost only a fraction of the price of their ready-made counterparts. Occasionally, it may be necessary to apply a cleaner and allow it to sit for a few seconds or minutes before wiping it off. You might also have to go over the area a second time to get the last traces of dirt. However, most homemade cleaning products are less caustic and more environmentally friendly.

Listed in this chapter are the recipes for various cleaning agents and solutions.

All-Purpose Cleaner

2 cups ammonia
2 cups distilled white vinegar
½ cup baking soda
11 cups warm water to fill a one gallon container

Pour all of the listed ingredients into a one-gallon container. Put the lid on the container and shake to combine. To use, pour the solution into a spray bottle and spray it on the soiled surface. Let it soak for a few seconds. Wipe. This cleaner works well for cleaning grimy dirt on many surfaces including kitchen appliances, walls, bathroom surfaces, and so on. Use this cleaner only with good ventilation. For stubborn dirt, use extra baking soda as a scouring powder. (Rinse with clear water to remove any remaining residue from the baking soda.)

Window Cleaner

1 cup ammonia
1 cup distilled white vinegar
½ cup rubbing alcohol
1 teaspoon dishwashing liquid
few drops of blue food coloring (optional)
13 cups of water to make one gallon

Pour all of the ingredients into a one-gallon container. Note: If you have very hard water, increase the amount of ammonia and vinegar to three cups each and add only nine cups of water. Properly label the container to indicate its contents. To use, pour the window cleaner into a spray bottle and spray it on the window. Wipe with a damp sponge or damp cloth to loosen any visible dirt. Use a rubber squeegee, clean dry cloth, or newspapers to remove all traces of the cleaner. Polish the window with a soft dry cloth to remove any remaining streaks.

Wall Cleaner

1 tablespoon clothes detergent
½ cup baking soda
1 quart warm water

Mix ingredients in a bucket. Use a sponge or cleaning cloth to apply the wall cleaner. No rinsing is necessary. To remove crayon or grimy areas, sprinkle extra baking soda on the sponge and gently rub the area. If baking soda is used as a scouring powder, remove all traces of the powder by rinsing well with clear water.

Furniture Polish and Bathroom Ceramic Tile Polish

1 cup vegetable oil
3 tablespoons lemon oil

Combine all ingredients and pour them into a fine mist spray bottle. Use this polish to clean and polish wood furniture. Spray the solution liberally on clean dry tiles. Wipe the tiles with a soft cloth to ensure that all of the tiles are covered with a thin coat of the polish. Use another soft dry cloth to polish them to a luster. The tiles will remain clean for a longer period of time. Do not use this solution on floor tiles. Use caution not to get any of the tile polish on the bathroom floor, bathtub, or shower floor—it will make them slick!

Dust Magnet Spray

water

To facilitate the removal of dust, lightly mist a clean, dry, lint-free cloth with plain water. This works every bit as well as the purchased product. To clean cobwebs from the ceilings, cover a broom or dust mop with a clean cloth or old towel. Secure it with a rubber band and lightly mist with water. The long handle of the broom or mop will make removal of the cobwebs "ladder-free."

Cleaning Television and Computer Screens

To remove the dust held in place by static electricity and further reduce its accumulation, dust the screen of a television or computer with a new fabric softener sheet. If the screen is dirty from fingerprints, clean it with a mixture of ½ teaspoon liquid fabric softener in two cups of window cleaner. No need to buy a special computer screen anti-static spray. Note: Always turn off and unplug the television or computer when cleaning or dusting the screen.

Carpet Deodorizer

Vacuum the carpet to remove all surface dirt. Lightly sprinkle baking soda over the entire surface of the dry carpet, and allow it to remain in place for at least 30 minutes. Use one 16-ounce box for each 20 × 20 foot room. For best results, leave the baking soda on the carpet overnight. Vacuum the carpet to remove all traces of the baking soda. Your carpet will be fresh smelling and odor free.

Floor Cleaner

½ cup distilled white vinegar
½ gallon warm water

This mixture is for use in cleaning no-wax and ceramic tile kitchen or bathroom floors. Baking soda works well when used as a scouring powder to remove heel marks and other stubborn marks. Because excess water can harm the finish of many brands of vinyl or no-wax flooring, use very little water.

Always consult the floor's manufacturer to determine the recommended cleaning method and adhere to those recommendations. Use of the wrong floor cleaner may void the warranty. Many floor manufacturers only suggest vacuuming and damp mopping with water.

Remove Built-Up Floor Wax

Full strength ammonia inexpensively and easily removes old wax from floors. Wear rubber gloves and always ventilate the room well. Allow the ammonia to remain on the floor for several minutes for best results. Work on a small area (3 feet × 3 feet) at a time. Scrub the area with a stiff bristled brush. Use a sponge to remove the excess ammonia and old wax. Rinse well with clear water to remove all traces of the old wax and any remaining ammonia. Always consult the manufacturer of your floor regarding its recommendation for the removal of wax on your floor. This method is not intended for use on wood floors.

Drain Opener and Monthly Cleaner

½ cup baking soda
½ cup distilled white vinegar
Boiling water

Sprinkle baking soda down the drain, followed by vinegar. Let it remain undisturbed for 30 minutes. Pour several cupfuls of boiling water down the drain. The vinegar and baking soda break down fatty acids into soap and glycerin, allowing the clog to wash down the drain or keep the drain open. This is safe for use with septic tanks. Note: Do not use this method if a commercial drain opener was used to try to open a clogged drain.

Brass Cleaner

Lemon juice
Baking soda

Using the listed ingredients, make a paste the consistency of toothpaste. Rub this paste onto the tarnished brass with a soft cloth until the tarnish is removed. Rinse with clear water and dry. To protect a newly polished brass item and keep it free from tarnish for a longer period of time, spray it lightly with hairspray.

Ceiling Stain Removal

Occasionally, a white ceiling becomes stained with water spots, sprayed champagne, or other stains of unknown origin. Instead of repainting the entire ceiling, try this tip first to remove the stain. Wet a sponge or cleaning cloth with undiluted chlorine bleach. Gently dab the stain with the sponge. There is no need to scrub the stain, the bleach will make it fade within a few minutes.

Reduce Static Electricity in Carpets

Combine one capful of liquid fabric softener with two cups of water. Spray a light misting of this mixture onto the carpet when static electricity becomes a problem.

Inexpensive Septic Tank Maintenance

To maintain the proper pH and alkalinity in your septic tank, flush one cup of baking soda down the toilet each week.

Bathtub, Sink, Counter Top, and Butcher Block Stains

Most bathtub, sink, countertop, and butcher block stains can be removed by applying undiluted bleach to the area. Allow the bleach to remain in place until the stain fades. This works on porcelain, fiberglass, tile, Corian, Formica, and wood butcher blocks alike and will not scratch the surface because bleach is not an abrasive.

Remove Rust Stains in Bathtubs or on Counter Tops

Pour hydrogen peroxide on the rust so it completely covers the rust stain. Sprinkle cream of tarter over the stain. Allow the solution to remain in place at least 30 minutes. Rinse with clear water. Repeat if necessary.

Toilet Bowl Cleaner

- Option 1: Pour ½ cup chlorine bleach into the toilet bowl. Allow it to soak at least 10 minutes. Scrub the bowl with a bowl brush to remove remaining stains.
- Option 2: Sprinkle ½ cup of baking soda or Borax* on the inside of the toilet bowl. Scrub briskly with a toilet bowl brush and allow the cleaning agent to soak at least 10 minutes. Scrub again and apply more baking soda or Borax to any remaining stains. This method is safe to use with septic systems.
- Option 3: Spray distilled white vinegar or lemon juice on the inside of the toilet bowl. Sprinkle Borax* over the areas sprayed and scrub with a toilet bowl brush. Allow it to remain for about 2 hours and then flush to rinse. Distilled white vinegar and/or lemon juice are effective in eliminating stains caused by hard water and some minerals.

*Borax is toxic. Handle it with care and store it safely. You can buy Borax brand (or its generic equivalent) in many grocery stores near the laundry detergent.

Cleaning Filmy Glass Shower Doors

Pour distilled white vinegar in a spray bottle. Spray the vinegar on the glass door and allow it to remain for a few minutes. Wipe the door with a cloth saturated with additional vinegar. Polish with another soft dry cloth. Use a paste made of baking soda and a small amount of water to clean any remaining stubborn areas. Rinse well with clear water.

Removing Soap Spots and Film from Bathroom Tile and Tubs

- Option 1: Use the All-Purpose Cleaner to spray the area. Allow the cleaner to remain on the tile or tub for about one to two minutes. Wipe with a damp sponge or cloth. Use baking soda as scouring powder for any remaining stubborn stains. Rinse well with clear water.
- Option 2: Mix a solution of one cup distilled white vinegar in two cups of water. Pour into a spray bottle. Spray the tile and wipe with a damp sponge or cloth. Repeat if necessary. Ventilate area well when using sprays.

Cleaning Grout

To clean grout between ceramic tiles, try using one of the following inexpensive methods after washing the tile floor as usual:

- Dampen the tile and grout with water and liberally sprinkle baking soda over the area. Scrub the grout with a recycled toothbrush and allow it to remain for a few minutes. Rinse well. Repeat if necessary.
- Spray the tile and grout with a solution that is half chlorine bleach and half water. Allow the solution to remain on the grout for several hours. Rinse well with water. This method will remove the discoloration from the grout if it is used daily for several days. To keep the discoloration from returning, re-apply the solution weekly. Use this method only with good ventilation.
- Liberally apply hydrogen peroxide to the tile and grout and allow it to remain at least 15 minutes. For particularly dirty grout, make a

paste of baking soda and hydrogen peroxide and use a recycled toothbrush to scrub the grout.
- Spray full strength distilled white vinegar onto the tile and grout. Allow it to soak at least 15 minutes. If necessary, scrub with a recycled toothbrush. Rinse with water.

Daily Shower Cleaner

Instead of buying one of the new daily shower cleaner products, use inexpensive rubbing alcohol. Fill a spray bottle with full-strength rubbing alcohol and lightly spray the interior of your shower after completing your daily shower. Of course, just like the commercially available products, it works best if it is used initially on a clean shower. Use care to keep this alcohol-filled spray bottle out of a child's reach, and DO NOT get any of the spray on your painted wall because the alcohol may alter the color!

Fog Free Mirrors

To make your bathroom mirrors fog free, wash as usual and dry thoroughly. Then, wipe a thin coating of liquid dishwashing soap over the entire surface of the mirror using a clean cloth. Polish with another clean dry cloth to remove the soap. If a haze remains, very lightly mist the mirror with window cleaner and wipe dry to remove the soap haze. You will have a fog free mirror for months to come.

Making Mold and Mildew Disappear

Mix ½ to 1 cup bleach with two cups water. Sponge the solution on the mold or mildew. If necessary allow it to soak for a few minutes. The mold will disappear before your eyes. For severe mold, you may need to re-apply the bleach solution and allow the bleach to remain several hours until mold and mildew are removed completely. (See the section "Bleach Precautions" later in this chapter.)

Remove Lime and Mineral Deposits

To remove lime deposits from faucets, soak paper towels in full-strength distilled white vinegar. Apply the wet paper towels to the lime deposits and leave in place for about one hour. The deposits will be softened and can easily be removed by brushing the area with an old toothbrush. Hard water spots (mineral deposits) can be removed by wiping them with a cloth moistened with distilled white vinegar. Dry and polish with a soft cloth. Spray full strength distilled white vinegar directly on lime deposits in showers or on walls. Allow the vinegar to remain on the area until the green lime has disappeared.

Showerhead clogged with mineral deposits? To remove mineral deposits, unscrew the showerhead. Place the showerhead in a bowl filled with distilled white vinegar and allow it to remain immersed in this solution until the sediment is softened and can be removed by rinsing or brushing with an old toothbrush. A second method is to pour ½ to 1 cup of distilled white vinegar into a watertight plastic bag. Tie this plastic bag over the shower head (without unscrewing the showerhead from the wall) so it is soaking in the vinegar. Allow the bag to remain in place for at least a half hour. Remove the bag and turn on the shower to clear out the mineral deposits.

To remove lime deposits in a teakettle, pour 1 cup distilled white vinegar into the teakettle and fill it with water. Allow it to soak until the deposits have disappeared.

To keep a drip coffee maker running freely, pour ½ cup distilled white vinegar into the carafe. Pour additional cold water into the carafe until it is full. Pour this vinegar-water into the reservoir as though you were making coffee and turn on the coffee maker. This solution will remove hard water mineral deposits from the tubing. Rinse the coffee maker by using several carafes of clear water in the same manner, until no trace of vinegar remains.

Room Deodorizer

To rid a room of cooking odors and cigarette smoke, place a small bowl of white vinegar or chlorine bleach in the room. Allow the vinegar or bleach to remain for several hours. DO NOT use bleach for this purpose if you have pets or young children.

Refrigerator and Freezer Deodorizer

We all know that baking soda works well to deodorize the refrigerator. However, a less expensive method is to use two or three charcoal briquettes, instead of an entire box of baking soda. Charcoal briquettes work just as effectively as baking soda. A box of baking soda costs 35¢ to 50¢. A piece of charcoal is about 2¢. Replace the charcoal every three months with fresh briquettes. After using them in the refrigerator or freezer, toss them in the barbecue grill to use for cooking supper. Note: Do not use the type of charcoal briquettes impregnated with lighter fluid, for example, Match-Lite brand.

Frugal Simmering Potpourri

An inexpensive and effective way to freshen and scent the air in your home is with simmering potpourri. There is no need to purchase potpourri from the store, you can easily make it from leftover cooking scraps.

Coarsely chop the leftover skin from oranges, grapefruit, and other citrus fruits. Place the skins in a small pan. Pour enough hot tap water into the pan to cover the skins with water. If desired, add a pinch of cinnamon. Place the mixture on the stove over the lowest heat setting. As you allow the mixture to simmer, the wonderful aroma will permeate throughout your house. The mixture can also be placed in a Crock-Pot and allowed to simmer. The Crock-Pot uses less energy than the stove, so it is the preferred method for maximum savings. Continue to add water as necessary to keep the potpourri from boiling dry. The mixture can be refrigerated overnight in a tightly sealed container and reused the next day.

The skin from one fruit and one teaspoon of cinnamon or imitation vanilla is enough to provide a wonderful aroma in your home. Apple skins or dried plants and herbs, such as lavender and pine needles, can also be used. This is a good use for fruit that is "past its prime." Chop up the entire piece of fruit and use it in your simmering potpourri pot. Experiment to find different combinations you like.

Drip Coffee Makers

Pour two tablespoons of baking soda in the carafe and fill it with cold water. Pour this mixture in the reservoir and turn on the coffee maker. Rinse the coffee maker by using several carafes of clear water in the same manner until no trace of the baking soda remains. Use baking soda as a scouring powder to remove coffee stains on the heating plate and other parts of the coffee maker. This method removes all traces of coffee stains.

Smooth Top Range

To clean the surface of a smooth top stove, use baking soda as scouring powder. Scrape off crusted burnt food with a single-edge razor blade. Rinse well with clear water to remove any residue or a white haze will be present when it dries. (Remove any remaining haze by rinsing again.)

Cleaning the Exhaust Hood and Filter

Use the All Purpose Cleaner to remove greasy dirt on an above range exhaust hood. Use baking soda as a scouring powder to remove any stubborn dirt. Rinse the area well with clear water if baking soda is used.

To clean the metal mesh filter, remove it from the hood, and place it in the bottom of a plastic basin or sink. Pour hot water over the filter until it is covered with water. Sprinkle 2 to 4 tablespoons of baking soda over the filter and watch the grease and dirt float away. Rinse with hot water, allow to air dry, and replace it in the hood.

Oven Cleaner

1 cup ammonia
Baking soda
Very fine steel wool

Pour ammonia in a bowl and place it in a cold oven. Close the door and allow it to remain overnight. The next day, wipe the interior surface of the oven with a damp sponge or cloth. Use baking soda and a very fine steel wool pad to remove stubborn burnt on food. Note: Do not use steel wool on self-cleaning or continuous clean ovens or if the manufacturer warns against its use. Wipe off baking soda residue with a damp sponge. Rinse well with clear water and dry.

Sparkling Stainless Steel Sinks

An inexpensive and effective way to clean a stainless steel sink is to use baking soda as you would scouring powder. Rinse well. Then, to make it shine like it did when it was brand new, apply a thin coat of mineral oil to the entire surface of the sink with a paper towel. Mineral oil can also be applied to the chrome faucet to make it shine too. Rub the mineral oil into the stainless steel until it is no longer visible. You will have to re-apply the oil every three to six days depending on the amount of dishes you wash because the liquid dish detergent slowly dissolves the mineral oil.

Clean Barbecue Grills Easily

Before using a barbecue grill, coat it with vegetable oil or spray it with cooking spray. The oil will prevent the food from sticking to the grill and makes cleanup easier. Place the oil-coated grill over the coals and use as usual.

To clean a dirty barbecue grill, mix equal parts of baking soda and water to make a paste. Apply the paste to the dirty grill with a wire brush or steel wool pad. Allow the paste to remain on the stubborn areas for a few minutes and rescrub. Rinse the grill well to remove all of the remaining baking soda.

Homemade Rinse Aid for Spot Free Dishes

Instead of using a commercial rinse aid in your dishwasher, add distilled white vinegar in the rinse agent dispenser. Your dishes will be spot free and sparkling clean.

No More Stinky Gym Bags, Lockers, Sneakers, and Diaper Pails

Minimize the offensive odors of clothing, shoes, and so on by sprinkling baking soda over the item(s). Sprinkle baking soda in a gym bag or place an open box of baking soda on the shelf in a gym locker or closet shelf. Sprinkle baking soda in shoes and let it remain overnight. In the morning, shake out the remaining baking soda. Odors will be neutralized. Add baking soda to the water used to soak cloth diapers to get rid of odors and help to whiten them.

Remove Perspiration Stains and Smells from Clothing

Soak the clothing overnight in a solution made of one-part distilled white vinegar and four-parts water. Wash as usual. The odors and stains will be gone. Another effective and inexpensive method is to hang the item outside in the sun to dry after laundering.

To Remove Various Stains from Garments

Use this solution only on machine washable clothing to remove a variety of stains. If you have any question about whether or not the colors may bleed, place a few drops of the presoak solution on a hidden part of the garment. Gently rub the wet area with a white cloth or towel. If any color rubs off onto the white material, or if a change in the color is noted, do not use the presoaking solution. This solution effectively removes a variety of stains including formula and baby food stains on infant clothing. It also whitens and brightens dingy socks.

LAUNDRY PRESOAK SOLUTION

½ cup household ammonia
½ cup *powdered* automatic dishwasher detergent
(The liquid or gel automatic dishwasher detergent contains bleach and should not be used.)
¼ cup laundry detergent (powdered or liquid)
¼ cup baking soda
4–5 gallons water

Place the water in a large bucket. Use warm water for white fabrics and denim jeans. Use cold water for colored fabrics. Pour the ammonia, dishwashing detergent, laundry detergent, and baking soda into this bucket. Use a large spoon to stir the solution until everything is well dissolved. Do not get the solution on your hands or in your eyes because dishwashing detergent can cause injury to skin. Keep children and pets away from the solution. Avoid breathing the ammonia vapors and use in a well-ventilated area.

Presort the fabrics by color. Do not mix colored fabrics with white fabrics. Do not place red garments with other colors of garments. Place the stained garment(s) into the solution and allow them to soak overnight or until the stains have disappeared. Place the garments along with the remaining solution in the washing machine, add the usual amount of detergent, and wash as usual.

If any stains persist after the garments have been machine washed, resoak them in the laundry presoak solution. (Do not dry the garment in the clothes dryer until the stain has been removed to your satisfaction or you will further set the stain.)

I have found that the least expensive brands of clothing detergent and dishwashing detergent work equally well in making this solution. Note: Powdered laundry detergents cost less than liquid detergents.

CLOTHING SPRAY SPOT REMOVER

½ cup vinegar
½ cup ammonia
½ cup liquid laundry detergent
½ cup warm water
½ cup baking soda

Mix the listed ingredients together and pour them into a spray bottle. Spray this solution on greasy stains, food spots, dirty collars, and cuffs. If necessary, scrub the sprayed area with an old toothbrush to facilitate the removal of the stain. Wash the garment as usual. Do not use this solution on garments that are labeled "dry-clean only." Pre-test this spray spot remover as described previously to ensure it won't cause the colors to bleed.

Laundry Stains

Everyone must deal with stains on their laundry from time to time. Following is a list of inexpensive ways to rid your clothes of various types of stains. Always test each of the following remedies on an inconspicuous area of the garment first. (If discoloration is noted when cleaning with baking soda or ammonia, neutralize the cleaning agent immediately by using lemon juice or vinegar (acids). If discoloration is noted when cleaning with an acid such as vinegar or lemon juice, use an alkaline solution like baking soda or ammonia to neutralize the acid.) After the removal of the stain, wash the garment as usual. To prevent from setting a stain that was not completely removed, avoid drying the garment in the clothes dryer. Instead, air dry the garment. Once dry, confirm that the stain is completely gone. Only after the stain is completely removed should you use the clothes dryer to dry the garment.

Blood: Clean it as soon as possible. Dried blood is harder to remove than blood that is still wet. Pour club soda or hydrogen peroxide directly on the stain. Repeat as needed until the stain is gone.

Coffee or tea: Pour distilled white vinegar and laundry detergent on the stain and gently scrub the area. Rinse and repeat until the stain is removed.

Chocolate: Make a paste of washing soda (or baking soda) and water plus any liquid clothes/dish detergent and rub it into the stain until it is removed.

Grass: Pour distilled white vinegar or rubbing alcohol and liquid clothes detergent on the stain. Rub this into the stain until it is removed. Rinse and repeat if necessary.

Grease or Oil: Rub the stain with a paste made from baking soda and liquid clothes/dish detergent. Repeat until the stain is gone.

Ink: Dab the stain with a paper towel moistened with rubbing alcohol until the ink is lifted from the garment.

Lipstick: Rub the lipstick with cold cream or shortening to dissolve the color. To remove the remaining grease, rub the area with a paste made from baking soda and liquid clothes/dish detergent.

Chewing gum: Rub the gum with ice until the gum flakes off, or use peanut butter to dissolve the gum. To remove any remaining grease residue left from the peanut butter, rub the area with a paste made from baking soda and liquid clothes/dish detergent.

Perspiration: Soak the stained area in distilled white vinegar.

Berries: Soak the stained area in distilled white vinegar or milk.

THE STORAGE AND USE OF CLEANING AGENTS

Always use and store cleaners safely. Although most of the ingredients in homemade cleaners are safe for use in cleaning the home, some may be toxic or harmful when mixed with other chemicals.

To ensure that cleaning agents are used and stored safely, remember and follow these guidelines:

- Use caution in mixing cleaning agents. Some solutions, such as chlorine bleach and ammonia, produce a toxic gas when mixed together that could cause injury to your lungs.
- Mix only one month's supply at a time. Over time, the cleaning agents may lose their effectiveness.
- Mix solutions in a well-ventilated area.
- Store all cleaning solutions out of the reach of children.
- Label the outside of the container indicating the contents. This is especially important if other people in your home clean or have access to the cleaners.

Bleach Precautions

All bleach is created equal. Therefore the cheapest brand works exactly the same as the most expensive. Bleach is very effective in killing germs. However, special precautions must be taken when using bleach.

- Do not mix bleach with ammonia.
- Read labels carefully to confirm that a specific solution can be added to bleach. For example, many dishwashing liquids indicate that they are not to be mixed with bleach. However, most laundry detergents can be mixed with bleach.
- Caution! Bleach can permanently remove the color from carpets, clothing, towels, and other materials.
- Use only in a well-ventilated area.
- Do not put bleach in a spray bottle. Sprayed bleach may be inhaled and therefore represents a health risk. Excess spray may damage surrounding fabrics and surfaces.
- Avoid contact with skin. Wear gloves and use caution not to get it in your eyes.

14

Health and Beauty Savings

Do you buy the "I'm worth it" shampoo? Yes, you are worth it. However, that does not mean you have to purchase an overpriced product to prove it. Instead, use a less expensive product or an alternative product to attain equally good results. Included within this chapter are a variety of ways to save money on your health and beauty including ways to pay less for eyeglasses, contact lenses, and orthodontic care as well as recipes for inexpensive homemade versions of commercially available products.

DON'T OVERLOOK CLEARLY VISIBLE SAVINGS ON EYEGLASSES

Have you purchased a new pair of eyeglasses recently? You can easily spend more than $200 on a single pair of eyeglasses. According to a report by the Federal Trade Commission, studies show that the price and type of eye practitioner are not necessarily indications of quality. In other words, paying a lot for an eye exam and eyeglasses does not guarantee a good quality pair of glasses or the appropriate prescription needed to correct your vision problems. Comparison shopping can assure the best quality eyewear and eye care specialist for the lowest price.

Insurance

Some health insurance policies cover the cost of eye examinations and eyeglasses. Contact your health insurance company to determine if this is a covered service. You may only need to submit a claim form for this service to be covered in full or in part by your insurance.

Eye Examinations

A refraction is the test performed by an eye care specialist to determine the prescription needed to provide normal vision. Only two types of eye care specialists can perform this test and write a prescription for eyeglasses: ophthalmologists and optometrists.

Ophthalmologists are physicians and are either medical doctors (M.D.s) or doctors of optometry (O.D.s). They specialize in the diagnosis and treatment of eye diseases. Ophthalmologists can prescribe medicines, examine the eyes, perform surgery on the eyes, and dispense eyeglasses as well as contact lenses.

Optometrists have a doctor of optometry degree from a school of optometry (O.D.s).They are not medical doctors, but are skilled at examining the eyes for vision problems and specific diseases of the eyes as well as dispensing eyeglasses and contact lenses. The laws in each state govern the scope of an optometrist's practice. Because laws vary from state to state, the extent to which optometrists can diagnose and treat eye disease also differs in each state.

To comparison shop for an eye care specialist, contact optometrists and ophthalmologists in your area and inquire about their usual charge for a refractory examination for a new eyeglass prescription. Be certain to ask for a listing of specific tests that will be performed for the given price. For example, does the examination include dilation of the eyes or a test for glaucoma? Depending upon your age, previous eye problems, general health, and other factors, it may be advisable to have these additional tests performed. (Your medical doctor and your eye care specialist can discuss with you your need for these tests.)

You may be surprised at the variations in price for the same service. When I recently contacted eye care specialists in my area, to evaluate the cost of a basic eye exam, I found the prices varied from the low cost of $35 to a high cost of $145. The lowest prices seemed to be consistently from optometrists.

The next step is to contact the local consumer affairs or consumer protection department and the professional licensing branch of the State

Department of Public Health. In most states, the state department of public health regulates the licensing of optometrists. They are usually located in each state's capital city. A quick phone call to these groups will reveal if any complaints have been lodged against the eye care specialist you are considering. This should provide a level of confidence in a new eye care specialist, especially if their price is the lowest in the area. You can also ask friends and acquaintances about their experiences with specific eye care professionals.

Your Legal Rights

Eye care specialists are required by the Federal Trade Commission's "Prescription Release Rule" to give you a copy of your eyeglass prescription at no extra cost immediately after an eye exam. Request a copy of your prescription if it's not automatically offered to you.

Low Cost Lenses

Opticians fill eyeglass prescriptions written by an optometrist or ophthalmologist. The law does not allow opticians to examine the eyes or prescribe lenses. In 21 states, they must be licensed. With your prescription in hand, call various optical stores in your area to inquire about their price to fill your prescription for the lenses only. Be certain to inquire if the price quoted is for glass or plastic lenses. The American Academy of Ophthalmology recommends that children have polycarbonate lenses to reduce injuries due to broken glass lenses. Once again, do a side-by-side comparison of your findings. When contacting various optical stores in my area, I was quoted prices ranging from $65 to $185 to fill the same prescription with the same type of lenses.

The quality of your eyeglasses is based upon the skill of the optician filling the prescription. If opticians are licensed in your state, inquire if the store has licensed opticians on staff and their level of supervision in filling your prescription. Contact the State Board of Opticians to inquire if any complaints have been lodged against the optician(s) at the store you're considering and to confirm the status of their license.

You can also contact the National Academy of Opticianry for a list of the State Opticianry Licensing Boards. Their street address is listed in the

"Schools of Opticianry" section. Its Web site at *www.nao.org/state.htm* lists the addresses and phone numbers of all state opticianry licensing boards.

Schools of Opticianry

The least expensive lenses are frequently available from schools that train opticians. Because students need experience, this service is frequently provided for only the cost of the materials. In addition to filling the prescription for the eyeglass lenses, they frequently sell eyeglass frames. When I contacted a local opticianry school, they informed me that the price to fill the prescription and put new lenses in my current frames would be $20. (A far cry from the $65 to $185 I had been previously quoted from optical stores.)

You may not be aware of the location of an opticianry school in your area. However, the monetary savings may make it more than worth your time and effort to investigate if one is near you and if it provides this service. Because students primarily staff these schools, the hours may be limited. Contact the school near you to inquire if it provides optical dispensing services, its exact hours of operation, and the price to fill your specific prescription. The supervision of the students that fill your prescription is quite rigid. Therefore, you can be assured a high-quality pair of eyeglasses.

Contact the following organizations for a complete list of all schools in your area. You may need to contact all of the sources listed because schools may be accredited by one group and not another.

National Academy of Opticianry
10111 Martin Luther King, Jr. Hwy #112
Bowie, MD 20720-4299
Phone: (800) 229-4828
www.nao.org/state.htm

The National Federation of Opticianry Schools
10342 Democracy Lane
Fairfax, VA 22030-2521
Phone: (703) 691-8355
www.nfos.org/nfos.html

Commission on Opticianry Accreditation
7023 Little River Turnpike, Suite 207
Annandale, VA 22003
Phone: (703) 691-8355
www.nao.org/coa.htm

Association of School and Colleges of Optometry
6110 Executive Boulevard, Suite 690
Rockville, MD 20852
Phone: (301) 231-5944
http://home.opted.org/asco/list.html

Low Cost Frames

We all want to wear a pair of eyeglasses that makes us look our best. Many "economy frames" available from optical stores enhance your pocketbook, but do nothing for your appearance. However, because many optical stores carry the same frames, comparison shopping is quite easy. Simply go to a store with a large selection of frames and try on frames until you find several you like. Have the optician or clerk write down the company name of the frames and their stock number, reorder number, or name of the frame. With this information in hand, you can call other optical companies (and schools of opticianry) to comparison shop.

Tips for Clearly Visible Savings

- You do not have to buy your frames from the same store that fills the lens prescription.
- To save the most money, you might have to buy the frames from one store and have the lenses put in at another store. If you comparison shop by phone, you can save money and time.
- Keep your old frames and simply replace the lenses. Children do not usually outgrow their frames yearly. Adults never outgrow their frames.
- Choose eyeglass frames with a great deal of care based not only on how they enhance your appearance but the quality of workmanship. The optician should be able to provide information based on his or her own experience regarding the durability of a frame.

- Trendy styles are usually higher priced and their popularity is transient. Therefore, it is best to choose a conservative style that is proven to be popular over the course of time. A well-chosen style is a good investment because you will be able to reuse the same frame many times
- Optical stores usually repair eyeglasses free of charge, even if they did not sell them to you. You may be able to reuse your frames if they are repaired properly.
- Does the optical store guarantee its work and provide for customer satisfaction in filling the prescription?
- Ask for a discount. Always ask the optical store if they can further reduce the price of the frames. Let them know that a competitor has the frame or a similar frame for a lower price, and ask if they can beat its competitor's price. I find this to be an interesting phenomenon, but stores frequently will not offer a lower price unless you ask for one. It is as though they only give discounts to savvy shoppers. Ask the salesperson if he or she will discount the price of the lenses if you buy the frames (at a discount, of course).

Pay Less for Contact Lenses

Federal laws require an ophthalmologist or optometrist to give a patient a copy of his or her eyeglass prescription. However, these federal laws do not mandate the release of a contact lens prescription. Some states have laws that require the release of a contact lens prescription, they include Alabama, Arizona, Colorado, Delaware, Florida, Georgia, Indiana, Iowa, Louisiana, Maine, Massachusetts, New Hampshire, New Jersey, New York, North Carolina, Ohio, Oregon, South Dakota, Texas, Vermont, Virginia, Washington state, and Wyoming. It is not uncommon for practitioners in the remaining states to release prescriptions upon patient request. Therefore, at your next visit, ask for a copy of your contact lens prescription.

Refer to Figure 14-1 for a list of questions to be asked of a new vision care specialist before your first visit. If you live in a state that does not require the release of a contact lens prescription and your new eye doctor does not release it, cancel the appointment and find another vision care specialist who does. If you are getting contact lenses for the first time, your vision care specialist will probably not allow you to purchase your initial

> **FIGURE 14-1**
>
> **Choosing a Contact Lens Vision Care Specialist**
>
> Determine the following information about any potential new vision care specialist:
>
> - Can I get a copy of my prescription?
> - What tests are included in the eye examination?
> - What are the charges for the examination, contact lens evaluation, fitting, lens-care kit, and follow-up visits?
> - Do you have a refund policy if I can't adapt to contact lenses?
> - What types and brands of contact lenses do you sell?
> - What is the charge for replacement lenses?

pair of contact lenses elsewhere. However, once he or she has you properly fitted, obtain a copy of your final prescription.

With prescription in hand, you can comparison shop for the best price for replacement contact lenses. You will be pleasantly surprised at the money you can save. Contact local opticians, discount stores, warehouse stores with optometry departments, and mail order contact lens companies or those with toll-free numbers. Look in the yellow pages of your phone book for these traditional and nontraditional retail outlets. Many of the mail order contact lens companies have Internet Web sites.

Determine all expenses associated with the purchase of your contacts including postage, handling fees, membership fees, and so on from each source. All ancillary charges should be figured into the cost of a pair of contacts to do an accurate side-by-side comparison. The following list contains additional factors to be considered.

- Does the contact lens company sell the contact lens prescribed by your doctor (including brand name, style, and size)? Accept no substitutions or changes in the prescription given to you by your eye doctor.
- Upon receipt of a replacement pair of contact lenses from a source other than your vision care specialist, examine them carefully to confirm that they are the correct lenses. They should be the same brand and size (i.e., the diameter and base curve should be the same). This information is found on your prescription. If there is any doubt, have the contact lenses examined by your vision care specialist.

- Before placing an order, confirm that the mail order source has a satisfaction guaranteed policy.

PAYING LESS FOR ORTHODONTICS

More than four million people in the United States and Canada are in the care of an orthodontist. Braces straighten teeth and provide a beautiful smile. Of course, the most important consideration for many is the boost in self-confidence that a better smile provides.

Without treatment, some orthodontic problems can lead to gum disease, tooth decay, bone destruction, and chewing or digestive difficulties. Misalignment of the teeth can also contribute to speech impairments or tooth loss. However, most people get braces simply because they want to enhance their appearance and not out of medical necessity.

An orthodontist is a dentist who specializes in moving teeth and helping the jaw to develop properly. The American Dental Association requires orthodontists to have at least two years of post-doctoral, advanced specialty training in orthodontics in an accredited program after graduation from college and dental school.

When Should a Child See an Orthodontist for the First Time?

The American Association of Orthodontists suggests that every child should see an orthodontist by age seven. Some problems are corrected more easily if detected and treated early, rather than waiting until jaw growth has slowed. Early treatment may allow a patient to avoid surgery or other more serious corrections later in life. However, healthy teeth can be moved at any age, so an orthodontist can improve the smile of almost anyone.

Choose an orthodontist that is a member of the American Association of Orthodontists (AAO). You can then be assured that he or she is properly trained and sufficiently qualified.

To obtain a list of orthodontists in your area who are AAO members, call

800-STRAIGHT, (800) 787-2444 or write:
American Association of Orthodontists
401 N. Lindbergh Boulevard
St. Louis, MO 63141-7816

The Cost of Orthodontic Treatment

The location of the orthodontist as well as the complexity of the treatment plan seem to be the two most important factors in determining the cost of orthodontic treatment. An orthodontist practicing in a rural area, where rents are low and malpractice claims are rare, may charge under $3,000. On the other hand, an orthodontist in a city with high rents and rampant malpractice cases may charge $7,000 or more for a complex case.

To determine the lowest cost in your area, compare the prices charged by local orthodontists. Many times, the orthodontist's office staff will provide this information over the phone. Ask parents of your child's schoolmates. Most parents are more than willing to share this information with you. It may be necessary to go to the orthodontist for an initial examination and treatment plan before he or she will tell you the anticipated cost. Be certain to inquire about the cost of this initial examination prior to the visit. Many times there is no charge for the initial examination. However, there will be a charge if the orthodontist has to take X rays. To avoid this cost, bring any recent X rays of your child's teeth that may have been taken by your dentist or any previously seen orthodontists.

Can I Negotiate Lower Fees with My Orthodontist?

The decision to reduce the cost of the treatment rests with the orthodontist. It certainly could not hurt to ask if he or she would be willing to reduce the cost. This may be especially important if, in fact, your dental insurance does not cover this expense. Ask him or her, "In view of the fact that I don't have insurance, are your fees negotiable?" Perhaps you can barter with the orthodontist by trading your services or a product from your business. I know of a man who sold the orthodontist a luxury car from the car dealership where he worked at a dramatic discount as barter for free orthodontic treatments for his child. Most orthodontists allow you to pay for your child's treatment in installments. Frequently, they do not charge interest on the unpaid balance.

What You Need to Know about Dental Insurance

Many dental insurance plans now include orthodontic benefits. Read your policy carefully to understand the details of your plan. Will you be responsible for a percentage of the bill? Will you be required to pay an additional fee each month for this coverage? Will the insurance company only pay if you see one of their preselected orthodontists? Are there restrictions limiting the orthodontic treatment? Are there certain conditions under which braces are not covered? Does your child's situation meet these requirements?

Insurance companies frequently negotiate contracts that require orthodontists to charge one half or two thirds of their normal fee. However, some insurance companies base the subscriber's co-payment on the normal, full fee, not the reduced fee that the insurance company is actually charged. The end result, in this instance, is that the insurance company pays less or nothing toward a subscriber's orthodontic bill, whereas the insured pays the entire fee through his or her co-payment.

For example, ABC Dental Insurance Company previously negotiated a reduced rate with Dr. Alyssa the orthodontist. She agreed to provide treatment to their subscribers for $2,400 instead of her normal fee of $4,000. The ABC Dental Insurance Company has an agreement with its subscribers to pay 40 percent of the cost of orthodontic care. The subscriber is to pay the remaining 60 percent as a co-payment. However, ABC Insurance Company bases the 60 percent co-payment on the normal, full fee of $4,000, not the reduced rate of $2,400, the actual fee charged by Dr. Alyssa. Therefore, the subscriber is required to pay a co-payment of 60 percent of $4,000, or $2,400. In this example, the insurance company pays nothing because the subscriber paid the full amount due, or $2,400.

If the "actual cost" is used to determine the subscriber co-payment, the subscriber would only pay $1,440 (60 percent of $2,400) and the ABC Insurance Company would pay $960 (40 percent of $2,400).

You, the subscriber, may not even be aware that the insurance company had negotiated this reduced amount and was not paying anything toward the treatment. Ask the orthodontist to notify you regarding the actual amount billed to the insurance company. If it appears that your co-payment is based on the normal fee and not the actual amount billed, talk with your insurance company. Try to get them to base the amount of your co-payment on the amount actually charged by the orthodontist. If the insurance company seems to be resistant to considering a change in this practice, contact your states Commissioner of Insurance and/or state attorney general to inquire if you can do anything further to rectify the situation.

Does Your Employer Offer a Flexible Spending Account?

Some employers allow their employees to set aside money from pretax dollars to pay for specific medical expenses not covered by their insurance plan. The money placed in this flexible spending account is excluded from the payment of income tax, Social Security, and Medicare tax. The tax laws allow employers to offer this benefit and employees never have to pay taxes on this money. Inquire at your place of employment to determine if you can put aside money for the payment of your orthodontist's bill. Paying this bill with pretax dollars will result in paying several hundred dollars less in taxes. A middle income wage earner will pay $852 fewer taxes if they place money in their flexible spending account for the payment of a $3,600 orthodontic bill. It's like getting an $852 discount on the orthodontist's bill.

Low Cost Orthodontic Treatment

If you live within reasonable driving distance from a dental school, contact the school to inquire if it also trains orthodontic students. Student orthodontists need to practice on real patients. Often the price is reduced when done by a student orthodontist. An experienced orthodontic instructor oversees all student work, so you can be assured that your child receives proper care and treatment.

To obtain a list of accredited orthodontic education programs and dental schools in your state, contact the American Dental Association at the following address:

American Dental Association
211 E. Chicago Avenue
Chicago, IL 60611
Phone: (312) 440-2500
www.ada.org

Facts to Consider When Selecting an Orthodontist

1. Ask your orthodontist if he or she recycles any part of the braces that will be used in your child's mouth. Insist that only new

materials be used. Indicate this requirement in writing on the consent form to ensure there is no misunderstanding regarding your intention.

Some orthodontists recycle orthodontic materials from one patient to another. It is estimated that in the U.S. as many as one orthodontist out of every three recycles brackets used in the treatment of a patient. Brackets are removed from one patient's mouth, cleaned, and then bonded onto another patient's teeth. Currently, there are no standards for the resterilization and reuse of brackets. All companies that manufacture these brackets specifically state on the original packaging that the brackets are for single use only. A study done by the University of Iowa confirmed that recycled brackets do not meet the manufacturer's original specifications. Unfortunately, there are no governmental guidelines that prevent this practice. If you have a managed care dental plan, confirm with the plan administrator that the orthodontist is required to use only new (not recycled) materials in your child's mouth. If your dental plan allows the dentist to recycle brackets from one patient to the next and you cannot convince your plan administrator to pay for new, not recycled, materials for your child, consider paying extra personally for these new materials to be used. Discuss this option with your orthodontist.
2. Ask the orthodontist about his instrument sterilization procedures and the specific methods used to sterilize everything that will be utilized in your child's mouth.
3. Inquire about the infection control procedures used by your orthodontist. Does the orthodontist, as well as his assistants, wear gloves and change them before examining a new patient? The orthodontist and anyone else examining your child's mouth should put on a new pair of disposable examination gloves before each treatment. The gloves do not have to be "sterile." Washing gloves between patients is not acceptable.

MONEY SAVING BEAUTY PRODUCTS

Make your own natural skin care products to have fresh, glowing skin and hair for a fraction of the cost.

"Cheap and Easy" Leave-In Hair Conditioner

To make your own leave-in hair conditioner for only a fraction of the cost, dilute your current hair conditioner with water. Place any brand of cream rise or hair conditioner into a spray bottle and dilute it with water using one part conditioner/cream rinse to six or seven parts water. Shake well before using. Lightly mist this solution on wet, shampooed hair. Allow it to remain on your hair undisturbed for about one minute to allow it to become evenly distributed. Then, comb and style as usual. You will find that you have fewer tangles, if any, and that your hair is soft and shiny. If your hair appears to be dull or heavy, further dilute your solution with more water until an acceptable dilution rate is achieved.

Deep Conditioning Hair Treatment

Use this treatment for dry, brittle, or damaged hair once a month to restore its shine. Combine two tablespoons oil (olive oil or vegetable oil) with one egg. Apply this mixture to your dry hair. Cover your hair with a plastic bag. The warmth of your head will enhance the conditioning treatment. Place a dry towel over the plastic bag and relax. Let the treatment remain on your hair for at least 15 minutes. Wash your hair as usual until all of the oil is removed.

Hair Conditioner

¼ cup olive oil
¼ cup vegetable oil
¼ honey
1 whole egg

Combine the oils and honey in a small pan and heat over low heat on the top of a stove until warmed and well blended. Allow the mixture to cool to room temperature and stir in the whole egg. Wet your hair and apply the conditioner to the ends of your hair. For severely damaged hair, apply the conditioner to your entire head. Wrap your hair loosely on top of your head and cover it with a plastic bag. Leave the conditioner on your hair for about one hour. Shampoo the mixture from your hair. Rinse and dry as usual. Store any unused portion covered in the refrigerator.

Make Your Own Vitamin Enriched Shampoo

Remove the liquid from six capsules of Vitamin E and add the oil to 16 ounces of your regular shampoo. Shake well to combine. Shampoo as usual with your new vitamin enriched shampoo. Purchase Vitamin E on sale at a discount store or pharmacy for maximum savings.

Eye Makeup Remover

Use baby oil or mineral oil to remove eye makeup instead of buying special eye makeup remover. Baby oil is mineral oil with a fragrance added.

Facial Cleanser and Exfoliator

Use 1–2 teaspoons of baking soda as a mild facial cleanser and exfoliator. Dampen face with warm water. Gently massage the baking soda into your face to remove makeup and dirt. Rinse well with warm water. If your skin is normally dry, use this no more than once a week.

Yogurt Facial Cleansing Scrub

When used as a cleansing agent, yogurt helps balance the pH of your skin. Sugar has antibacterial properties that can help troubled acne prone skin to heal more quickly. Sugar also sloughs off any dry facial skin so it looks fresh and healthy again.

Moisten the entire face with very warm water. Massage about one tablespoon of plain yogurt onto the face and neck. Place about 1 teaspoon of sugar in the palm of your hand. Gently mix ½–1 tablespoon of yogurt with the sugar. Massage this sugar mixture over the entire face and neck. Rinse well with warm water. A scrub should not be used more than once a week.

Yogurt alone can be used to clean the face after makeup has been removed with oil as described in the next section "Natural Makeup Remover."

Natural Makeup Remover

Use olive oil or safflower oil to remove makeup gently and naturally. Place a few drops of the oil in the palm of your clean hand. Gently rub your hands together to warm the oil. Using your fingertips, massage the oil onto your face. Remove the oil with a wash cloth or cotton balls dampened with warm water. Repeat, if necessary, to remove all traces of makeup. The oil leaves the skin moisturized and smooth feeling.

Organic Facial Scrubs

Use one tablespoon of any of the following as a facial scrub: oatmeal, cornmeal, dry yeast, or sea salt. Splash warm water on your face and scrub gently with the desired scrub. Rinse with warm water and pat dry. Do not use a facial scrub more than once a week. For added cleansing, mix the scrub with your normal facial cleanser and use as described.

Fruit Facial Mask

1 small apple, peeled and chopped, or 4 strawberries, or ½ banana, or ½ peach
2 tablespoons honey

Puree the chosen fruit in a blender or food processor only until mashed. Combine the fruit and honey in a small bowl. Apply the mixture to your face. Allow the mask to remain on your face for at least 10 minutes. Rinse with cool water. Pat dry. Store unused portion in the refrigerator.

Strawberry Skin Moisturizer

1 tablespoon vegetable, olive, or coconut oil
3 strawberries
1–2 drops Vitamin E oil

Wash the strawberries and remove the green top. Use a fork to mash the strawberries into a pulp. Add the oil and vitamin E. Stir to combine. Apply the mixture to your face and skin. Store unused portion covered, in the refrigerator.

Herbal Facial Mask

1 tablespoon honey
1 whole egg
1 tablespoon dried chamomile
1 teaspoon fresh mint, finely chopped

Combine all of the listed ingredients in a small bowl. Apply the mixture to your face and neck. Allow it to remain on your skin for at least 10 minutes. Rinse with cool water. Pat dry. Store unused portion covered in the refrigerator no more than 24 hours. This mask cleans and tightens pores.

Lemon Moisturizer

1 egg yolk, beaten
¼ cup olive oil
¼ cup vegetable oil
1 tablespoon lemon juice

Combine egg yolk and lemon juice in a medium bowl. Add the oils while stirring the egg yolk mixture with a wire whisk. Mixture will thicken. Apply the mixture to face and neck. Allow the moisturizer to remain on your face at least 10 minutes. Rinse with cool water. Pat dry. Store unused portion covered in the refrigerator no more than 24 hours.

Cucumber Facial Mask

1 tablespoon instant nonfat dry milk
½ cucumber, peeled and chopped into large chunks
2 tablespoons plain yogurt

Puree all of the ingredients in a blender or food processor until smooth. Apply the mixture to your face and neck. Allow the mask to remain on your face for at least 10 minutes. Rinse with cool water. Pat dry. Store unused portion covered in the refrigerator. This mask cleans and moisturizes.

Egg Facial Mask

Eggs have been used for many years as a natural, healthy, facial treatment. For dry skin, use the yolk of the egg to nourish it and make it glow. For tightening and to degrease oily skin; use the white of the egg. With this information, you can make a mask to meet the needs of your skin.

Allow the egg to come to room temperature. Break the egg and separate the yolk from the white. Place each in a separate small bowl. Use a fork to beat the needed egg yolk and/or egg white. For combination skin, apply the white to the oily areas of your face and the yolk to dry areas. Allow the egg to dry on your face. Rinse thoroughly with warm water.

Vinegar Skin Toner

Skin toner or astringent restores the skin's pH balance after cleansing and it removes all traces of the cleanser. To make this all-natural skin toner, use only apple cider vinegar. Do not use distilled white vinegar. Combine ½ teaspoon of apple cider vinegar with one cup of tap water or rainwater. Pour the toner into a clean container with a lid. For dry skin, use less vinegar; for oily skin, increase the amount of vinegar. To use, apply the toner with a cotton ball or tissue. Do not rinse.

Smooth Shaving

Women can effectively use hair conditioner instead of shaving cream when shaving underarms and legs. After washing the area, rub one tablespoon of hair conditioner on the damp skin. Shave as usual and rinse thoroughly. The skin feels smooth and will be less prone to dryness because of the moisturizing benefits of the hair conditioner. Even the most inexpensive hair conditioners will work equally well. If a man runs out of shaving cream, he too can use hair conditioner when shaving his face.

Breath Fresheners

Gargle with baking soda to freshen your breath inexpensively. Stir ½–1 teaspoon of baking soda into ½ cup of water. Gargle with the solution.

Treatment for Yellow Fingernails

Fingernails frequently turn yellow with repeated application of fingernail polish. Apply undiluted lemon juice or hydrogen peroxide to bare fingernails with a cotton ball or tissue. Allow the lemon juice or peroxide to remain on the nails until the yellowing disappears. Repeat as necessary.

Deodorizing Bath Powder

Make your own bath powder to control odor and to maintain a dry, comfortable feeling, even in hot weather. Combine ¼ cup cornstarch with ¼ cup baking soda. Stir well. Pour the powder into a container with a shaker top. Use as a body powder after a shower or bath. It works as well as a commercial product and can be made for just pennies.

15

Say Hello to Good Buys

When many people need a given item, they go to a retail store and buy it. At best, to save money, they may wait until it goes on sale to purchase the item. However, there are many ways to reduce living expenses and pay less for luxury items. This chapter explores nontraditional methods, such a bartering or cooperative buying to obtain services and products at reduced prices or at no cost. The secrets of having a lucrative yard sale as well as shopping techniques at yard sales are also shared.

BARTERING, THE BUCK STOPS HERE

Most of us first became familiar with the concept of bartering when we were in grade school and traded a bag of chips for a candy bar. To barter is to trade, or to buy and sell without exchanging cash. We are now seeing a more formal resurgence of this form of commerce. Today there are groups of businesses in many communities that have organized to buy and sell their products and services as payment instead of cash. These bartering groups develop their own form of currency, like barter bucks, or use a credit card system to track a member's barter money.

This is how it works. Let's say you own a restaurant and belong to a barter group. Another member of the group could come in and use some of his or her barter bucks to pay for a meal in your restaurant. If the meal totaled $50, you would receive $50 in barter bucks. As the owner of the restaurant, the actual cost to you for this meal is only $20. You therefore receive $50 worth of barter bucks, at a cost to you of only $20. You could now take these barter bucks to another member of the bartering group and buy something you need. For example, you could go to a printer in the group and pay for the printing of new menus with your $50 in barter bucks. This formal method of bartering is primarily available to businesses that have products or services of value to the current members of the bartering club.

Even if you do not own a business, you can still use the concept of bartering to reduce your living expenses or get services you might normally have to purchase. For example, a group of friends can establish a babysitting cooperative, or co-op. For every hour a member watches your child, he or she gets one hour of sitter credit. You would be able to take advantage of this service by turning in the sitter credit you earned by sitting for other members' children. The "barter hours" in this case are earned at one credit per child per hour. So, if you watched two children for one hour, you would receive two hours of sitter credit.

Another bartering arrangement is a family meal exchange group. In this instance, seven families with similar diets and food preferences get together to plan menus for one week at a time and use the meals as barter. Each member only prepares one evening meal each week, and then distributes this same meal to all members of the meal exchange. For example, let's say Mrs. Morgan's day is Monday and the meal she has agreed to prepare is lasagna. She prepares seven pans of lasagna, which includes one pan for her family's supper, and delivers the other six to members of her meal exchange group for Monday night's supper. This is the only night she cooks supper for the week. On the other six nights, supper is delivered by the other members of the exchange. In this bartering group example, the members trade their cooking talents and the form of exchange is the prepared food. All members meet regularly to plan menus that everyone enjoys and to ensure that each member spends an equal amount on food.

Buying as a Member of a Cooperative

According to the International Cooperative Alliance, "a cooperative is an autonomous association of persons united voluntarily to meet their common economic, social and cultural needs, and aspirations through a jointly-owned and democratically-controlled enterprise. They are based on the values of self-help, self-responsibility, democracy, equality, equity, and solidarity. In the tradition of their founders, cooperative members believe in the ethical values of honesty, openness, social responsibility, and caring for others."

There are over 700 million members in the worldwide cooperative movement in agricultural, banking, credit and savings, energy, industry, insurance, fishery, tourism, housing, and many other areas. Cooperatives give consumers and workers control over the places they bank, shop, work, and live in an effort to improve the quality of their lives and reduce their living expenses. Members receive price reductions as a result of purchasing in large quantities. For example, members of a home heating oil co-op pay less per gallon for the oil used to heat their homes than an individual using the same vendor. The per gallon price for the co-op members is based on the expected sale of thousands of gallons of oil to all members of the co-op, as opposed to selling only a few hundred gallons to one individual. The heating oil dealer is able to buy home heating oil at a reduced rate when buying in larger quantities and can therefore pass the added savings on to the co-op members.

The Center for Cooperatives at the University of Wisconsin provides information and support to groups with a desire to start a cooperative. At their Web site, *www.wisc.edu/uwcc*, you can link to directories listing various cooperatives in the United States and Canada. Perhaps you can find one that you might want to join.

The address and phone number of The Center for Cooperatives at the University of Wisconsin is:

UWCC
230 Taylor Hall
427 Lorch Street
Madison, WI 53706
Phone: (608) 262-3981

Informal Cooperatives

To benefit from the concept of a cooperative, you do not need to formally establish a cooperative. Anytime two or more people are interested in buying the same product or service, they can join together to negotiate a lower price based on buying in volume. For example, if three neighbors need to have their driveways paved, they could negotiate a lower rate with the asphalt contractor by approaching him as a group. The contractor's expenses should be less because all three neighbors live in the same geographic location. These savings can be passed on in a lower price to each homeowner in the group. To get the best possible price for your group, comparison shop with as many vendors as possible.

PRECAUTIONS WHEN ORDERING MERCHANDISE BY PHONE, ONLINE, OR MAIL

At some point, we have all taken advantage of the convenience of ordering merchandise over the phone, online, or via the mail. These nontraditional ways to buy merchandise are becoming increasingly popular. However, unless specific precautions are taken, you could lose your money or be stuck with an inferior product destined for your next garage sale.

Questions to Ask Before the Purchase

Determine the answers to the following questions anytime a product is purchased from a nontraditional source:

- When can you expect delivery?
- How much is the postage?
- Are there any special handling fees?
- What is the company's return policy?
- How are returns handled?
- Is there a warranty or guarantee for the product being purchased? Is this in writing? Can you get a copy of it in writing?
- Can you get a written copy of any supporting information to back up any unusual marketing claims made by the company?
- When ordering perishable goods (flowers, food, etc.) will the company replace the item or refund the payment if the goods are spoiled upon arrival?

Shopping Tips

- Carefully evaluate the company to determine if it is reputable. Contact the Better Business Bureau (BBB) in the city where the company is located. Call the Council of Better Business Bureaus at (703) 276-7060 for an office near you.
- Read any printed literature very carefully—especially the fine print. The photograph you see in the catalog or promotional literature may make the product look larger than it really is.
- If available, read the warranty, refund, and exchange policies. If a written copy is not available, ask for this information verbally. Take written notes regarding what the representative tells you as well as the name (first and last) of the person that reports this information to you. Are these policies acceptable? If not, do not purchase merchandise from this source.
- If you are unable to determine the previous information, or if there is any information that makes you suspicious, do not place the order.
- Never send cash in the mail. Sending a check, credit card number, billing information, or money order will provide a written record of your payment.
- Keep the advertisement to which you are responding and a copy of the order form. If there is no order form, keep a record of the company's name, address, phone number, date, amount paid, the item you purchased, and any delivery date that may have been promised. Also include the first and last name of the person who took your order (or his or her employee identification number).
- Never provide your credit card, debit card, or bank account number to the person taking your order until you have confirmed that you are dealing with a reputable, established company.
- If you are ordering something to be delivered by C.O.D., write out the check to the seller, not the post office. If necessary, you can then contact your bank and stop the check if there is an immediate problem with the merchandise. You cannot stop payment on the check if it was made out to the U.S. Post Office.

Your Legal Rights When Shopping from Home

Your state may have more specific laws that protect you from home shopping problems. The following federal laws offer some protection when ordering merchandise from your home.

- Your order must be shipped within the time frame given by the company. If your order cannot be filled within this period of time, you must be given the following two options: to continue to wait or be allowed to cancel your order with a full and prompt refund issued.
- If the company cannot or will not give a shipping date, you have the right to cancel the order due to nondelivery 30 days after you placed the order.
- If you paid for the purchase with a credit card, you do not have to pay for the bill that is in dispute until the problem is resolved.
- The seller must give you a full refund within seven business days of receipt of your request.

You Have the Right to Refuse a Delivery of Damaged or Spoiled Items

If a package received is obviously damaged, write "REFUSED" on the outside of the package at the time of delivery and return it to the shipper. You cannot open the package to inspect the contents if you intend to refuse the shipment.

The Fair Credit Billing Act

Whether you are buying online, by phone, mail, or in person, using your credit card to pay for the purchase offers additional protection because your transaction is protected by the Fair Credit Billing Act. Some credit cards offer an extension to the manufacturer's warranty or other protection benefits.

Disputes or Billing Errors

What do you do when you receive three gizmos, yet you only ordered one? On occasion, people have problems with their orders for one of the following reasons.

- Being overcharged for the merchandise.
- Nonreceipt of an item for which they were charged.
- Merchandise was received damaged.
- False or misleading advertising was used in the marketing of the merchandise.

Gather together all of your supporting documents including copies of canceled checks, the order form, advertisements promoting the product you ordered, names of people that you have talked to in the past, and so on. Immediately write to the company explaining your concerns and ask for a specific resolution to the problem.

Be sure to include:

- Your name.
- Your address.
- Your daytime phone number.
- If known, include the order or invoice number.
- Always include a copy of the canceled check, or credit card statement indicating the charge made to your account.
- A copy of the original order form.
- Any other helpful information about your purchase.

NOTIFY YOUR BANK OR CREDIT CARD ISSUER

If your purchase was charged to a credit card, or the payment was to be automatically withdrawn from your bank account, send a copy of the complaint letter to your bank or the credit card issuer. Write to the credit card company at the special address indicated on your monthly statement for "billing inquiries." Include your name, address, credit card number, and a brief description of the billing error.

You have only 60 days after receipt of the credit card bill to file a formal dispute. The credit card company has 30 days to respond to your complaint. They must completely resolve the dispute within 90 days. If you used a debit card, the issuer must respond within 10 days to your dispute and cannot take more than 45 days to resolve the problem.

UNAUTHORIZED CHARGES

If your credit card is used without your authorization, you can be held liable to pay for the first $50 in unauthorized charges per account. However, if you report the loss of your card before it is used, you are not liable for any unauthorized charges.

The rules governing the use of a credit card do not apply to debit cards. You are liable for $50 to $500 for the unauthorized use of a debit card, depending on when you report the loss or theft. If you do not report an unauthorized transfer or withdrawal within 60 days after your statement is sent to you, you risk unlimited loss.

Promptly review your monthly bank and credit card statements for billing errors or unauthorized purchases. Notify your credit card or debit card issuer or bank immediately if your credit card, debit card, or checkbook is lost or stolen.

Cybershopping

Placing an order on the Internet is fast and convenient. However, this new shopping experience requires special precautions to protect your personal security. Your Internet browser is the software that acts like a telephone to receive the information from the Internet. Unsecured information sent over the Internet can be intercepted. Ensure that you are using a secure browser, which will encrypt or scramble information that you want to keep private: your credit card number, address, social security number, and so on.

Make certain the Web site where the order is placed is using a Secure Sockets Layer (SSL) or Secure Hypertext Transfer Protocol (S-HTTP).

The credit card industry is also developing enhanced levels of security using Secured Electronic Transactions (SET). The SET protocol provides highly encrypted communication between card issuers, merchants, and card members.

If you question the security of your credit card information, call the company direct, fax your order, or send your check or money order via the U.S. mail.

Be wary if personal information such as your Social Security number is requested. This information is not needed to purchase merchandise. Although many reputable companies sell merchandise on the Internet, it also serves as a way for con artists to attract consumers to their scams.

Double-check all information when you are placing an order on the Internet. A simple typographical error could bring ten of the given product to your door instead of only one. Double-check all calculations to ensure that there are no errors. Print out a copy of your order and confirmation number for your records.

The same laws that protect you when you shop by phone or mail apply to shopping in cyberspace.

CYBERSHOPPING FOR BARGAINS

Much has been said about the dramatic increase in consumer spending over the Internet. However, shopping over the Internet is much different from walking into a local department store. Unless specific precautions are taken, consumers could not only pay too much for a given product, but may not receive the merchandise they ordered.

A storefront on the Internet, unlike a store made of bricks and mortar, can be set up in a matter of hours with only a minimal financial investment. Consumers may make false assumptions regarding the stability of a given merchant based on the sophistication of its Web site. The following sections contain information every consumer should take into consideration before purchasing anything via the Internet.

Comparison Shop and Try to Negotiate a Lower Price

Prices vary widely on the Internet. Look for sales. Some Internet merchants post clearance sales on their Web sites. Others use their Web sites to sell excess inventory or out-of-season merchandise at deep discounts.

Always determine the local retail price for the item and compare it with the Internet price for the same item. If you can find a given product on the Internet at a lower price than that offered by a local merchant, print the Internet offer. Take the offer to the local merchant and ask if he or she can meet or beat the Internet price. You may be surprised how often local merchants will reduce their price to compete with the Internet price. Although you may not have to pay sales tax for an Internet purchase, you will probably have to pay shipping and handling. Some Internet companies do not charge for shipping.

Take all of the charges into consideration when comparing prices. Shipping and handling charges vary greatly between online companies. Online sales are not bargains if handling and shipping fees are excessive. Some online merchants automatically charge the rate for two-day delivery. If possible, choose a less costly delivery option.

Confirming the Reliability of an Internet Merchant

Verify the reliability of an Internet merchant before making a purchasing decision. You can do this by contacting the Better Business Bureau (BBB) and/or the Biz Rate Web sites.

Contact the Better Business Bureau in the city where the online merchant is located. Visit the BBB Web site at *www.bbb.org* for links to local offices.

Talk to friends, colleagues, and family members to inquire about their personal experiences with Internet merchants and their recommendations. If you have a complaint against an online merchant, report it to the Council of Better Business Bureaus at their Web site. The specific URL for information regarding the proper procedure to file a complaint is *www.bbb.org/bbbcomplaints/welcome.asp*.

Read customer ratings of online merchants at the Biz Rate Web site. Biz Rate provides customer ratings of various online merchants and compares their services. Before placing an order with any online merchant, review their rating at *www.bizrate.com*.

Never Give Your Internet Password to Anyone

If an Internet merchant requires that you create an account with a password, never use the same password used for other accounts or Web sites.

Be Wary of a Merchant If You Are Asked to Supply Personal Information

Never give out your Social Security number or personal bank account information to conduct a transaction over the Internet. Personal information is seldom necessary and represents a risk to your personal safety and security.

Keep Written Records of Every Internet Purchase

Anytime an order is placed, keep a written record of the purchase by following these steps.

1. Write down the URL of the site where the item was purchased.
2. Print out a copy of your order immediately before it is sent, so you have a written record of your actual order.
3. Keep a record of the confirmation number of your order.

This information is extremely valuable if you have any problem with the receipt of your merchandise. The copy of your actual order is your only proof that you did not order 12 copies of a best selling novel, you only ordered one copy.

Read Your E-Mail

Confirm that you gave the correct e-mail address to the merchant at the time of your order. The merchant may send you important information about your purchases that requires a timely response.

Problem Resolution

If your problem cannot be resolved using the methods listed in this chapter, contact the state or local consumer protection office where you live. It may be listed in the "self-help" or government section (usually the blue pages) in your telephone directory. These agencies may be able to help resolve your complaint.

THE NATIONAL FRAUD INFORMATION CENTER

This nongovernment service gives free advice by phone to consumers who suspect fraud or misrepresentation. The phone number is (800) 876-7060.

TREASURE HUNTING AT YARD SALES

Avid yard sale shoppers thoroughly enjoy swapping tales about the best "deal" they got at a yard sale. One purchased an antique sofa valued at over $3,000 for only $2, another purchased a $45 food blender for only 50¢. Most view a yard sale, tag sale, garage sale, flea market, or estate sale as the location of a modern day treasure hunt. The "treasure maps" are found weekly in the classified ads, posted on community bulletin boards, or on "Yard Sale" road signs.

The best items sell first, so plan to arrive as soon as the sale begins. Classified ads or posters advertising the sale indicate the specific hours of the sale. Consider returning near the end of a sale when sellers are motivated to get rid of any remaining items. Frequently, sellers reduce their entire remaining inventory by as much as 50 percent toward the end of the sale.

Preplan your driving route to the various sales to maximize your time, energy, and gasoline. Do not overlook the yard sale signs of unadvertised sales.

If your time is limited and you are unable to spend the entire weekend going to yard sales, be selective in the sales you do attend to increase your chances of finding valuable treasures. Use the following guidelines to choose the "best" sales to attend:

- Multiple family sales or those sponsored by church groups or members of civic organizations are frequently rich sources of many hidden treasures. The more families or people contributing merchandise to the sale, the larger the selection of merchandise.
- Attend sales that list the specific items you are seeking in their classified ad.

Professional Estate Sales

Estate sale professionals can be hired to hold a sale on behalf of an individual or family. Although these sales usually have a great deal of merchandise, the prices are almost always higher than a "nonprofessionally run" sale. In fact, the prices are frequently comparable to those charged in an antique store.

Come Prepared to Shop

- Wear comfortable shoes and clothing appropriate for the weather.
- Dress casually. Wear clothes that can be easily laundered because you may get a little dusty or dirty digging through boxes of books, clothes, and so on.
- Do not wear expensive clothing or jewelry or drive a high-priced car to yard sales. These symbols of wealth put you at a disadvantage if you try to haggle with the seller to reduce the price.
- Come armed with the sizes and measurements of each family member. Bring a tape measure to determine the size of a garment if the size is not apparent.
- Bring snacks and drinks to keep up your energy.
- Have lots of change and one dollar bills available. You put yourself at a disadvantage if you try to haggle a price down from $3 to 50¢ for an item, and then pull out a $10 bill to pay for it.
- Bring along a few AA and C batteries to test battery operated items.

Buyer Beware

- Always test an item to ensure it is in working order: ride a bicycle, test working parts, open boxes to make certain all parts are present, and so on.
- Inspect items carefully, especially clothing. Yard sales do not traditionally give refunds. Buying stained clothing is risky because the stain may have set and be difficult to remove. Check for missing buttons and rips in the material. Assure that zippers work correctly.
- Compare the asking price with the retail price of the item when it was new to determine if the asking price is fair.

The Hunt

- Although most sales have merchandise neatly displayed on tables, occasionally, you will come across a disorganized sale with merchandise tossed in boxes or bags. These sales can be frustrating and time consuming—but don't give up and don't be shy. (Remember—this is a treasure hunt!) Look under tables, in boxes, and in bags. You may be rewarded with an unbelievable treasure.

- Some sellers do not mark individual prices on merchandise, instead they post a sign stating "make an offer." In these instances, use the tactic antique dealers have used successfully for years when they buy antiques—offer one lump sum for everything you are buying. The seller will focus on the total amount and usually not question the individual prices. Therefore, wait until you have chosen everything you want to buy before offering a price. Take the items to the seller and offer him or her one price for everything you have chosen.
- Offer to purchase clothing by the bag. Pack the bag as full as possible, double bag it if necessary to hold the most clothing for the dollar.
- Do not be shy or afraid to offer less for an item you think is overpriced. The worst thing a seller can say is "no."
- If you see something you like, pick it up before someone else does. You can always put it down later if you decide not to buy it. Simply because you were the first person to see an item does not give you the right of first purchase.
- If you see a piece of furniture you want to buy, immediately talk to the seller to negotiate a price or someone else might beat you to the treasure. Furniture that is priced right sells quickly at yard sales—so do not hesitate or it may be lost.

The Secrets of Holding a Profitable Sale

Sell unneeded items taking up space in your home by having a yard sale. To have a successful sale, various factors must be considered. With these few simple tips you should not only have fun but you will make some extra money from items you no longer need.

PERMITS

Contact your local town hall to determine if a permit is needed and if your community has any restrictions regarding yard sales.

INSURANCE

Review your homeowners' insurance policy to confirm you are adequately covered should an accident occur.

BEST TIMES

In most areas, yard sales are most frequently held between Memorial Day to Labor Day. Choose a date well in advance. Allow at least two weeks for adequate preparation. Most sales start at 8:00 or 9:00 A.M. and end by 3:00 or 4:00 P.M. If you live in an area where the afternoon temperature can exceed 90°F, plan to end the sale before the temperature peaks.

LOCATION

A sale can be held just about anywhere: the yard, driveway, under a tent, the garage or basement, in an apartment, inside a room in your house, and so on.

INVENTORY

You can sell just about anything at a yard sale. Large ticket items can also be sold at yard sales. These include cars, motorcycles, and even the house where the sale is being held. Of course, smaller items are most frequently sold: plants, clothes, toys, dishes, curtains, tools, rooted cuttings, small appliances, and so on. Get the entire family involved in collecting the inventory (i.e., "stuff" you want to sell). The more inventory, the greater the opportunity for a successful sale. Ask friends and relatives if they have something to sell at your sale. They may be willing to share advertising costs and help with the sale.

If an item is more than 25 years old or considered "collectible," contact antique shops to determine the resale value of the item. Unless you know the current value of an item, you might underprice it dramatically and lose a significant amount of money. For example, lunch boxes are highly collectible. I recently saw a Partridge Family lunch box for sale at an antique store for $85. The dealer probably bought it at a yard sale for under $1. Most antique dealers get a significant amount of their inventory from yard sales.

An electrical outlet should be handy for customers to test electrical items.

Clean all inventory to make it look its best. Dusty, filmy glassware won't sell for as much as shiny, clean glassware. Display everything attractively at eye level. Do not put various items in a large box and make customers dig through it. Many customers will simply not bother.

Organize items by putting similar things together so customers can easily find items of interest. For example, place all kitchenware together in one area, all tools together in another area, all gardening supplies and plants together in a third area, and so on.

TIPS TO PROPERLY DISPLAY INVENTORY

- If available, place items in their original boxes and/or attach the instruction manuals. You can charge more for these items if they are in good condition.
- Locate expensive items close to the area where you will be sitting, so you can keep an eye on them and prevent theft.
- Do not put anything for sale on the ground or under a table. It may be overlooked or, worse yet, damaged by someone stepping upon it.
- Tables are the best way to display most items. Borrow folding tables or card tables from friends, family, church, and so on. Use a piece of plywood or take an interior door off its hinges to serve as a tabletop. Two saw horses or large, sturdy cardboard boxes can function as table "legs."
- Hang clothes on hangers if at all possible, or neatly fold and display them on a table sorted by size and type of clothing. Be certain all clothing is labeled with its size.

ESTATE SALES

If you are cleaning out grandma's attic full of old "stuff," do not sell the items at a yard sale without knowledge of the current value of each item. Few of us have the desire or time to become overnight experts in the retail price of "collectibles" and antiques. To receive the most money for these items, contact a reputable antique dealer and sell the items on consignment through his or her store, or use the services of an estate sale professional to conduct the entire sale.

PRICING

The success or failure of a sale can depend upon the prices charged. There are no hard and fast rules about pricing at yard sales. Many find it difficult to determine prices. Of course, if you are experienced at going to yard sales, you already have a good idea of the routine prices charged. The best advice is to charge what the market will bear (i.e., whatever you think people will be willing to pay).

The following list contains a guide that is used by many to price their yard sale merchandise:

- If an item sells for less than $50 at a retail store, sell it for 10 to 15 percent of the current selling price. For example, if a blender is in good condition and sells for $25 at a retail store, mark it at $2.50–$3.75.
- If an item currently sells for more than $50 in a retail store and is in good to excellent condition, you may be able to charge 25 to 50 percent of the retail price. Pricing these more expensive items on the higher end allows you to reduce the price, if necessary.
- Price your high quality clothing at no less than half the price they would sell for at a consignment shop. If sold at a consignment shop, you receive half of the selling price. Consignment shops only accept clothing in excellent condition. Reduce the price of garments that can't be "consigned." For example, if you paid $25 for a blouse, the consignment store would probably sell it for half the retail price or $12.50. Of this $12.50, you would receive half or $6.25. Therefore, do not price the blouse for less than $6.25 unless it is in less than excellent condition. If it is a little worn, reduce the price dramatically because your only other option would be to donate it to a nonprofit organization, such as Goodwill or the Salvation Army.

To make it easier to total each customer's purchase, round the prices to the nearest 25¢, 50¢, or $1. Clearly mark all items with a price. Make an inexpensive price sticker from a one-inch piece of masking tape. Write the price on the tape with a bold marker. For a multiple family sale, place a letter on the tape to indicate who is to receive the money. When the item is sold, pull off the tape and place it on a piece of cardboard or in a notebook under the appropriate seller's name.

Do not put items in large containers with signs indicating "Everything in box 10¢ each." Too often, items are moved between containers, and you risk selling them for the wrong price. Mark all items individually.

NEGOTIATING PRICES

Many customers ask for a reduction in the price of an item. Just because someone asks you to lower the price does not mean he or she would not buy it for the stated price. Nor does it mean that he or she thinks the price is genuinely too high.

If the sale is to last for only one day, do not reduce the price of an item within the first two to three hours of the sale. If a customer is interested in buying an item for a reduced price at the beginning of a sale, chances are another interested buyer will come along that will buy the item for its posted price. If a sale is to be held for two days, you may want to wait until the second day to reduce any prices. The most dedicated yard sales shoppers start out early in the morning. They are also the ones most likely to ask for a price reduction.

You cannot always believe a customer when he or she tells you the "going price" of an item. For example, a customer may comment, "I buy these old canning jars all the time at yard sales and never pay more than 25¢ each. You have them priced at $1 each. Will you take 25¢?" Actually, the blue canning jars (like the ones you have for sale) sell for more than $6 each. I have heard some pretty exaggerated claims about the "going price" of a particular item told in an effort to make a naïve yard sale holder lower a price. If you think you are asking a fair price for an item, do not reduce the price just because a customer tells you differently. Someone else will probably come along and gladly pay your asking price.

Consider reducing the prices of all items the last one or two hours of the sale to get rid of any remaining inventory. Post a sign stating, "½ off price listed 3:00–4:00 P.M. today," to bring customers back a second time.

EARLY BIRDS

Frequently antique and resale dealers go to the home of a yard sale one or two hours before the stated opening time. By doing so, they are able to get the best items. Many people post signs in the yard or state, "No early birds," in their classified ads. Others charge double the stated prices on any purchases or selections made prior to the opening time.

SIGNS

Signs are very important for any yard sale. In fact, if your house is easily accessible via a major road, you can have a very successful sale by simply placing signs out for motorists without using any other method of advertising.

The following list contains important details to consider when making signs:

- Use only black ink for all lettering.
- Letters and numbers should be at least 1½ inches or higher in size. The words YARD SALE should be twice as large as any other word.
- Use block, capital letters printed in a bold manner, so signs can be easily seen from a distance.
- Use bright colored backgrounds to catch the eye of potential customers driving by.
- Attach two or three balloons (nonhelium) to draw attention to your signs.
- Make all of your signs look similar to make it easier for customers to follow them to your house.
- Place a bold arrow on each sign, pointing in the direction customers should drive to attend your sale.
- Signs should be at least 12 × 12 inches in size, but preferably much larger.
- Indicate the following three pieces of information on each sign:
  - The words: "Yard Sale," "Garage Sale," or "Tag Sale."
  - An arrow pointing in the direction of the sale.
  - The address of the sale. Optional: If the sign is large enough, include the dates and times of the sale.
  - All signs should be double-sided so they are visible to motorists driving in either direction.

Placement of Signs
- Place signs on all major roads leading to your house and at every corner, further directing motorists. The more signs the better. Do not forget a sign in your front yard stating "YARD SALE HERE" with the date(s) and time(s).

- Cut tall grass or large weeds that might block your sign.
- Seek permission before placing a sign on private property.

Using Signs

Put signs out immediately before the sale and take down all signs at the end of the sale. If the date(s) and time(s) of the sale are on the signs, they can be put up two or three days prior to the sale date.

Check signs periodically during the sale to assure they did not fall down. Ask customers if they had any problem following the signs. Make any necessary changes as soon as possible, so people can find you easily.

Contact your town clerk to determine if there are any local ordinances about the placement and use of signs.

MARKETING

Make your sale look enticing by displaying some inventory, so it is visible from the road.

If a passing motorist cannot see your garage, consider holding the sale in the yard, closer to the street. Park your personal car(s) in the driveway or along the road to make it look like you already have a lot of customers. Those driving by will think they must be missing something because there are so many other people already there.

If you have lots of children's items to sell, ask the director of a local day care center to hang one of your posters advertising the sale in the day care center.

Multifamily or multigenerational yard sales are popular because they usually have a wide variety of items for sale. Be certain to advertise your sale as a multifamily or multigenerational sale on signs and in the classifieds.

I know of one neighborhood where all of the families have yard sales on the same weekend every year. They receive good coverage in the newspaper because it is such a novel idea—so they do not even need to run classified ads. A television news crew even came one year. Even if you do not get free advertising, the cost of a classified ad can be divided among all families, so your advertising expenses are reduced.

ADVERTISING

If you live near a busy intersection or road, you probably won't need to advertise in the paper. Your signs alone will draw in plenty of customers.

If you do place a classified ad, be brief and general in nature to keep the costs down. Do not list specific items unless you have something expensive to sell. Instead, list categories of items for sale that will appeal to many potential customers. Always include the date(s), time(s), and street address in every classified ad. Do not put your phone number in the paper. Use words like "HUGE" or "BIG" to encourage people to come. If your house is hard to find, do not put directions in the paper—it will make the ad too expensive. Instead put, "Follow signs at . . ." and list a major intersection where your signs are posted.

FREE STUFF

If you have "stuff" that cannot be sold but may be of use to someone else, toss these items in a box labeled "FREE." Make a sign for this box that is big enough to be seen from the street as people pass by. This alone will make some people stop at your sale.

GET THE KIDS INVOLVED

Your children can be helpful by collecting, sorting, and cleaning the inventory. The best way to get them motivated is to let them keep the money from the sale of their own toys. The second best way to get them motivated is to let them have a drink stand at the sale. This will keep them busy most of the day, so you can focus on the sale. It is also a great way for them to make some extra money and learn a little about running a business.

DETAILS, DETAILS

The following list contains details to consider when having a sale:

- Newspaper, cardboard boxes, and plastic bags should be available to wrap and package items.
- Small bills and coins should be available to make change.

- Determine your policy about accepting personal checks before the sale. (I do not recommend that you accept checks—I accept cash only at my sales.)
- Never leave the money on a table in a container. Have one person be the money holder and keep it in hand at all times.
- Do not allow anyone into your home. A potential "customer" may be checking out the valuables inside your home to determine the best way to break-in at a later date.
- Have a good working calculator (or two) handy.
- Determine a method to keep track of the money owed to individual sellers. A notebook or piece of cardboard works well in tracking what has been sold. Pull off the price sticker and place it next to the seller's name.
- Use a sheet or tarp to cover things in your garage or in the general area, that are not for sale to avoid confusion and to ensure that customers are not distracted.
- Remember to sell, sell, sell! Be friendly to your customers and allow them to look around at their own pace. However, a little encouragement on your part will increase your sales!

CLEAN UP

Too often, people simply throw unsold items in the trash. Please do not do this with your leftover items. The following list of options is much better for the environment and your community:

- Clothing or housewares can be taken to consignment shops to be sold.
- Donate items to local nonprofit charities, such as the Salvation Army or Goodwill Industries. Ask for a written receipt on the charity's letterhead, so it can be used as a tax deduction (if you itemize your income tax return). For more information about charitable contributions, call the IRS at (800) 829-3676 and ask for publication #526 or visit its Web page at *www.irs.ustreas.gov.*
- Offer unsold items to a local group or church holding a yard sale to raise money.
- Donate books to your local library (or other organization) for its annual used book sale.

- Give books, clothing, housewares, furniture, toys, and other usable items to a day care center, homeless shelter, battered women's shelter, and so on.
- Many local newspapers have a FREE section that lists items that will be given away at no cost.
- Place items in front of your house with a large sign stating FREE. Chances are good they will be gone in the morning.

16

A Diaper Bag of Tricks

Just like Humpty Dumpty in the nursery rhyme, many parents are of the opinion that their ability to control their living expenses fell apart after the birth of their first child. As children become older, their needs seem to carry an even higher price. Yes, raising children can be expensive. However, it does not have to be. In this chapter, practical advice and specific methods are given to put the shattered pieces of your budget back together and still meet the needs of your children.

USED CHILDREN'S ITEMS

New parents can save a great deal of money by purchasing used children's items and clothing at yard sales, consignment stores, or via classified ads in the newspaper. Friends and relatives may also give you their unneeded children's items.

Children's car seats, baby beds, cribs, and so on are frequently recalled for safety reasons. It is illegal for a retail store to sell recalled merchandise. Yet, there are no laws governing selling such items at yard sales, so you could possibly obtain a used, unsafe item. Contact the Consumer Product Safety Commission at (800) 638-2772 to determine if a specific item was subject to a recall and is safe for use by your child. (Some manufacturers will give you a new item to replace the recalled one, regardless of its condition.)

For safety reasons, retailers can no longer sell children's clothing with pull strings in the hoods, around the waist, at the bottom of the garment, and so on. Children have been killed when the strings were caught on bus doors, slides, and so on. Yet, you can still buy clothing at yard sales with the strings still in place. Simply remove the strings and the garment can be safely worn.

BABY FORMULA

The best nutrition for your baby is breast milk. Breast milk is also the most economical because it is free and requires no special preparation (no measuring or reconstitution) or equipment (no bottles, nipples, or bottlebrushes). Only 10 percent of new mothers are unable to breastfeed their children. Therefore, this option remains open to most mothers. Another overlooked advantage is the passive immunity that is transferred to a baby from his or her mother through the breast milk. The natural antibodies that are transferred have been shown to help build the immune system and reduce the number of illnesses experienced by breast-fed children.

BABY FOOD

Making your baby's food is very easy and inexpensive. Best of all, yours will not contain added sugar, starch, salt, or preservatives. Use a food blender, food processor, or baby food grinder to puree the chosen food to a consistency that is appropriate for the baby's level of physical development. Very small infants require food that is more finely ground or pureed to the smooth consistency of pudding. Once a toddler has teeth, the food need only be a ground texture, not smooth. Do not add additional spices, herbs, or sugar to the baby food. Some spices and herbs may cause indigestion or diarrhea.

Cook raw or frozen vegetables or fruit to make baby food by boiling or steaming the vegetable or fruit until tender. Canned vegetables and fruits do not require cooking. Puree the cooked or canned vegetables or fruit. If the pureed vegetables are too thick, add water until the desired consistency is achieved. Place a single-serving portion of the pureed vegetables or fruit into small freezer safe containers. Refrigerate or freeze until needed. Store your baby food in the refrigerator for no more than three days. Freeze it if longer storage is needed. I used zip-top (sandwich size, not freezer) plastic storage bags and placed the premeasured serving of baby food in one bag, compressed all of the air from the bag, and then quickly sealed the bag. The sandwich bags are less expensive and hold up well in the freezer or refrigerator.

I also prepared combinations of baby food that could be used as a main dish for the baby's meal.

Some combinations include:

- Chicken, pasta or rice plus a combination of vegetables: peas, green beans, and/or carrots.

- Lean roast plus a combination of vegetables: carrots, green beans, and/or potatoes.
- Lean roast, pasta or rice, carrots, and green beans.
- Chicken plus a combination of vegetables: carrots, zucchini, peas, green beans, and/or potatoes.

Use this ratio to prepare a combination baby food: one pound of uncooked poultry or meat, three cups vegetables of choice, one cup pasta (before cooking) or a half cup rice (before cooking). To prepare a combination baby food, place the raw or frozen vegetables and raw meat in a large pot as though you were making soup. (Note: If canned vegetables are used, do not add them to the pot—simply add them to the baby food immediately before it is pureed.) Place only enough water in the pan to cover the food. Cook over low to medium heat and cover with a lid until the vegetables and meat or poultry are tender and done. Allow the baby food to cool to room temperature, and remove any bones or obvious fat. If desired, place it in the refrigerator overnight so you can easily remove the fat that rises to the surface. If pasta (spaghetti or macaroni) or rice is to be added to the dish, prepare it according to the package directions immediately before the baby food is pureed. Drain all liquid from the mixture and set this liquid aside. Place the remaining meat/vegetables (and drained noodles or rice, if desired) into a blender or food processor. Puree this mixture. If the mixture is too thick, add the reserved cooking liquid until the desired consistency is achieved. (If desired, stir ¼ to ½ cup dry, undiluted baby cereal into the pureed mixture to ensure your baby gets a serving of cereal with the meal.) Separate this pureed mixture into individual serving-size containers or zip-top bags and refrigerate or freeze.

I prepared all of the food for both my children until they were old enough to eat with the adults. I usually prepared an entire month's worth of food at one time to make it easier and more efficient. The baby food I prepared was very nutritious because it had no added fillers, such as starch or added sugar. Read the labels of commercially prepared baby food. They usually contain starch and sugar.

BABY WIPES

The least expensive way to clean a baby when changing a diaper is to use a washcloth that can be laundered and reused many times. Commercially prepared diaper wipes are expensive to purchase. Instead, buy a large package of washcloths that you can dedicate solely to this task. Recycle old T-shirts by cutting them into 12 × 12-inch squares and use them for this purpose. The T-shirt washcloths can be washed repeatedly and discarded when they wear out. Keep the washcloths handy for your use when needed. Place the used washcloth in a diaper pail that contains a soaking solution until they can be laundered.

Homemade Baby Wipes

1 roll of paper towels (Bounty, VIVA, or other premium quality towel seems to work best)
2 cups tap water
1 tablespoon baby bath or baby shampoo
1 teaspoon mineral oil or baby oil

Use a long sharp knife to cut the roll of paper towels into two equal-size rolls. Remove the cardboard center tube. Combine the remaining ingredients listed. Place the half roll of paper towels into a container with a lid. Pour the liquid into this container until the paper towels are completely covered with the liquid. To use, pull out a paper towel from the center of the roll and tear it from the roll. Reserve any remaining liquid until it is needed for the second half of the roll. Recycle commercial baby wipe containers to use in making your own. If you primarily use baby wipes for wiping hands and faces when away from home, omit the mineral or baby oil.

THE 9 GOLDEN RULES OF BACK TO SCHOOL SAVINGS

Regardless of the age of your student, he or she needs some basic supplies for school. With a little advanced planning and common sense, the savings can be measurable.

Make a List of Needed School Supplies Before Going to the Store to Shop

Advanced planning will reduce the chance of buying unneeded items on impulse. Many schools provide a basic list of school supplies for elementary age children. Providing your children with only those items on the list will adequately satisfy their needs. If no list is provided, be conservative and use common sense. Your child does not need a pencil featuring a favorite cartoon character at 89¢ each. Most children lose pens and pencils easily, so do not buy expensive items.

Review What You Already Have

Retrieve school supplies leftover from the previous school year. Go through drawers, pencil cases, desks, and any other places in your home where excess school supplies may be stored. Use these recycled supplies before even thinking about buying new school supplies.

Purchase Only Those Items on Your List

Do not allow yourself to be lured into buying the latest gizmo for use in school. Stick to your list and your bank account will love you for it.

If Possible, Do Not Take Your Child with You to Buy School Supplies

If you take your child with you, he or she will try to influence your decision regarding the purchase of an item that costs more than a similar item for less. However, if your child remains at home, he or she will not "know what he or she is missing" and will be pleased with your choices when you return home.

Take Advantage of Sales

From the first week in August until mid-September, stores dramatically reduce the cost of various supplies needed for school. For example, you may be able to buy 10 pencils for 10¢. Purchase school supplies at these dramatically reduced prices for optimal savings

Frequently, stores limit the total number of products that can be bought at the sale price. Simply go through the line more than once to stock up on items that will be needed throughout the year, such as pens, pencils, and paper. Some companies offer rebates when their product is purchased. Take advantage of these rebates only if the price of the product plus the cost of postage to mail in the rebate reflects genuine savings when compared to a similar product. Then, of course, do not forget to mail in the necessary forms and receipt to obtain the refund.

Stock Up on School Supplies

The back-to-school season reflects the only time during the year that stores have sales on office and school supplies. Therefore, stock up now for savings throughout the year.

Ignore the Latest Cartoon Character or Popular Star When Choosing School Supplies

Products with these characters cost more than their "plain vanilla" counterparts. Visit a yard sale and look at the large number of discarded products featuring characters like Popples, Smurfs, Care Bears, Tamigachi's, or Superman to learn the fate of similar items. Products decorated with these characters are usually discarded because the character is no longer "in" not because they become too worn to be used. Most parents would agree that one of the certainties in life is that what is popular with kids today will not be popular tomorrow.

Buy School Supplies at Yard Sales and Factory Closeout Stores

It is not unusual to find a variety of good quality used or lightly worn school supplies at these locations.

Quality Counts When Considering the Purchase of a New Backpack

Backpacks take a lot of abuse from a child. My personal experience has taught me to always consider the quality of the backpack when making this purchase decision. Spending extra money on a high-quality backpack will pay off because your child will be able to use it for more than one year.

To determine if a backpack will endure the rigors of school life, carefully examine its construction and materials. Is it made of thick, durable canvas or lightweight plastic? Is the zipper well sewn into the canvas and made of thick metal or nylon? Are the seams double sewn? The easiest and most efficient way to choose a durable backpack is to read its warranty. Most backpacks come with no warranty at all. Do not buy a backpack that does not have some type of extended warranty or guarantee unless you want to buy your child more than one backpack this school season.

There are several companies that make backpacks with "lifetime warranties." Read the warranties to determine any restrictions. If you limit your search to one of these backpacks, you will be able to secure a backpack that will last not only the entire school year but perhaps a second or third year as well. Be certain to keep the original receipt and the written warranty in a secure location so you have it readily available if needed, should the zipper break or seams tear. These backpacks are more expensive than those without warranties. Yet, if you watch the sales, you may be able to buy one at a reduced price.

The two brands of backpacks that I am aware of with such warranties include JanSport and L.L. Bean.

JanSport provides a "limited" lifetime warranty that covers only defects in workmanship, but not damage caused by "typical wear and tear, unreasonable use, or neglect." The company will replace a zipper under the warranty. The JanSport Web site can be found at *www.jansport.com* and the toll-free number is (800) 426-9227.

L.L. Bean is known for their 100% satisfaction guarantee on all products that it sells. If at anytime you are not satisfied with a product purchased from L.L. Bean, return it and the company will "replace it, refund your purchase price, or credit your credit card as you wish." To obtain an L.L. Bean catalog or place an order, call (800) 221-4221 or visit the Web site at *www.llbean.com*.

L.L. Bean distributes sale catalogs only twice yearly; after the first of the year and at the end of June. To determine if it has an item discounted, refer to the sale catalog or call the 800 number listed in the catalog. Note: L.L. Bean has two factory outlet stores, one in North Conway, New Hampshire and the other in Freeport, Maine. If you happen to be in the area, stop by.

17

Wrap Holidays in Good Wishes and Merriment

Celebrating the various holidays throughout the year can be fun and inexpensive with a pinch of planning and a large spoonful of creativity. Within this chapter, you will find cupfuls of ideas and pounds of creativity to use in making your holidays very special, but not very expensive.

THE CHRISTMAS HOLIDAY

Most of us vividly remember the anticipation, excitement, and warmth we felt as children during the holiday season. The smell of the Christmas tree, the warm glow of holiday candles, and the sound of seasonal music may come to mind. As parents, we strive to provide a memorable holiday for our children. Yet, many falsely assume the only way to have such a holiday is to buy mass quantities of expensive gifts. In reality, the peace, joy, and love you felt as a child was not directly proportional to the amount of money your parents spent. Instead, it was, and continues to be, the traditions and shared activities that define the holiday.

Children (and other loved ones in your life) do not equate the monetary value of the gifts they receive with the degree of love you feel for them. Why would they? Many of the gifts do not even come from their parents. Instead, they came from a total stranger dressed in a red suit. Consider the experiences of a child. A child has no genuine appreciation for the value of a dollar because they lack any frame of reference. He or she has no concept of the true cost of daily living or what is involved in earning a dollar. Money comes from a machine at the mall or a bank. A toy comes from the store or from Santa Claus. To show your feelings for someone, give them the most precious gift of all—your time. Children and other loved ones do correlate the amount of time you spend with them with the degree to which you love them. From the time of birth, a child is conditioned to understand that a caregiver's time is extremely valuable. How often have you said to your son or daughter, "Not now, I'm busy," "Maybe later," "Go play with your toys while I do this," and so on.

Gift giving during the holidays should not be allowed a prominent position in the celebration of the season. If the primary event during the holidays is the opening of the gifts, your children will experience a great deal of anticipation and excitement associated with this activity. If, on the other hand, every year your family does several activities and attends various seasonal events, everyone will look forward to participating in these traditions. The opening of the gifts will be relegated to a position of less significance.

Every year, people complain about the increasing commercialization of the Christmas holiday. This pattern can be stopped by placing the true purpose for the season first in your personal celebration. There is no need to go into debt to celebrate the holiday. Carefully chosen gifts that are wanted and needed by the recipient do not have to carry a high price tag. In fact, many of the best gifts have no monetary cost.

The following list contains a variety of specific things you can do to reduce your holiday gift giving expenses:

- Reduce the size of your holiday list. Many families get together during the summer for a reunion. When you are together with your family members, approach the subject of exchanging gifts during the holidays. As the children in a family grow up, leave home, and begin families of their own, there comes a time when it becomes impractical (as well as too costly) to try to continue to exchange gifts with all siblings, nephews, nieces, cousins, aunts, uncles, and in-laws. Approaching the subject during a summer reunion will encourage an open discussion so other options can be explored. You may decide to stop exchanging gifts altogether or to simply exchange family gifts (i.e., a gift for the entire family). Many families draw names from a hat or only exchange gifts among the children. In discussing the true meaning of the holiday and the intent of exchanging gifts, you may also decide to restrict the total cost of each gift to a specific amount.

- Set a budget for your children's gifts and let them know the amount you plan to spend. We began this with our children after they passed the "Santa" stage of development. (When younger, we explained that Santa gave each child a specific number of gifts, so they should choose their list carefully.) They now know our spending limits and prioritize their Christmas list to make the best use of this limited amount of money. They even watch for sales for those items on their lists.
- Frequently, coworkers within an office setting draw names and exchange gifts. Instead, the office can adopt a needy family or child. Office staff can donate gifts or money to this family with the knowledge that the money is being put to good use. (The donation may even be tax deductible.) Every year, various nonprofit organizations in all large cities have adopt-a-family programs. Other options include donating the money to a homeless shelter or battered women's shelter serving your community.
- Make some or all of your gifts. Go to the public library and review craft books and magazines for suggestions. Visit stores that feature handmade items for additional ideas. Many people are opposed to considering this option because of the low quality homemade gifts they have received in the past. Choose the gift(s) you will make with great care. Make something that is wanted and needed by the recipient. Take your time to find something that you can make that does not look "homemade." Do your very best work to ensure that your gift is of the highest quality.
- Make gifts of food. Just about anyone can prepare a food item that is appropriate as a gift. Because we all have to eat, food makes the perfect gift. Many kinds of candy are easy to make. Most public libraries have many cookbooks with gift and candy recipes. Holiday magazines frequently feature candy recipes. Keep your homemade gift costs at a minimum by purchasing the ingredients when they are on sale. Always consider the price of the ingredients when choosing the food gift you will make. Do not make something with elaborate, expensive ingredients. Make large quantities of only two or three recipes, and then give everyone an assortment. This allows you to buy in bulk. An important consideration when giving food is its presentation. For example, by placing your homemade truffles on an inexpensive crystal-like glass plate from the dollar store, they will

look elegant. Plan your food gifts in advance so you can pick up various containers when you find them on sale throughout the year.
- Set a reasonable spending limit for each gift and stick to it.
- Give a family gift all can enjoy instead of individual gifts. Fruit baskets make good family gifts and can be inexpensive if your make it yourself. Best of all, they do not look homemade.
- Buy your holiday gifts well in advance. Begin buying your holiday gifts for next year immediately after the holiday. Watch for sales in which items are dramatically discounted.
- Stock up on holiday decorations and wrapping paper immediately after the holidays during clearance sales.
- Get family members to agree to a "handmade holiday." Only handmade items or gifts of your time can be given. Someone remodeling his or her house would appreciate an "IOU" for one weekend to help paint a kitchen or a bedroom.
- Shop for bargains to give nicer gifts for less money. Shop at end of season sales. Scour factory outlet stores and consignment shops to find great gifts for a fraction of their original cost. Thrift stores, used book sales, flea markets, and yard sales sometimes sell brand new items or things so lightly worn they look new. Give a collection of books that is "no longer in print" (i.e., used). "Collectible" (i.e., yard sale) stemware is also a lovely gift. Pour homemade jelly in a stemware glass and top it with a layer of melted wax for a unique, inexpensive, and tasty gift.
- Make the following pre-holiday promise, "I will not pay retail for any gift."
- Pay cash for all gifts. Do not charge any holiday purchases.
- Do not compete. It's ridiculous to go into debt trying to keep up with the Jones's.
- Remind yourself, "It's the thought that counts." The amount of thought that goes into a gift is what one sees when he or she opens your gift, not the price.
- Shop before the Christmas rush when selection is best.
- Shop alone. Friends and kids cause distractions and fatigue. When tired, you may make reckless (and expensive) purchases.
- Do not shop in crowded stores, you will be too frustrated to look for bargains.

- Keep all receipts in a special envelope so items later found to be damaged, ill fitting, or that do not wear as expected, can be promptly returned.
- Instead of buying individual gifts for special friends, invite them to your home around the holidays for a special evening to celebrate the season. Don't go overboard on the food served or you have defeated the purpose. Look through holiday magazines for decorating ideas to make everything look special.
- Give photographs as gifts. Enlarge favorite pictures of family and friends the next time a local photo shop, drug store, or mail order film developer has a special sale. Use yard sale frames to display this one-of-a-kind gift.
- If mailing the gift, give only lightweight, smaller gifts to save postage.
- Use free product samples as stocking stuffers. Many manufacturers offer free samples of their products. These smaller sizes are perfect for a Christmas stocking and best of all—they are free. To secure an ample supply of free products, use your computer to browse the Internet. Many companies offer free products online. You will find links to many Web sites offering free products on The Frugality Network Web page at *www.frugalitynetwork.com/freestuff.html.*

COOKIE AND CANDY EXCHANGES

Homemade cookies and candy are welcome gifts during the holidays. Recipients can be coworkers, relatives, friends, teachers, and so on. You can always make cookies and candy for less than those bought from a bakery or a candy store. Yet, making several different kinds of cookies and candy can take a lot of time. The expenses associated with buying the unique ingredients required to make a variety of cookies or candy are also greater. Making only one type of cookie or candy allows you the option of buying in bulk. Wouldn't it be a welcome option to make only one kind and exchange or trade your cookies for an equal number of different types?

This is certainly not a new concept. People all across America hold cookie and candy exchanges and have for many years. Those unfamiliar with this concept should read on to get the basic information necessary to take advantage of this practical, efficient, and inexpensive way to increase your enjoyment of the holidays.

What Is a Cookie or Candy Exchange?

In a cookie or candy exchange, each person brings one type of cookie or candy, so there are as many different types of candy or cookies as there are participants. You are usually expected to bring one dozen cookies or one plate of candy per participant. Most groups exchange either cookies or candy, not both, depending upon the interest and talents of the members.

Steps to a Successful Exchange

Discuss the idea with friends, family, neighbors, church members, coworkers, and so on to determine those people interested in participating. The exchange can be as big or small as you like. A good size for an exchange is six to 10 participants. However, if more than 10 are involved, the number of cookies or candy a participant is expected to bring should be limited to 10 dozen cookies or 10 plates of candy. Even in a large cookie exchange, each member should take home an assortment of the same amount of sweets that they bring.

Choose a date for the actual exchange that is agreeable to everyone. The coordinator should send invitations with details regarding the date and location of the exchange. It is best to provide a few weeks notice to allow participants adequate time to make their cookies or candy.

The exchange members should be asked to contact the coordinator of the cookie exchange in advance to indicate the type of cookie or candy they are bringing so duplicates can be avoided.

The Exchange

To prepare the treats for the actual exchange, each participant should divide their cookies into the predetermined amount to be exchanged with each member. For example, if each member is to receive one dozen cookies, arrange this amount on a sturdy disposable plate and cover it well with plastic wrap. In a large cookie exchange of more than 10 members, a half dozen cookies could be placed on each plate so each member receives a wider variety of cookies.

Use masking tape or a permanent marker to write the name of the cookie on the outside of the plastic wrap. Because many people are allergic to nuts, indicate the specific type of nut used, if they were added.

The actual exchange of the treats can take place in a variety of ways:

- Host a cookie or candy exchange party for members only. Each member can bring an extra dozen cookies or one extra plate of candy to be served for refreshments at the party.
- Sweets are dropped off in the morning or during the day at a designated member's house. The goodies are divided into equal portions before the members return later that day or the next day to pick up their assortment of cookies or candy.
- For a small exchange with members living near one another, participants can personally deliver one dozen cookies to each member's home.

Types of Cookies or Candy

Ask members to prepare cookies and candy based on the following criteria:

- Choose cookies and candy that do not need to be refrigerated and require no special handling.
- Prepare cookies and candy that look as good as they taste when displayed on a platter with other cookies.
- Tint the frosting of cookies in holiday colors.
- Neatness counts. Take your time to do your very best when preparing the cookies.
- Do not prepare the cookies too far in advance so they will be fresh when brought to the exchange.
- If appropriate, cut the candies into bite-size pieces and place them in small fluted paper cups made especially for candy. Larger pieces of candy, brownies, and bar cookies can be placed in cupcake papers. When displayed in this manner, candy and bar cookies look extra special.

WELCOME THE NEW YEAR
(BUT DON'T KISS YOUR BUDGET GOODBYE!)

The biggest budget busters in celebrating the New Year are contained in the following sections. These ideas and solutions will keep your celebration within reasonable limits.

I Have Nothing to Wear

Shop at a consignment shop or buy a dress on sale. This time of year many stores have sales on evening wear. (Shop after the first of the year at New Year clearance sales for next year's dress.) Buy a classic, simple design that can be worn more than once without going out of style. Black is always a good color for an evening affair (and has a slimming effect). Consign last year's dress at the shop, and use the money to buy another one.

Re-examine all of the clothes in your closet. Perhaps a dress can be updated or embellished by adding a gold belt, new jewelry, vest, or floral scarf. Try putting a velvet jacket over a basic A-line dress. Add a sequin blouse to a basic black skirt. Old shoes can be made more dramatic by adding pearls, sequins, buckles, or bows.

Borrow a dress from a friend. Let her borrow the dress you wore last year.

Tips to Save Money When You Are the Hostess for the New Year's Celebration

The following list contains some tips to keep your entertaining costs to a minimum when you are the hostess:

- Have a potluck party or an hors d'oeuvre only party with each guest bringing a part of the meal or a plateful of hors d'oeuvres.
- Ask guests to BYOB (bring your own bottle of liquor). Better yet, have a nonalcoholic New Years party.
- Plan all aspects of your party carefully and well in advance. Do you need a new tablecloth? Before buying a new one, ask friends and family if they have one you can borrow. Surely someone you know has a punch bowl as well as extra drinking glasses, serving trays, folding chairs, and tables. Careful planning will prevent hurried, last minute (expensive) purchases or rentals.

- Make everything yourself. Prepared hors d'oeuvres are expensive. Prepare food in advance, over the course of several days or weeks. Keep the food frozen until party time. Many professional caterers serve hors d'oeuvres and even main dishes that were previously frozen. Look for inexpensive recipes that freeze well. You will probably find a nice selection of recipe books on the topic in your local library. Ask friends for their favorite party recipes.
- Choose the party menu based around sale items at the grocery store. Carefully consider the cost to prepare each dish before adding it to your menu.

Miscellaneous Reduction Strategies for Your New Year's Celebration

A little creativity and planning can result in saving money without any loss of enjoyment.

- Stay home and invite good friends over for a casual evening. Put on your favorite CDs for dancing. Turn down the lights and use candles to create your own in-home nightclub. Send the kids to the basement or another room for their own special party. Or, have all of the children at one house (with a shared sitter) and the adults at another house.
- Stay home and have a New Year's popcorn and soda party with your kids.
- Celebrate the New Year the day before or after when prices are not inflated.
- Be moderate in your drinking. Alcohol is always expensive and the prices go up on New Year's Eve.
- BYOB—Some restaurants and clubs will allow you to bring your own liquor. Individual drinks are very expensive.

CELEBRATE VALENTINE'S DAY INEXPENSIVELY

Valentine's Day is the day set aside to express our feelings for those we love. On Valentine's Day more than any other holiday, it is truly the thought that counts. It is not necessary to spend a great deal of money to express your emotions for another. Therefore, the frugal gift suggestions listed here are primarily gifts from the heart.

- Prepare a simple, tasty lunch and take your Valentine "out" for an old-fashioned picnic. Go to the park or beach if you live in a warm climate. If you live in a colder climate, go to a botanical garden/greenhouse, a mall, or an art museum. Show up at his or her office and plan a picnic lunch on the desk. Bring a tablecloth and everything necessary to establish the mood (maybe even a few plastic bugs).
- Decorate your Valentine's car with messages of love. Use red or pink craft paint and heart-shaped sponges to stamp hearts on the inside of his or her car windows. (Caution—craft paint permanently stains upholstery, fabric, and plastic. It can easily be scraped off windows, but cannot be removed from other surfaces.)
- Give your sweetheart a "heart attack." Cut out dozens of hearts of various sizes. Write simple, short messages on each heart, "I love you," "You're the best," and so on. Place them in various locations so your sweetheart will find them throughout his or her day: the bathroom mirror, the computer screen, car windows, clothing pockets, briefcase, and so on.
- Give the biggest Valentine of all. If you have snow on the ground outside your home, walk in the snow, impressing the pattern of a heart into the snow. Place water in a spray bottle and add red food coloring. Spray this solution on the snow to tint your heart red. If your climate is warmer, cut the grass into the shape of a heart to accomplish the same objective.
- Write a long, detailed love letter to your Valentine. Scent it with your favorite cologne or perfume.
- If you feel that you must go out to eat on Valentine's Day, go out for breakfast. It is the least expensive meal to eat at a restaurant.
- A warm bubble bath by candlelight can be a part of a Valentine's Day gift. A body massage is frequently a welcome gift.
- Make a pizza or a monster cookie in the shape of a heart.
- Make your Valentine a romantic candlelight dinner for two. Serve it on your best china with a tablecloth. Write up the menu (like people do for an exclusive dinner party) and place the menu on his or her plate. Do not forget the romantic background music and candles.

- Instead of giving your loved one a dozen red roses, give her only one rose with a handwritten copy of the Robert Burns poem, "A Red, Red Rose." Because this poem was written in the eighteenth century, you will demonstrate to your Valentine that you are just an old-fashioned, romantic kind of guy. Tell her that your love is as distinct as this single rose. Explain how a rose cannot be appreciated for its beauty when it is one of a dozen. It can best be appreciated when it is separated from the rest. Only then can you smell its unique fragrance and appreciate its individual beauty. She too is like the rose, beautiful in her own unique, wonderful way. (After you tell your Valentine this, you will never have to buy a dozen roses again, just a single rose will suffice.)
- Fill the inside of your Valentine's car with pink or red balloons. Write a message on each balloon with a permanent marker. Use lung power to blow up the balloons, not helium.
- Use a prop to describe your feelings for your Valentine. Every time he or she sees the object, he or she will be reminded of you. Give a card expressing this sentiment as well as the object. For example, on the outside of the card write, "Happy Valentine's Day." On the inside, write "My love for you burns like a hot fire—only you can light my fire." Then, attach a package of matches to the card. Other examples of sentiments and gifts include:
    - "Your love keeps me warm": Give your beloved a pair of gloves.
    - "You add color and beauty to my life": Include a box of crayons.
    - "You are the light of my life": Enclose a flashlight key chain.
- Instead of cut flowers from a florist, give your Valentine an indoor houseplant from the discount store. You will pay less, and it will last longer than cut flowers.
- Refill the empty heart-shaped box of chocolates you received last year with candy kisses or a favorite candy of your beloved and give it to him or her on this day of love.
- Use your favorite sugar cookie recipe to make a dozen heart-shaped cookies. Decorate with pink, red, and white icing. If you do not have a cookie cutter, simply use a sharp knife to cut the cookie dough into a heart shape.

HAVE A HAUNTINGLY HAPPY AND FRUGAL HALLOWEEN

Adults and children alike celebrate Halloween. Although most children wear costumes to go trick-or-treating, many adults also dress up on Halloween. There is no need to rent a costume or buy expensive masks and clothing. With a little imagination and creativity, you can put together a costume for very little money. The following list contains a variety of costume ideas for every age. Simply modify the size for each individual.

Beach Bum

This costume is easy to assemble and comfortable to wear. Swim trunks (or swimsuit for a girl), a T-shirt, sandals, sunglasses, and a straw hat are all that is needed. Put zinc oxide or white grease paint on the nose of the wearer to complete the "look."

Witch

Witch costumes are easy to fashion from any black dress, blouse, and skirt or even a black graduation gown. Make, borrow, or buy a pointed witch's hat. Make hair white or streaked with baking soda. Use green grease paint to make the witch's face green.

Sports Figure

Dress up in a sport uniform. If you play softball (or another sport), simply wear your uniform for your Halloween costume. Do not forget to bring props, like a softball and mitt.

Professional

Borrow uniforms or clothing from friends and relatives. A mechanic's uniform, overalls, hospital scrubs, waitress uniform, and so on. Do not forget to bring props with you to accompany your costume: a waitress tray with glasses, a stethoscope, tool belt, and so on.

Static Cling

Use safety pins to secure socks and dryer sheets randomly to the outside of your clothing. Use a bobby pin to secure a dryer sheet and/or sock to the top of your head like a hat.

Halloween Face Makeup

1 tablespoon solid shortening
2 tablespoons cornstarch
food coloring

Combine shortening and cornstarch in a small bowl until it is well blended. Add liquid or paste food coloring until the desired color is achieved. Use paste food coloring for a deeper, darker shade. To make brown face makeup, substitute powdered cocoa for cornstarch and omit the food coloring. Store unused face makeup in the refrigerator. Apply with fingers to the face. To remove, wash your face with soap and water.

EASTER CELEBRATIONS

Easter is a welcome holiday in my home because the celebration of Easter means spring is not far away. New England winters can be long and cold. The hope of spring returning invigorates us as we look forward to a warmer, greener season. Therefore, we always decorate the house and celebrate the season.

Easter Baskets

The most traditional decoration is an Easter basket. Just about any basket can be made into an Easter basket. Baskets can be purchased inexpensively at yard sales, garage sales, and thrift stores throughout the year for less than 25¢ each. Many families have special Easter baskets for each child, like Christmas stockings, that are reused each year. My dear grandmother used to make each grandchild an Easter basket from a green plastic strawberry basket. She filled the basket with Easter grass, and then placed various types of candy in the basket. A recycled pastel Christmas bow was occasionally placed on the rim of the basket as added decoration. Even as a teenager, I looked forward to receiving this token of her love.

Easter Grass

Easter grass goes on sale every year after the holiday. Instead of paying 79¢ per bag, I buy 10 bags at a clearance sale for $1. I use the Easter grass when I make fruit baskets. It is a colorful, inexpensive filler for many different types of gift baskets. I also save the Easter grass used in Easter baskets from year to year. For a little added sparkle, mix Christmas tree tinsel with the Easter grass. Recycled paper from a paper shredder can also be used as Easter grass. Pastel colored paper looks best. Don't have a paper shredder? Cut paper into ¼-inch strips. Put junk mail to a good use by cutting it into strips for Easter grass. For the best results, wrinkle the strips by rubbing them between your hands so they look "fluffy."

Coloring Easter eggs

Do not buy egg coloring kits! You probably already have all of the necessary ingredients to color Easter eggs in your kitchen cabinet. Two methods for coloring Easter eggs are listed here.

TRADITIONAL METHOD

1 cup hot boiling water
1 teaspoon distilled white vinegar
Food coloring of choice

Pour one cup hot boiling water in a suitable container, such as a deep bowl. Add one teaspoon of vinegar and a few drops of food coloring. Stir to combine. Place the hard-boiled egg in the mixture, and allow it to remain until it is dyed to a satisfactory color. If necessary, add more food coloring to make the egg's color more intense.

FAST, EASY, FRUGAL EGG COLORING METHOD

1 plastic zip-top sandwich bag
¼ teaspoon distilled white vinegar
2–4 drops food coloring of choice

Pour the vinegar and food coloring in the plastic zip-top sandwich bag. Place the hard-boiled egg in the bag. Close the bag and gently move the egg around in the bag so it is completely coated with the food coloring. This only takes about a minute. Add more food coloring as necessary for a more intense color. This method works well with small children because it doesn't use boiling water and is certainly not messy.

Regardless of which of these two methods you use, remove the dyed egg from the food coloring and allow it to air dry. The lid of a soda bottle is just the right size to hold an egg upright until it is completely dry.

Homemade Stickers

Make stickers to include in a child's Easter basket or to decorate Easter eggs, stationary, photo albums, and so on. Cut and paste various clip-art images onto a sheet of paper and make a copy of the page. If you have a computer with clip-art images included in a software program, you can do this by simply printing the final page using your printer. Images can also be drawn by hand or traced from a coloring book or comic book onto a sheet of paper. Color the images with marking pens, colored pencils, or crayons. Paint the back of the page of stickers with sticker glue using the recipe and directions as listed next.

STICKER GLUE

2 tablespoons white craft glue
1 tablespoon distilled white vinegar

Combine the glue and vinegar. Use a paintbrush to paint this glue onto the back of each sticker. Allow it to dry thoroughly. If desired, paint a second coat of the sticker glue onto the back of each sticker and allow it to dry. Cut out each individual sticker. Then, moisten the back of the sticker with water and adhere it to the desired surface.

18

Pinch a Penny and Make It Smart

Pinching pennies is not a new Olympic event. If it were, you would have adequate knowledge and skills to compete by using the information within this chapter. An important way to demonstrate an appreciation for the life force you trade for the money you earn is to ensure that you get true value for every dollar. This chapter provides specific techniques to ensure that you get the most for every dollar you earn.

INCREASE YOUR PAYCHECK WITHOUT GETTING A RAISE

Would you like to receive $1,000 more per year in your paycheck? The federal government allows for the payment of specific benefits offered by an employer before withholding taxes are deducted from an employee's paycheck. As a result, the total amount of wages used to calculate withholding taxes is reduced. In other words, you pay fewer taxes because your gross wages are reduced.

The federal government allows employers to offer this benefit to employees. However, many employees do not or are unable to take advantage of this opportunity either because they do not understand how they can personally profit or because their employer does not offer this option. If this benefit is not offered, by reading this chapter, you will have the necessary information to discuss this with your employer and encourage participation in this program.

Withholding Taxes: The Basics

All employees pay taxes to the federal government based on their total earned income. The percent of income taxes paid is dependent upon several factors. However, the main determinant is the employee's gross wages.

We have a progressive income tax rate in the United States. This means that the more you make the higher percent of income taxes you pay. However, simply because you are in the 31 percent tax bracket does not mean you pay 31 percent taxes on all of the money you earn. Instead, taxes are withheld at a lower income tax rate until the upper limit of the wages within the given tax bracket are earned. Only the wages earned above this amount are taxed at the higher rate. For example, a married employee, Mr. Crabapple is paid $93,000 per year (before taxes are deducted) and is therefore in the 31 percent tax bracket. The following list contains a summary of how his employer will determine the amount of income taxes to be withheld from his paycheck based on our progressive tax system:

- The first $6,450 earned is not included in the withholding tax. Therefore, no money is withheld
- The next amount earned up to $45,450 (i.e., a total of $39,000 in wages) is taxed at 15 percent. Therefore, a total of $5,850 is withheld from the first $45,450 earned by Mr. Crabapple for the payment of income taxes.
  $45,450 − $6,450 = $39,000
  15% of $39,000 = $5,850   or $39,000 × .15 = $5,850
- Wages of $45,450 to $92,850 (i.e., a total of $47,400 in wages) is taxed at 28 percent. Therefore, a total of $13,272 is withheld from the next $47,400 Mr. Crabapple earns.
  $92,850 − $45,450 = $47,400
  28% of $47,400 = $13,272   or $47,000 × .28 = $13,272
- Any wages Mr. Crabapple earns over $92,850, but under $156,000, is taxed at 31 percent. Because his gross wages are $93,000, only $150 is taxed at 31 percent.
  $93,000 − $92,850 = $150
  31% of $150 = $46.50   or $150 × .31 = $46.50
- The total taxes withheld from Mr. Crabapple's wages of $93,000 per year are $19,168.50.
  $5,850 + $13,272 + $46.50 = $19,168.50

Employment Taxes

Regardless of the employee's tax bracket, 7.65 percent of the gross wages are deducted to pay employment taxes including Social Security and Medicare taxes. (Note: Beginning with the tax year 1997, only the first $65,400 earned is subject to the withholding of Social Security Tax). The specific amount withheld for each employment tax is:

- Social Security Tax 6.2%
- Medicare Tax 1.45%

Figure 18-1 represents the typical taxes paid on gross wages of $4,000 per month. (In this case, Mr. Richards is married, paid monthly, and has three withholding allowances and yearly gross wages before taxes of $48,000, therefore, his tax bracket is 28 percent.)

Various deductions are routinely subtracted from the after tax wages including contributions to retirement plans, health insurance, dental insurance, and so on. The amount remaining after these deductions is the amount the employee receives in his or her paycheck.

Figure 18-1
Mr. Richards' Typical Deductions

Gross wages	$4,000.00	After tax wages	$3,271.00
Income tax withheld	−423.00	Health insurance	−300.00
Social Security, Medicare	−306.00	Take home pay	$2,971.00
Total taxes	$729.00		

What Can Be Paid with Pretax Dollars?

Employers are allowed to provide fringe benefits as part of an employee benefit program in which specific benefits are paid with pretax dollars. In other words, employees pay for their portion of these benefits before income tax and employment taxes are deducted. The employer is not required by law to provide this benefit to employees. It is left to the discretion of the employer as to whether or not this option is available to his or her employees.

The following list contains benefits that can be paid with pretax dollars:

- Group health plans provide medical care to employees. The portion paid by the employee for group health insurance or the amount an employee contributes to a medical savings account can be excluded from the payment of income tax, Social Security, and Medicare taxes.
- Group term life insurance premiums paid by the employee are excluded from the payment of income tax, Social Security, and Medicare taxes. The maximum amount of life insurance that can be excluded from the payment of taxes is $50,000. Premiums for life insurance in excess of $50,000 of coverage are subject to all withholding taxes.
- Adoption assistance programs are not subject to federal income tax. However, Social Security and Medicare taxes are to be deducted before the payment of these programs.
- Dependent care assistance programs includes day care for a dependent child. Up to $5,000 of an employee's annual wages can be excluded from the payment of income tax, Social Security, and Medicare taxes.
- Educational assistance programs including an employees' education expenses: books, equipment, fees, supplies, and tuition. Unfortunately, after June 30, 1996, the cost of graduate level courses are excluded. Up to $5,250 of an employee's annual wages can be excluded from the payment of income tax, Social Security, and Medicare taxes.

Note: This information was obtained from IRS publication #535, "Business Expenses" section 5, Employee Benefit Programs. Refer to this publication for more detailed information about the establishment of an employee benefit package offering this option. A copy of this publication is available on the IRS Web site at *www.irs.ustreas.gov* or by calling the IRS at (800) 829-1040.

Increase Your Take Home Pay

Let's look at the financial impact of paying for one of these benefits with pretax dollars compared to paying for them after taxes have been deducted. In the previous example, Figure 18-1, Mr. Richards' take home pay was $2,971 when his health insurance was paid with after tax dollars.

Figure 18-2
Health Insurance Paid with Pretax Dollars

Gross wages	$4,000.00
Health insurance	−300.00
	$3,700.00
Income tax withheld	375.00
Social security, Medicare	+283.05
Total taxes	$658.05
After tax wages	**$3,042.00**

Illustrated in Figure 18-2, Health Insurance Paid with Pretax Dollars, is the impact of paying his health insurance premium of $300 from gross wages before taxes are computed and subtracted (i.e., the insurance premium is paid with pretax dollars). As a result, Mr. Richards' take home pay would be $3,042. This reflects an increase in his take home pay of $71.00 per month compared to paying the benefit with after tax dollars. Over one year, Mr. Richards' take home pay would be increased by $852.

Child day care expenses can also be paid with pretax dollars. Figure 18-3 illustrates the financial impact of paying for day care expenses in the traditional manner with after tax dollars.

Figure 18-3
Day Care Paid with after Tax Dollars

Gross wages	$4,000.00
Income tax withheld	423.00
Social security, Medicare	+306.00
Total taxes	$729.00
After tax wages	$3,271.00
Day care	−415.00
After tax wages	**$2,856.00**

In Figure 18-4, deducting the maximum of $415 per month for daycare from pretax dollars increases Mr. Richards's take home pay by $97.75 per month or $1,173 per year.

If Mr. Richards's employer offered the benefit to pay for health insurance and day care with pretax dollars, and he chose to take advantage of this

Figure 18-4
Day Care Paid with Pretax Dollars

Gross wages	$4,000.00
Day care	−415.00
	$3,585.00
Income tax withheld	357.00
Social security, Medicare	+274.25
Total taxes	$631.25
After tax wages	**$2,953.75**

opportunity, he would increase his annual pay by $2,025. Because he is in the 28 percent tax bracket, he would normally have to earn $2812.50 more per year to receive $2,025 more in his paycheck.

This benefit offered by Mr. Richards' employer is similar to giving him a 6 percent or $2,812.50 annual raise.

What Can You Do?

Review the benefit package offered by your employer carefully to confirm that you are taking full advantage of it by paying for any desired benefits with pretax dollars. If your employer does not offer this option, survey fellow employees to determine their level of interest. Your employer may be more likely to consider adding this employee benefit if he or she is aware of a high degree of interest among employees.

What's Your Tax Bracket?

Figure 18-5 contains the annual wages for the various tax brackets

Figure 18-5

Single Person		Married Person	
Annual wages	Tax bracket	Annual wages	Tax bracket
$2,650–$26,150	15%	$6,450–$45,450	15%
$26,150–$55,500	28%	$45,450–$92,850	28%
$55,500–$126,150	31%	$92,850–$156,000	31%
$126,150–$272,550	36%	$156,000–$275,300	36%
$272,550–	39.6%	$275,300–	39.6%

19

Pennywise Gardening and Pest Control

Yes, you can save money on your grocery bill by growing your own vegetables. To keep costs to a minimum, you must be conservative in your gardening practices and the supplies used. In this chapter, we will examine the main expenses associated with a garden and provide frugal options to reduce these costs. Regardless of whether you have a half-acre garden or only a few tomatoes on the patio, this chapter will provide you with inexpensive, earth friendly options to garden successfully.

THE FRUGAL GARDEN

Growing your own vegetables can save money on your grocery bill. All too often, I hear of people planting gardens with the intent of saving money, only to lose money in the long run because they purchase unnecessary, expensive garden tools, equipment, fertilizers, and/or plants. After all costs are factored into the actual vegetables harvested, it may cost them $10 or more per tomato. Of course, you can buy tomatoes much cheaper at the local grocery store. If you enjoy gardening, have a plot with adequate sunlight, and the time to care for a garden, you have the potential of growing a profitable vegetable garden.

Let's look at some of the main expenses associated with a garden and some frugal options to reduce these costs.

Water

Gardens need water. If you have to pay for municipal water, carefully monitor water usage to keep gardening expenses to a minimum.

- Know the water requirements for each type of plant. Some require more water than others. The amount of sand in the soil also affects how much and how often water is required. Many times, water is wasted because plants are either given too much water or are watered during the hottest part of the day.
- Dig a trench around the base of each plant so the water can collect where it is needed.
- Set up a rain barrel. Long ago, people had rain barrels to collect the rain as it drained off the roofs of their houses. This rainwater is free water for your garden.
- Recycle water. Save the water used to boil vegetables and pasta. The nutrients in the water are a free added benefit. Recycle the water from a fresh water fish aquarium each time the water is changed.
- Mulch, mulch, mulch. Place two to four inches of mulch around the base and between all plants. Mulch retains the moisture in the soil so you will not have to water as often. Inexpensive or free sources of mulch material include grass clippings (make certain no weed killer has been used on the grass before it was mowed), newspapers (black and white pages only), leaves, pine needles, shredded wood or bark (contact landfills or utility companies for free wood chips), old carpets, hay, and sawdust (do not use sawdust from pressure treated wood).

Amending the Soil

Instead of buying chemical-based fertilizer to enhance the quality of your soil, use organic matter and compost. Some mulch adds nutrients to the soil. Kitchen scraps, like coffee grounds, potato peels, and eggshells can be finely chopped (by hand or in an electric blender) and mixed into the soil. Wood ashes from a fireplace are high in potassium. Cow manure and horse manure is usually free from a dairy farm or horse barn. Refer to the section "Garden Pest Control and Fertilizers," for specific tips.

Soil Preparation

To adequately prepare the ground for a garden, turn over the top six to 12 inches of soil in the spring. If your garden is small, you can easily do this with a shovel. Do not buy a rototiller unless you plan to have a sizable vegetable garden for at least 10 years. It may take about 10 years for you to recover this sizable initial investment and make your gardening efforts profitable. Many rental companies rent rototillers for a small fraction of the price to purchase and maintain one.

Pests and Weed Control

Do not buy chemicals to control weeds, diseases, or bugs. Instead, use organic methods. Organic methods are less expensive than chemicals and they are nontoxic to you and the environment. The best way to control weeds is to cover the ground around your plants with two to four inches of mulch. The mulch will prohibit the weed seeds from germinating by denying them sunlight. Pull out any persistent weeds that do pop up through the mulch.

Pest control can be accomplished by simply picking off the offending bug and dropping it in a bucket of soapy water. Refer to the section "Garden Pest Control and Fertilizers" for various concoctions you can make yourself to rid your garden of unwanted visitors.

Location

Vegetables require full sun for a significant part of the day and earth, rich in organic matter. Compost is the best free source of organic matter for your garden. Any good organic gardening book will provide detailed information about starting and maintaining a compost pile.

Most of us have only a limited space for a garden. Fewer of us have the extra hours required to plant and maintain a large garden. Careful planning and management of the available area with crops evenly distributed over the entire growing season will greatly increase the yield.

Tools

The number of tools needed depends on the size of garden and personal gardening style. Many times, used tools are sold at yard sales or auctions.

Buy tools at a discount during end-of-season sales. Most frugal gardeners find the only tools they need are a hand trowel, long handled shovel, and an iron rake. A child's red wagon can easily perform double duty as a garden cart and a recycled plastic gallon milk jug works well as a watering can. Recycled window cleaner spray bottles can be filled with organic fertilizing spray or organic bug spray. Large recycled plastic buckets have many uses in the garden including capturing rainwater or making "liquid organic fertilizer." Powdered laundry detergent, cat food, and other products come in these buckets. You can also get them at no cost from a deli or restaurant.

Seeds and Plants

Plants are more expensive than seeds. The price to purchase one small tomato plant may be 50¢ or more. Better yet, get free seeds by saving some of the seeds from the current crop of nonhybrid vegetables to plant next year. Vegetable seeds can be planted directly in the ground outside as soon as the weather permits with very good results. Place sheets of clear plastic (not black plastic) over the ground after planting the seeds outside. This helps warm the soil and speeds germination.

Interplanting

Interplanting or square foot gardening is the practice of growing two or more crops in the same area at the same time. This method saves space and increases the harvest. Well-planned crops discourage pests and disease. Although this technique works well with raised beds, it can also be used in traditional gardens. However, too little space between plants can encourage disease, insects, and competition for light, air, nutrients, and water. Therefore, the types of vegetables and planting techniques should be carefully considered.

In his book, *Square Foot Gardening,* Mel Bartholomew explains this method in detail, so that even a beginning gardener will be successful. This book covers all aspects of growing a vegetable garden. Many libraries have this book available for your use.

Crop Rotation

To further maximize your limited space, replant the area with another crop as soon as the first one has been harvested. Your choice of the second crop is limited by the required days to maturity and the length of your growing season. Seed companies base the estimations printed on the package regarding the number of days to maturity on the assumption that the seeds are planted in the spring. A midsummer sowing will mature much more rapidly because the earth is warmer. When possible, sow crops for the second and third plantings from entirely different plant families. Nematodes and other pests tend to build up in the soil when the same crop is grown over and over in the same place. For example, plant carrots or lettuce after snap peas. Do not plant broccoli in the space where cabbage was grown. Instead, plant tomatoes.

GARDEN PEST CONTROL AND FERTILIZERS

Many gardeners prefer not to use chemicals in their gardens to kill bugs or fertilize their plants. Others look for inexpensive homemade alternatives to save money. Regardless of the reason, the following gardening tips may be helpful in making your garden more bountiful and pest free. Best of all, they will save you money.

All-Purpose Pest Spray

This spray has multiple uses in a frugal garden; it gets rid of various pests, controls fungal diseases, and keeps out larger pests, like raccoons. Vary the quantities of the given ingredients for better results. For example, to keep out raccoons, increase the cayenne pepper or chili powder to ¼ cup or more.

- 1–3 whole garlic bulbs
- 1 small yellow onion
- 1 tablespoon cayenne pepper or chili powder
- 1 cigarette
- 1 quart of hot tap water
- ½ teaspoon liquid nondetergent soap.

Add one cup of hot water to a blender or food processor. Add garlic and onion. Puree. Pour this mixture and the remaining hot water into a jar with a lid. Add cayenne or chili powder and the tobacco from one cigarette. Shake to mix well. Place the solution in a warm place out of the sun for about 12 hours. Strain the mixture and add soap. Spray plants thoroughly with this solution, paying particular attention to the undersides of leaves. Rinse the residue off the leaves of delicate plants a few hours after application. (Use this solution with caution on delicate plants, the soap may burn them. If necessary, omit the soap from the recipe.) Do not add tobacco if the spray is to be used on tomatoes or roses. This recipe yields one quart. Store the solution in a tightly sealed container in the refrigerator for up to one week.

Red Cedar Spray

Red cedar spray controls Mexican bean beetles, Colorado potato beetles, cucumber beetles, squash bugs, mealy bugs, and spider mites. If sprayed daily on the corn silk of sweet corn plants, corn earworm moths are repelled from laying eggs on the ears of developing corn. Purchase cedar shavings at discount stores in the pet department or in pet stores. Cedar sawdust, chips, or chopped twigs can be obtained at lumberyards, lumber mills, or landscape suppliers.

1 gallon very hot water
2–3 cups cedar sawdust, shavings, chips, or chopped twigs

Place the cedar in a two-gallon container. Pour one gallon of very hot water over the cedar. Place the solution in a warm place for at least three hours. Strain to remove the cedar. To use the mixture, pour it into a spray bottle and mist the affected plants to thoroughly wet all leaf surfaces.

Garlic Oil Soap Spray

Garlic is an effective antibiotic and fungicide. It also repels insects. Use garlic oil sprays to rid your garden of cabbage moths, cabbage loopers, earwigs, leafhoppers, mosquitoes, whiteflies, aphids, squash bugs, tarnished plant bugs, slugs, and hornworms. It does not seem to control bigger insects, such as Colorado potato beetles, grasshoppers, ants, and grapeleaf skeletonizers. This recipe makes a half pint of concentrate—when diluted it will make one to two gallons of spray.

10–15 cloves garlic
3 teaspoons mineral oil
1 teaspoon liquid nondetergent soap
1 cup warm water

Place the unpeeled garlic in a food processor or blender. Add the mineral oil and water. Blend or chop until the garlic is in small pieces. Pour the mixture into a jar with a tight fitting lid. Add the soap and place the mixture in a warm place for about 24 to 36 hours. Strain the solution and pour it back into the jar with a lid. The mixture can be stored in the refrigerator for several weeks.

To use the garlic oil spray, dilute 1 to 2 tablespoons concentrate in one pint of water. Spray this diluted mixture on the affected plants, being sure to spray the underside of leaves.

Mildew Spray

Baking soda controls mildew on various types of plants. Mix the baking soda in the correct concentration as listed in the following instructions with water and spray it on the leaves of the affected plants. Add one teaspoon of any mild soap to help the spray adhere to the leaves. Use only pure soap that does not list whiteners, perfumes, deodorants, or dyes as ingredients. Reapply the spray after rain.

- Mix two teaspoons of baking soda in one gallon of water to control mildew on beans, muskmelons, cucumbers, strawberries, and eggplants.
- Mix two teaspoons of baking soda in two quarts of water to control mildew on grapes.
- Mix one tablespoon of baking soda in two and a half gallons of water to control mildew on roses.
- Mix one tablespoon of baking soda dissolved in one gallon of water to control black spot on roses.

Moles

For many years, gardeners have planted castor beans around the perimeter of gardens to deter moles and shrews. Use this castor oil mixture as another effective way to rid your garden of these pests.

¼ cup castor oil
1 gallon warm tap water

Mix the oil and water in a one-gallon container. Sprinkle this solution around the perimeter of your garden as soon as mole activity is noted.

Snails

Snails can cause a lot of damage to flower and vegetable gardens. Try these nontoxic and inexpensive methods to control snails.

SNAIL AND SLUG BAIT

4 teaspoons sugar
1 teaspoon baking yeast
4 cups water
8 saucer-type containers (½–1 inch deep)—tuna cans work well

Mix all ingredients in an adequately sized container. Bury the saucers in the soil where slugs have been seen. The top edge is to be flush with the surface of the ground. Pour ½ inch of the solution into each saucer. Slugs are attracted to the mixture and will drown when they fall in. Check the saucers daily and remove any slugs. Replace the solution every two days.

SNAIL TRAPS

Slugs and snails feed on plants mainly at night. Trap them by placing the outer leaves of lettuce or cabbage, hollowed out melon rinds, or large pieces of bark on the ground around affected plants. In the morning, lift the leaves or other trappings and remove any snails or slugs hiding underneath. Kill trapped pests by dropping them into a pail of soapy water.

Slugs, Snails, Rabbits, Squirrels, Carrot Root Flies, and Cabbage Root Flies

Sprinkle dry wood ashes around plants to deter carrot root flies and cabbage root flies. Add chili powder or cayenne pepper to wood ashes—sprinkle on foliage and around plants to deter slugs, snails, rabbits, and squirrels.

Deer

To keep deer away from plants and bushes, hang strong scented deodorant soap at three- to four-foot intervals. This provides protection of plants within a two- to three-foot radius of where it is located. Many gardeners believe that original scented Irish Spring works best. Replace the deodorant soap about every three months, when the scent begins to fade.

Liquid Organic Fertilizer and Fungus Control

Fill a large bucket, barrel, or other container one-fifth full of fresh poultry, horse, or cow manure. Fill the container to the top with water, cover, and allow this solution to sit for one to two weeks. Strain out the solids with old pantyhose, cheesecloth, or other loosely woven fabric. Remove one cup of this liquid and further dilute it with water until it is the color of weak tea. Water vegetables with one cup of this diluted liquid at their base. Many gardeners report dramatically increasing their vegetable yields with this liquid organic fertilizer. Use this every one to two weeks to maintain good growth throughout the season. This liquid may be used on young plants as a starter fertilizer.

Spray this liquid organic fertilizer on the leaves of all plants including fruit trees, annuals, perennials, roses, and vegetables that are prone to attack by fungus. For example, it works well for black spot on roses and early blight on tomatoes. Mix one part of the concentrated liquid to five to 10 parts water. To enhance it further, add two tablespoons of blackstrap molasses to each gallon of diluted spray.

Homemade Starter Fertilizer

This starter fertilizer helps plants recover quickly from the shock of being transplanted.

½ cup fish emulsion
½ cup seaweed extract (liquid kelp)

Combine the fish emulsion and seaweed extract in a jar or plastic bottle with a well fitting lid. Shake the jar well to combine. Label the container. Store the solution in a cool, dark place. To dilute the fertilizer for use, place three tablespoons of the starter fertilizer in one gallon of water. Water each transplant with a half cup of this diluted solution. The diluted fertilizer can also be sprayed directly onto the plant because it is well absorbed through the leaves.

Make Your Own Planting Mix

Planting mix can be made inexpensively with supplies readily available from a garden nursery.

SEEDLING MIX

Combine all of the following ingredients in a large bucket. The seedling mix can be used immediately. Store in a closed plastic bag until needed.

1 gallon peat moss
1 gallon vermiculite
1 tablespoon superphosphate
1 tablespoon ground limestone

POTTING SOIL

This recipe makes a good all-purpose soil for most indoor and outdoor plants. Plants that require special potting soil, such as African violets, cacti, and ferns should not be placed in this potting soil. However, container grown annuals and vegetables as well as many houseplants will do well in this easy to make potting soil.

8 cups sterile rich topsoil or compost
4 cups peat moss
4 cups perlite or vermiculite

Combine all ingredients in a large bucket. The potting soil can be used immediately. Store it in a closed plastic bag until it is needed.

SOIL STERILIZATION

Garden soil and compost can be easily sterilized in your oven. Place four to six cups of soil in a large flat pan. Sprinkle one half to one cup of water over the soil and mix well until it is evenly damp. Bake the soil in a 200°F oven. Use a meat thermometer to maintain the temperature of the soil at 170°F for 30 minutes. Try not to let the soil temperature rise above 180°F. Allow it to cool and use the soil for potted plants.

Plant Propagation via Cuttings

An easy way to save money in the garden is to propagate plants from cuttings of existing plants. Instead of buying a flat of 36 annuals for $10, spend less than $1.50 to buy only one container of six plants and take cuttings from these plants. Within a few days, you will have more than 36 free plants.

Many different plants can be propagated via cuttings. This propagation method requires very little time or effort on your part. In fact, many of the plants you buy in a nursery are started from cuttings.

PREPARATION OF A CUTTING FOR PROPAGATION

Cut a two- to four-inch segment of new growth from the end of a stem. Plants root best when a cutting is taken during the time of active growth. Remove any buds or flowers. Leave at least one or two leaves on the stem. Remove any leaves from the lower half of the cutting that will be submerged in the rooting medium or water. Immediately place the cutting in water until you are ready to place it in the chosen rooting substance. Figure 19-1 includes a partial list of plants that can be propagated by a cutting.

Figure 19-1

Plants that Propagate by Cutting

Ageratum	Heleniums	Morning Glories	Scabiosa
Alyssum	Herbs	Oleander	Sedum
Asters	Hibiscus	Pachysandra	Snapdragon
Chrysanthemum	Hydrangea	Petunias	Tomatoes
Coleus	Hypericum	Philodendrons	Vinca
English Ivy	Impatiens	Phlox	Viola
Fuchsias	Lemon Verbena	Rambler Roses	Willow
Geraniums	Marigold	Salvia	Yarrow

ROOT A CUTTING IN WATER

Place the prepared cutting in an opaque container of clean, lukewarm water. Make certain that none of the remaining leaves are submerged in the water or they will decay. Check the water level daily to ensure that the ends of the cuttings remain submerged in water. Change the water if it becomes foul-smelling or has a change in color.

When roots are visible on the cuttings, plant them in potting soil and keep moist. The newly potted plants should not be placed in direct sunlight until the plants are well established—at least five days. The "recipe" for appropriate potting soil is listed in the "Make Your Own Planting Mix" section. Fertilize the newly potted cuttings with a liquid fertilizer.

ROOT A CUTTING IN VARIOUS MATERIALS

Some plants will not root in water or just seem to do better in a rooting medium. If cuttings fail to root in water, try taking another cutting of the plant and root it in one of the materials in the following list. Some cuttings root best if they are placed directly in the rooting medium, whereas others require the use of a hormone powder.

Rooting mediums:

- Course, clean sand
- Peat moss and course sand (1:1 ratio)
- Vermiculite
- Vermiculite and course sand (1:1 ratio)
- Perlite
- Garden soil
- Potting soil
- Peat moss

To use rooting hormone powder, dip the end of the prepared cutting in water. Immediately place the wet end in hormone powder. Poke a hole in the medium using a pencil. Gently insert the powder-covered end of the cutting into the medium. Use care so that none of the rooting powder becomes dislodged from the cutting. Firm up the soil around the cutting. Water with lukewarm water and keep the soil moist until the cutting has developed roots. Hormone powder can be purchased at garden centers and nurseries.

Geraniums root best without hormone powder. Roses and hydrangeas root best when hormone powder is used. A hydrangea will also root well in water.

Roses are easy to propagate. To root a rose cutting, place the cutting directly into the soil in a shady area of your garden. Cover the cutting with a large glass jar. If excess humidity is noted on the glass, remove the jar for a few hours. Leave the glass jar in place until it's well rooted with several new sets of leaves. It may take one full summer for a rose cutting to develop roots. Transplant the rose to its permanent location the following spring.

SOURCES OF CUTTINGS

Look around your garden to determine if you currently have any plants that can be propagated using one of these methods. Ask friends for cuttings of their plants to propagate. Many gardeners have found this to be their primary source for new flowers. They call their gardens "friendship gardens."

Any good gardening book with detailed planting and growing information about specific plants will indicate propagation methods for the listed plants. Experiment on your own to determine if the plant can be propagated via a cutting. Have fun and enjoy your free flower filled garden.

STARTING SEEDS INDOORS

The late winter months are a good time to start vegetables and annual flowers indoors. Not only does this give you a jumpstart on the growing season, but it also provides an easy way to save money. It is always cheaper to start a plant from seed than to purchase it as a seedling from a nursery or other supplier. For example, you may receive 50 cucumber seeds in a package for 69¢. Even if only half of these seeds germinate, you will have 25 plants for 69¢ or less than 3¢ each. You will always pay more per plant if they are purchased as seedlings. You may have to pay $1.50 for six cucumber plants or 25¢ each. By growing them from seed, you can save 22¢ per plant.

Containers

Seeds can be started in a variety of containers. However, regardless of the container used, there are two basic methods. One approach is to place one or two seeds directly into an individual container. Here the seedlings will grow until they are large enough to be transplanted into the garden. The second method is to grow many seeds in one single, large container (called a starter container). The seedlings will grow together for a few weeks until each is large enough to be transplanted into its individual container. Each method has its pros and cons. The method you use should be based on the type of seeds planted and your own personal preferences.

Regardless of the container used, it should be cleaned with soap and water and sterilized using a weak solution of common household bleach before any soil is added. Refer to the section "Sterilization of Containers, Tools, and Pots" later in this chapter for specific instructions.

Look around your house (especially at those things discarded in the trash) to determine if anything can be modified for use as a container. Be certain to puncture holes in the bottom of recycled plastic containers to allow for adequate drainage—or your seeds will rot. The following list includes some containers that can be used for starting seedlings:

- Flats from a garden center
- Clear plastic take-out food containers
- Plastic jugs and bottles cut to size
- Yogurt containers
- Frozen whipped topping containers
- Plastic frozen juice containers
- Recycled plastic plant cell-packs

Growing Medium

The growing medium used for starting seeds must be free of diseases, insects, and weed seeds. It should be loose and fine-textured and allow the water to drain freely. Never use soil from your garden for raising seedlings. If the soil is contaminated, the seedlings may die from damping-off or other diseases. (There is no way for you to determine if your garden soil is contaminated.)

Use caution to minimize the chance of contaminating the seedling mix. Keep the seedling mix in the original container until needed. When making your own seedling mix, sterilize the container and tools to ensure that the mixture remains disease free. The instructions for an inexpensive seedling mix is listed in the "Make Your Own Planting Mix" section.

Sterilization of Containers, Tools, and Pots

To prevent the newly planted seed from becoming infected with diseases and insects from a plant that was previously planted in the container, you must sterilize the container and any items that come in contact with the seed or soil. This process is really simple and takes only a few minutes. Do not skip this step. Few things are more frustrating than to have your little plants suddenly die from damping-off or another disease.

Use a solution of one part common household bleach combined with nine parts water. Allow the tools, containers, and pots to soak in this solution for 10 minutes, and then air dry. If a container is too big to soak, wipe this solution over its entire surface. Repeat as necessary so the surface remains wet for 10 minutes, then allow it to air dry. (Do not rinse the solution off the item, just let it air dry.)

Planting Seeds

To plant seeds, fill the previously cleaned and sterilized container with seedling mix. Allow ample room at the top so the seeds can be watered appropriately. The general rule regarding how deep to plant a seed is based on its size. Seeds as big as a match head or larger germinate best in the dark. Cover the seeds with soil twice as deep as their width. For example, if a seed is $1/8$ inch wide, cover it with $1/4$ inch of soil ($1/8 + 1/8 = 1/4$ inch). Pat the dirt gently over the seed to ensure it is secure in the soil. Tiny seeds require light to germinate so it should not be covered with soil. Most seeds are of intermediate size with some needing darkness and others requiring light. Refer to the seed package for more specific information regarding the planting depth and light requirements of the seeds you are planting.

SOWING SEEDS INTO INDIVIDUAL CONTAINERS

It is best to sow large seeds that grow quickly (melons, squash, cucumber, dahlias, sweet peas) and those with brittle roots (okra and hibiscus) in individual containers. Follow the directions on the package regarding the depth to plant the seeds. Plant one to two large seeds and three to four small seeds in each container. Some herbs and annuals do well if several seeds are grown in a single container because they tolerate being transplanted into the garden as a clump.

SOWING SEEDS IN A STARTER CONTAINER

A starter container should be shallow with one half to two inches of seedling mix spread evenly across the bottom. The seeds can be sown around the edge of the pot, in rows, in a checkerboard pattern, or sprinkled in a random fashion.

LABELING CONTAINERS

Be certain to label each pot to indicate the seeds it contains. Never rely on your memory to remember what seeds were planted.

LIGHTING NEEDS OF SEEDS

Fluorescent light fixtures are ideal for providing light to seeds and seedlings. However, if you have a room in your home with a southern exposure that receives a great deal of light during the day, you should be able to start seeds indoors without the use of additional lighting.

WATERING SEEDS

Immediately after planting the seeds, water the container thoroughly with lukewarm water or place it in a shallow tray of tepid water. When the surface of the seedling mix looks dark and glossy, remove the tray from the water, and allow extra water to drain from the bottom. Cover the containers with a tent of clear plastic (vegetable bags from the grocery store or plastic cooking wrap work satisfactorily) or a pane of glass. Covering seeds dramatically reduces the evaporation of the water and helps to ensure a constant moist environment necessary for germination. If covered as described, no additional water may be needed until the sprouts emerge. If the seedling mix becomes dry to the touch, remove the plastic or glass and spray the top of the soil again with tepid water.

SOIL TEMPERATURE

The temperature of the soil effects the germination rate of seeds. Some seeds sprout best in warm temperatures, whereas others have increased vigor in a cooler soil. The seed package should provide suggestions regarding the best temperature for the seeds you have chosen.

Do not place your planted seeds on a radiator. The temperature of a radiator or heating register is too hot for the germination of seeds. Many gardeners find that the top of a refrigerator works well in providing consistent warmth for sprouting seeds.

Once the shoots emerge, immediately remove the plastic or glass cover and move the sprouts away from the heat source. Extra heat and humidity can weaken tiny seedlings.

LIGHTING NEEDS OF SEEDLINGS

Move the sprouted plants to an area where they will receive plenty of light. If a fluorescent light is used, position the seedlings about six inches away from the light. This keeps the plants compact and healthy. If the light source is too far away from the seedlings, their stems will be forced to stretch toward the light. This weakens the overall plant. If you are using natural light and notice they are becoming elongated in appearance with the leaves spaced too far apart, they are not getting enough light. Move them to a location that receives better light for a longer period of time during the day or place them under a fluorescent light to supplement the natural light for several hours a day. As the plants grow, continue to readjust the fluorescent light so it remains only a few inches above the leaves.

WATERING AND FERTILIZATION OF SEEDLINGS

Once sprouted, check the seedlings for dryness at least two or three times each day and water as needed. Never allow seedlings to dry out or wilt. Push your finger gently into the soil, if particles of soil cling to your finger when it is removed, the soil is adequately damp. If no soil is clinging to your finger or if the soil feels dry, water the plant.

Overwatering is the most common reason seedlings develop diseases and die. Plants that have been overwatered have a tendency to develop damping-off diseases. The primary symptoms of damping-off disease are a plant falling over from the base and/or the development of a lesion near the base of the stem. Remove the affected plants immediately and discard them. Excess water in the container, water standing under a container, poor light, and high temperatures stimulate the development and spread of disease in seedlings.

To encourage rapid growth, give the seedlings regular applications of a very dilute fertilizer. Use only ¼ of the recommended amount of a soluble houseplant fertilizer, such as 20-20-20 or 15-30-15. Note: Miracle Grow or its generic equivalent is a 15-30-15 fertilizer. One teaspoon of fish emulsion also works well. Apply the chosen fertilizer once or twice each week when watering. Over fertilizing can kill the seedlings or promote damping-off disease.

PREVENT DAMPING-OFF OF SEEDLINGS

Damping-off causes the sudden wilting and death of new seedlings. Frequently, it begins when a soil borne fungus attacks the new seedlings. Pre-sterilization of the containers before planting the seeds will kill any fungi on the pots. Using only sterilized potting soil will further reduce any risk of fungus coming in contact with your seedlings.

Gardeners have successfully used various other preventive methods for years.

- Sprinkle a thin layer of milled sphagnum moss over the soil surface of newly planted seeds. Sphagnum moss contains helpful bacteria that prevent the development of damping-off.
- Garlic also contains helpful chemicals that prevent damping-off and other insects from harming plants. Place one good-sized garlic bulb in a blender along with one cup of water. Blend well. Combine this solution with seven more cups of water. Place the mixture in a jar with a lid. Allow it to remain at room temperature for 24 hours.

Immediately after the seeds have been planted, use this solution to water them for the first time. This solution can also be strained and then sprayed on the seedlings after they have begun to sprout.
- Dried chamomile tea prevents damping-off. Combine two tablespoons of dried chamomile leaves with one quart boiling water. When cooled to room temperature, place the mixture in a jar with a lid. Allow it to remain at room temperature for 24 hours. Strain the solution and use it when watering newly germinated seedlings.

TRANSPLANTING SEEDLINGS FROM A STARTER CONTAINER TO INDIVIDUAL CONTAINERS

If the seeds were sown in a starter container, the seedlings must be transplanted into individual containers. When the seedlings have at least one pair of true leaves, gently remove them and transplant each seedling into an individual cell or small pot. Do not allow seedlings to become overgrown or overcrowded before transplanting them. Fill a new individual container or pot with growing medium. Poke a hole in the center of the medium and set the seedling in at the same depth it was previously growing. If several seeds were sown in an individual container, thin out the weaker seedlings when the seedlings have at least one pair of true leaves. Water the seedlings immediately after transplanting or thinning.

HARDENING-OFF PLANTS AND TRANSPLANTING THEM OUTDOORS

Your seedlings can be transplanted outside after all danger of frost has passed. Consult your local garden nursery or county extension office to determine this date in your area.

NEVER TRANSPLANT SEEDLINGS DIRECTLY TO THE GARDEN AFTER BEING GROWN INSIDE YOUR HOME

A sudden change from the protected environment of your home to the harsh weather outside will kill tender seedlings. Instead, give them time to adjust to the real-world temperatures and weather conditions. Hardening-off is the process of gradually adjusting tender plants to the outside environment. Allow one to two weeks for the plants to become hardened-off.

The process involves gradually exposing the seedlings to the change in temperatures, the brighter light, drying wind, and overhead watering from the rain. At first, set the plants outside in a sheltered, shaded area for several hours each day. Bring the plants back inside to the protected environment each evening. Extend the total time they are left outside by about one to two hours per day. Gradually move the plants from the shade into the sunlight for a few hours each day. Do not place the tender transplants outdoors on windy, rainy days or when the temperature drops below 45°F.

During this time, monitor the soil moisture of the plants twice daily because they will dry out more quickly when outside. They may need to be watered twice daily when outside for extended periods of time.

As soon as they are able to tolerate being outdoors 24 hours a day without wilting in the sun or wind, they can be transplanted outside.

TRANSPLANTING SEEDLINGS OUTSIDE

When planting seedlings outside, several rules should be followed. Avoid transplanting in the midday sun and water the plants well before transplanting. Their root systems will take awhile to develop sufficiently to "forage" for water on their own. Transplant on a cool overcast day if possible, and water them well again after transplanting. Minimize root disturbance as they are taken out of their containers by keeping as much growing medium around the roots as possible. In removing the plant, thousands of tiny root hairs are broken off. Plants take a great deal of water in through these tiny roots, so it is best to keep them intact. Place the transplant into the ground at their previous depth in the container.

FERTILIZING TRANSPLANTS

Fertilize young transplants soon after transplanting using a starter fertilizer. A commercially available 10-52-17 fertilizer can be diluted and used as starter fertilizer. Place one tablespoon of the commercial fertilizer in a gallon of tepid water. Apply about one cup of the liquid starter fertilizer to each plant immediately after planting it into the ground. Refer to the "Garden Pest Control and Fertilizers" section for a recipe to make your own starter fertilizer. Happy gardening!

The Frugality Network
www.frugalitynetwork.com

I founded the Frugality Network to make the money-saving resources of the Internet easily accessible to its members. Knowledge is the most powerful resource you can use to reduce your living expenses, and the Internet is very effective in the dissemination of this knowledge. Yet, its vast scope and ever-increasing size makes finding the location of this pertinent information on the Internet frustrating and extremely time consuming. With more than five thousand links, the Frugality Network is the primary source for those with a desire to reduce their living expenses. To save time, the listed links take you directly to the desired information.

Through the Frugality Network, members share their experiences as well as specific Web sites they have found to help them save money. I am excited to provide this new avenue for those kindred souls out there, like myself, with a genuine respect for their money and a desire to spend it in a responsible manner. I sincerely hope that you find this information to be a powerful resource to lead you toward financial independence!

Best regards,
Cindy McIntyre

Index

A

Adjustable-rate mortgage (ARM), 89–90, 91
Air conditioners, 167–69
Air leaks, 165–66
All-purpose cleaner, 188–89
All-purpose pest spray, 277–78
Annual percentage rate (APR), determining, 90
Appliances, 175–79
Appraisal, 97
Assumable mortgage, 92
Attorney fees, 99
Auctions, 128
Automobile
    buying new versus used, 120–37
    insurance for, 137–46

B

Baby food, 246–47
Baby wipes, 247–48
Backpack, 250–51
Barbecue grills, cleaning, 199
Bartering, 222–25
Bath powder, 221
Bathroom, cleaning, 190, 193, 194
Beauty products, savings on, 215–21
Billing errors, 228–29
Bills, lack of money for, 7–9
Bleach, precautions with, 203
Brass cleaner, 192
Breath fresheners, 220
Butcher block, removing stains from, 193

C

Carpet deodorizer, 191
Carpets, reducing static electricity in, 192
Catalog outlet stores, 152
Chain cooking, 106–8
Children
    clothing for, 160
    used items for, 245
Christmas holiday, 252–56
Cleaning products, 188–203
Clearance stores, 152
Clothes, 147–61
    children's, 160
    information listed on labels of, 154
    laundering, 160

    reducing costs of, 148–61
    returning defective, 155
    stain removal from, 200–202
Coffee makers, 198
College tuition, reducing high cost of, 180–87
Computer screens, cleaning, 190
Consignment store, 148–49
Contact lenses, savings on, 209–11
Containers, 286, 287
Cookie and candy exchanges, 256–58
Cooling, methods of, 166–72
Cooperatives, 223–25
Counter tops, removing stains from, 193
Coupons, clipping, 111–16
Credit report, getting in shape, 76–78
Cuttings, plant propagation via, 283–85

D

Daily living expenses, 34–35, 41–42
Debt, 28–32, 76
Delivery, refusing damaged or spoiled items, 227
Deodorizer, refrigerator and freezer, 197
Department store clearance centers, 152
Diaper pails, cleaning, 199–200
Discounts, asking for, 12–13
Discount stores, 149–50
Dishes, rinse aid for spot free, 199
Dishwashers, 177–78
Disputes, 228–29
Down payment, saving for, 75
Drain opener and cleaner, 192
Ducts, 170
Dust magnet spray, 190

E

Easter celebrations, 264–66
Employment taxes, 269
Energy audit, 162–75
Escrow, 101
Estate sales, 233, 237
Expenses, developing internal control for, 45–47
Eye examinations, 205–6
Eyeglasses, savings on, 204–11
Eye makeup remover, 217

F

Facial cleanser and exfoliator, 217
Facial mask, 218, 219–20

INDEX

Facial scrubs, 218
Factory outlet shopping, 151
Fair Credit Billing Act, 227
Fans, 167
Fertilization of seedlings/transplants, 289–90, 292
Fertilizer, 281, 282
Finances, accepting responsibility for, 18, 24–32
Fingernails, treatment for yellow, 221
Fireplaces, 172
Fixed expenses, 34, 36–41
Fixed rate mortgage, 88–89, 91
Flea markets, buying clothes at, 150
Floor cleaner, 191
Floor wax, removing built-up, 191
Free Application for Federal Student Aid (FAFSA), 180–81
Freezers, deodorizer for, 197
Frugality Network, 293
Furniture polish, 190

G

Garage sales, buying clothes at, 150
Gardening, 273–92
Garlic oil soap spray, 278–79
Grocery dollars, stretching your, 102–19
Grout, cleaning, 194–95
Growing medium, 286–87
Gym bags, cleaning, 199–200

H

Hair conditioner, 216–17
Halloween, 263–64
Heating, methods of, 166–72
Heat pumps, 170–71
Holidays, 252–66
Home, legal rights when shopping from, 227
Home inspection, 96–97
Housing, 69–101
    choosing closing date, 99–101
    choosing new, 81–87
    determining amount to spend on, 72–81
    financing, 87–99
    renting versus buying, 69–72

I

Income, determining monthly, 33–40
Informal cooperatives, 224–25
Inspection
    of car, 130–35
    of home, 96–97
Insulation, 163–65

Insurance
    automobile, 137–46
    eye examinations, 204–5
    housing, 74–75, 235
    private mortgage, 98
    title, 98
Internet, buying car on, 129–30

L

Laundry, 174–75
    stain removal from, 201–2
Lemon moisturizer, 219
Lighting, 174
Lime deposits, removing, 196
Living expenses, reducing, 22
Loan application, filling out, 95–96
Lockers, cleaning, 199–200

M

Mail, ordering merchandise by, 225–32
Makeup remover, 218
Meal planning, 102–6
Mechanic, inspection of car by, 134–35
Menu cards, 103–4
Mildew, removing, 195, 279
Military, getting education through, 184
Mineral deposits, removing, 196
Mirrors, fog free, 195
Mold, removing, 195
Money
    acting socially responsible for, 23
    attitudes toward, 1–23
    taking control of, 22, 44–54
Money management account, 40–42
Monthly expenditures, 34–39, 44–45, 53–54
Monthly house payment, determining, 73
Mortgages, 88–94

N

National Fraud Information Center, 232
Needs, separating, from wants, 70–71
New Year, celebration of, 259–60

O

Off-price store, buying clothes at, 149–50
Online, ordering merchandise by, 225–32
Orthodontics, paying less for, 211–15
Oven cleaner, 198–99

P

Paycheck, increasing, 267–72
Pell Grant, 181
Perspiration, removing stains from clothing, 200
Pest control, 275, 277–81
Planting mix, 282–83
Plant propagation, 283–85
Points, 90–91
Potpourri, 197
Pre-qualification/pre-approval, 79–81
Pretax dollars, 269–70
Price cards, grocery comparison shopping with, 108–11
Private mortgage insurance, 98
Private sellers, 128–29
Problem resolution, 232
Property survey, 97

R

Ranges, 178–79
    cleaning smooth top, 198
Real estate taxes, determination of, 74
Red cedar spray, 278
Refrigerators, 178
    deodorizer for, 197
Rental car companies, 129
Room deodorizer, 196

S

Salvage stores, 152
Scholarships, 181–84
School supplies, saving on, 248–51
Seeds, starting indoors, 285–92
Septic tank maintenance, 193
Shampoo, 217
Shaving, 220
Shopping styles, 18, 55–68
Showers, cleaning, 194, 195
Sinks, cleaning, 193, 199
Skin moisturizer, 218
Skin toner, 220
Sneakers, cleaning, 199–200
Soap spots and film, removing, from bathroom tile and tubs, 194
Soil, 274, 275
Solar heat gain, 169–70
Special assessments, 74
Stain removal, 192–94, 200–202
State grants, 181
Static electricity, reducing, in carpets, 192
Supplemental Education Opportunity Grant (SEOG), 181

T

Tag sales, buying clothes at, 150
Tax bracket, 272
Taxes, real estate, 74
Telephone, ordering merchandise by, 225–32
Television, cleaning, 190
Thermostats, 171–72
Thrift stores, bargain hunting in, 151
Title insurance, 98
Toilet bowl cleaner, 193
Transplanting, 291–92
Transportation costs, lowering, 120–46

U

Utility and maintenance bills, 162–79

V

Valentines Day, 260–63

W

Wall cleaner, 189
Wants, separating needs from, 70–71
Wardrobe, planning, 155–59
Warranty on car, 132–34
Water for gardens, 274
Water heating, 173
Wealth determination factor, 27–28
Weatherization, 165–66
Weed control, 275, 277–81
Wholesale clubs, 116–19, 150
Window cleaner, 189
Withholding taxes, 268
Work study, 185
Worth, determining, 24–28

Y

Yard sales, 150, 233–44
Yogurt facial cleansing scrub, 217